125-32
134 146
176 260
270

EARLY
WESTERN PENNSYLVANIA
POLITICS

This Book is one of a series relating Western Pennsylvania history, written under the direction of the Western Pennsylvania Historical Survey sponsored jointly by The Buhl Foundation, the Historical Society of Western Pennsylvania and the University of Pittsburgh.

ALBERT GALLATIN
From a portrait in pastel by James Sharples

EARLY WESTERN PENNSYLVANIA POLITICS

RUSSELL J. FERGUSON

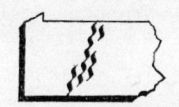

UNIVERSITY OF PITTSBURGH PRESS
1938

COPYRIGHT, 1938, BY UNIVERSITY OF PITTSBURGH PRESS

MANUFACTURED IN U.S.A.

PREFACE

THIS study of the first half-century of western Pennsylvania politics essays to trace the main thread of political behavior and thought of the people in the region from 1773 to 1823. It recounts the incidents of local politics in a segment of the frontier; it relates them to the economic and social problems of the time and place; and it coördinates them with the broader policies of the colonial, and later state and national governments. In other words, it attempts to portray the efforts of the people in a predominately pioneer agricultural society to find a solution for their economic and social problems through political action.

The author is indebted to many institutions and individuals for aid in the preparation of this monograph. The Western Pennsylvania Historical Survey, sponsor of this study, and the members of its staff; the Historical Society of Western Pennsylvania and its director, Mr. Franklin F. Holbrook; and the library staffs of the New York Historical Society, the Historical Society of Pennsylvania, and the Darlington Library at the University of Pittsburgh were generous with their services and advice. Many graduate students at the University of Pittsburgh made valuable contributions through the medium of master's theses and historical papers. Mrs. John B. Sellers, of the Historical Society of Western Pennsylvania, and Dr. Leland D. Baldwin and Miss Mary Jo Hauser, of the University of Pittsburgh Press, gave indispensable editorial assistance; Mr. and Mrs. John E. Reynolds, of Meadville, extended the courtesy of their home and library for several weeks of research; and finally my wife gave unsparingly of her time in clerical work and literary criticism.

Russell J. Ferguson

CONTENTS

Preface		vii
Chapter One	A Pioneer Agricultural Society	1
Chapter Two	Revolutionary Politics	20
Chapter Three	Back-Country Democracy Organizes	38
Chapter Four	Back-Country Democracy in Opposition	63
Chapter Five	The Challenge of Federalism	101
Chapter Six	The Struggle for Supremacy	132
Chapter Seven	Jeffersonian Democracy Organizes	155
Chapter Eight	Conflicts and Confusion	176
Chapter Nine	Passing the Baton	209
Chapter Ten	The American System	231
Chapter Eleven	The End of an Era	260
Bibliography		275
Index		293

ILLUSTRATIONS

PORTRAITS

Albert Gallatin	*frontispiece*
William Findley	*facing page* 48
Hugh Henry Brackenridge	" " 112
James Ross	" " 160
Henry Baldwin	" " 192
Walter Forward	" " 224

MAP

Western Pennsylvania in 1800	xiii

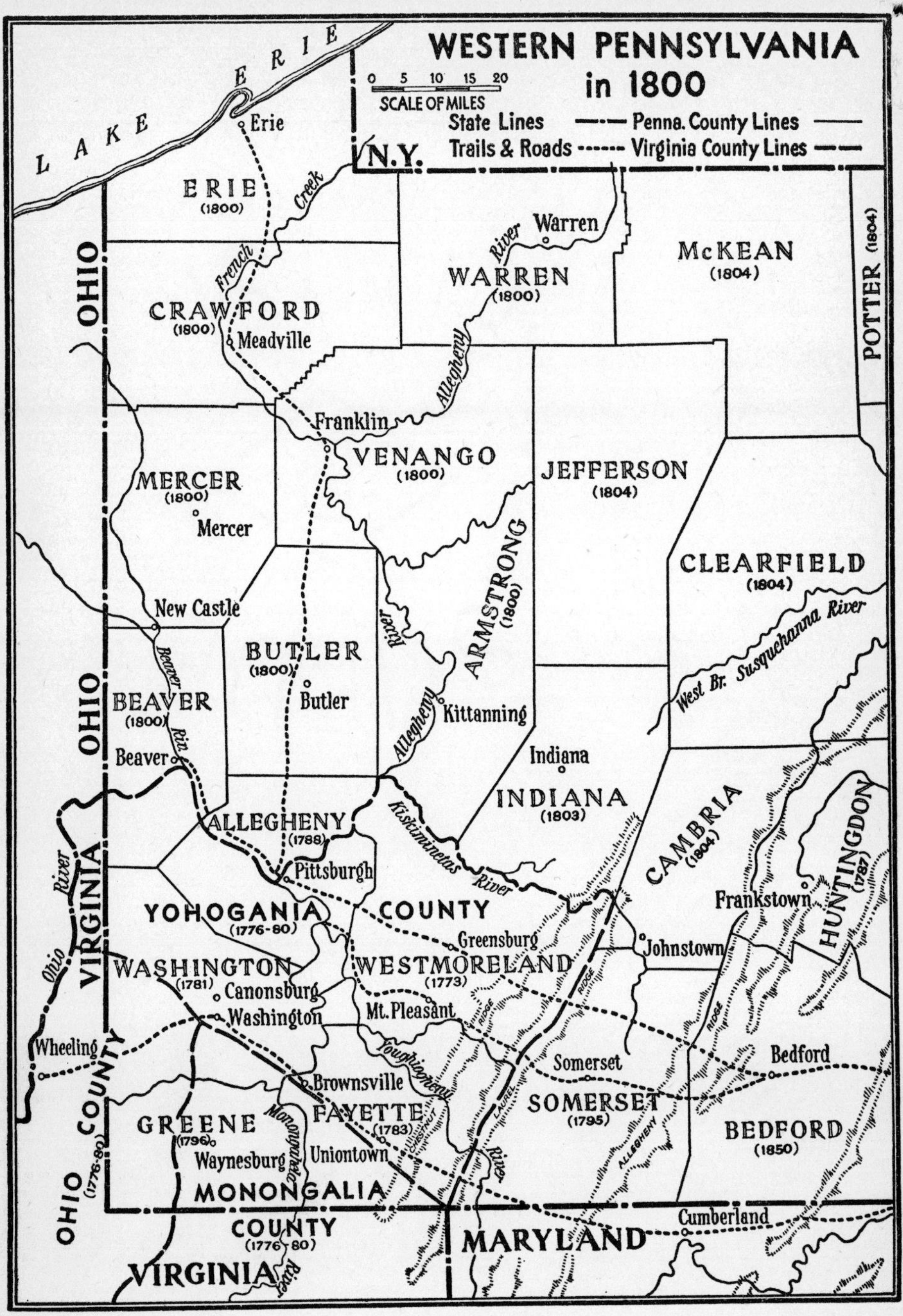

WESTERN PENNSYLVANIA
in 1800
0 5 10 15 20
SCALE OF MILES
State Lines
Penna. County Lines
Trails & Roads
Virginia County Lines
LAKE ERIE
N.Y.
Erie
ERIE
(1800)
French Creek
CRAWFORD
(1800)
Meadville
Warren
WARREN
(1800)
Allegheny River
McKEAN
(1804)
POTTER (1804)
Franklin
VENANGO
(1800)
MERCER
(1800)
Mercer
JEFFERSON
(1804)
CLEARFIELD
(1804)
West Br. Susquehanna River
ARMSTRONG
(1800)
New Castle
BUTLER
(1800)
Butler
Kittanning
Beaver Riv.
BEAVER
(1800)
Beaver
Indiana
INDIANA
(1803)
CAMBRIA
(1804)
HUNTINGDON
(1787)
Frankstown
ALLEGHENY
(1788)
Pittsburgh
Kiskiminetas River
YOHOGANIA
(1776-80)
COUNTY
Greensburg
Johnstown
WESTMORELAND
(1773)
WASHINGTON
(1781)
Canonsburg
Washington
Mt. Pleasant
Ohio River
Wheeling
Youghiogheny River
Somerset
Bedford
Brownsville
FAYETTE
(1783)
SOMERSET
(1795)
BEDFORD
(1850)
GREENE
(1796)
Waynesburg
Uniontown
Monongahela River
MONONGALIA
COUNTY
(1776-80)
OHIO
COUNTY
(1776-80)
OHIO
VIRGINIA
MARYLAND
Cumberland

EARLY
WESTERN PENNSYLVANIA
POLITICS

A PIONEER AGRICULTURAL SOCIETY

CHAPTER ONE

WESTERN PENNSYLVANIA in 1773 contained a group of some fifty thousand pioneers living in a part of the American frontier that was segregated from the Atlantic seaboard by the Appalachian Mountains. The political boundaries were not yet surveyed nor even defined. The colonies of Pennsylvania and Virginia, both under the jurisdiction of the king of England, advanced conflicting claims to the land. In addition, the Indians, as natural occupants, had refused to yield all their rights to ownership and possession. Only the French claims had been eliminated. But, despite the lack of certainty with regard to the ownership of the territory, despite indefinite boundaries, and in the face of many obstacles, a nascent pioneer agricultural society existed. Between 1773 and 1790 this turbulent and, at times, almost violent young society made accretions and underwent modifications.

Geographically, western Pennsylvania is a portion of a great plateau that slopes westward from the Appalachian watershed and extends far enough to include the territory now contained in the eastern counties of Ohio and the northwestern counties of West Virginia. The plateau is a corrugated, wooded highland, separated from the seaboard by a mountain barrier and drained by the Monongahela and Allegheny rivers and their tributaries, and is a geographical unit that belongs more to the Mississippi basin and the West than to the seaboard and the East. All its physiographical features—the mountains, rivers, texture of the soil, and climatic conditions —served as determinants in producing an early society of farmers.

The parallel ranges of the Appalachian Mountains, which extend in a southwesterly direction along the Atlantic seaboard from Maine to Georgia and Alabama, pass through central Pennsylvania and separate the eastern seaboard from the western plateau. The eastern approach to the various ranges is comparatively abrupt and difficult because of the steep slopes or escarpments, whereas the western approach is more gradual and less difficult because of the more gently sloping plateau. Early settlers traveling westward in Pennsylvania encountered successive ranges, each separated from the other by a fertile valley, each with a steep eastern ascent, until they reached the Allegheny Front, after which they descended gradually, except for the scaling of two ranges, Laurel Hill and Chestnut Ridge. The mountains were passable; there were water gaps and wind gaps. But two features of the ranges retarded the growth and development of western Pennsylvania: the eastern escarpments, which discouraged westward migration, and the fertile valleys between the ranges, which induced the weary travelers to settle rather than brave the difficulties of crossing another ridge.

The barrier of the Allegheny Ridge influenced the development of society in western Pennsylvania in a negative way. It retarded migration and transportation; it restricted communication; it prevented an easy exchange of ideas between the people of the East and those to the west of the mountains; it deprived the western inhabitants of eastern conveniences and advantages; it localized the transmontane pioneers and engendered a cultural and political ideology which became manifest in their political behavior.

The rivers and the river systems, on the other hand, made positive contributions to the expansion and growth of the people in the area. Rivers that were not integrally a part of western Pennsylvania aided in peopling the region and in the development of transportation, communication, and commerce. Of these the Susquehanna and the Potomac were the two most important. The West Branch of the Susquehanna, with some of its tributaries, rises west of the Allegheny Front, flows eastward to central Pennsylvania, and then strikes boldly southward through the mountain ranges to a junction with the North Branch, whence the Susquehanna continues in a southerly direction to the head of Chesapeake Bay. The mountain streams of this river system were not completely navigable in all places and at all times during the last quarter of the eighteenth century but they were available in places for canoes and small boats and they designated water gaps in the mountains through which settlers might go.

The Potomac River, like the Susquehanna, has tributary sources along the Allegheny Front and flows through the mountains in a southeasterly direction to Chesapeake Bay. The Potomac, however, lies almost entirely to the south of Pennsylvania. A few of its less significant tributaries rise above the fortieth parallel, but its main course is so close to Pennsylvania that only a relatively short trail was necessary to transfer travelers from it to the Youghiogheny River or even to the Monongahela. The old Nemacolin Trail had bridged that gap before the coming of the settlers, and the Braddock Road, constructed during the French and Indian War, supplemented the Potomac River in facilitating the progress of settlers into southwestern Pennsylvania for two decades before 1773. The Susquehanna and Potomac systems were avenues of commerce as well as channels of westward migration; they tended to promote an eastward movement for trade and thereby aided in tying the new commercial West to the older commercial East. The fact that the termini of the rivers were in Chesapeake Bay rather than at Philadelphia created a commercial affiliation between western merchants and those of Baltimore. As a result, a commercial sectionalism arose, which legislators from eastern Pennsylvania attempted to overcome by sponsoring the development of transportation and communication between Philadelphia and the West.[1]

The network of rivers that actually drained western Pennsylvania was even more significant to the people already settled there and to the internal development of the economic and social life of the region. With the exception of the tributaries of the West Branch of the Susquehanna, located in the north central part of the state, the waters of the rivers eventually reached the Ohio and thereby became a part of the vast Mississippi system. The Allegheny and Monongahela and their tributaries, which spread in every direction and into all sections of western Pennsylvania, converged at Pittsburgh and tended to point the commerce and the interest of the rural settlers in that direction. Furthermore, the Ohio, formed by the junction of the Allegheny and Monongahela, created a natural gateway toward the West for settlers, for certain types of commerce, and for the political interest of many people of the region. In addition to the larger streams, there were countless small creeks and runs which acted as byways along which settlers founded their homes.

The soil in the region varied in fertility. Along the beds of rivers and streams a rich alluvial soil had been deposited during the flood stages. The width of those fertile bottom lands varied from a few feet in some instances to several miles in some of the broader valleys. On the higher plateaus the soil was of a less fertile nature and sandy or rocky. It was adapted to profitable farming, however; and southwestern Pennsylvania, comprising the territory south of the Ohio and west of the Monongahela, which contained a great amount of such soil on its rolling hillsides, was very attractive to settlers. The soil of even the more mountainous areas was quite capable of producing vegetation, although for the most part such land was covered with trees and shrubbery and was not satisfactory for farming. There was an abundance of available fertile land in the region—enough to attract a host of settlers in the last quarter of the eighteenth century and to produce a pre-

[1] Lincoln, *Revolutionary Movement in Pennsylvania*, 55-73.

dominately agrarian society. Adequate rainfall and good climatic conditions supplemented the fertility of the soil in the advancement of agriculture. The rainfall was sufficient to produce the crops but was not so great that it created many swamps or unhealthful conditions. The climate was temperate, with cold winters and hot summers of about six months' duration, ideally fitted for the growth of the grain crops.[2]

There was plant and animal life in abundance for the immediate needs of the settlers. Hardwood trees were indigenous to the region, and great tracts of them stood scattered over the green-thatched plateau. Sturdy oak trees, both red and white, grew throughout the district and were available for homes, wagons, and firewood; the maple everywhere offered its sap for syrup or to be refined into a somewhat crude form of sugar; the chestnut trees on the hills of the southern part of the region, and the walnut and hickory in the valleys yielded their nuts for food and their trunks for fence rails and timber. The ash, valuable for tools and implements; the wild plum; the sycamore; and the tulip, with its regular leaves and beautiful blossoms, were other trees that studded the landscape. Soft pines and hemlocks were intermixed with the deciduous trees and at a later date became marketable commodities. Shrubs and vines vied with the larger trees for existence and although they won out on some of the hillsides, lost the fight in the denser forest tracts because of the lack of sunshine and light. In the small meadows and "clearings," after the trees had been removed, food crops could be grown in ample quantities for domestic consumption and, within a short time, at least by 1790, for exchange. Corn and small grains—wheat, barley, and rye—were grown by nearly all farmers in the southern half of the region. Hemp and flax were common and profitable products. Grass grew readily; vegetables common to that time yielded good returns; and everywhere wild berry bushes flourished. The domestic plants guaranteed a substantial diet for an industrious individual.

[2] Hutchins, *Topographical Description*, 1-20.

Wild animals in great numbers and of many varieties inhabited the woodlands or built their homes along the streams. Bears, deer, elk, and bison, available for both food and furs, were common to the whole region. Less valuable to the settler were the minks, otters, beavers, and raccoons that infested the streams. Although they were not readily edible, their furs were nevertheless desirable as a commodity of exchange. Wild turkeys, quail, and wild pigeons, all contributed to the larders of the pioneers. Fish of many kinds were to be found in the streams and were ever accessible to the angler.

Western Pennsylvania, at the time of the coming of the white man, was thus ideally constituted for the purpose of maintaining a pioneer agricultural society. The mountain barrier retarded the influx of the ideas and products of a more advanced society along the seaboard; the rivers facilitated transportation for settlers and for commerce and provided fish for food; the fertility of the soil, a temperate climate, and adequate rainfall encouraged agriculture; and the forests furnished timber for fuel, tools, and homes. There was plenty of food and plenty of land. It was a wilderness of plenty and promise, but it was not a wilderness Eden. The pioneers faced trials and hardships. The necessity of struggling with the soil for a livelihood, the menace of savage Indians lurking in the woods, the vicissitudes of cold hard winters, and the lack of medical facilities were some of the more unsatisfactory conditions on the frontier. Yet to this wilderness, with its advantages and disadvantages, settlers came to build a pioneer society.

The settling of western Pennsylvania was not sudden nor was it a matter of a continual flow of a small stream of settlers over the mountains into the new country. Rather, it may be likened to a succession of waves beating against a wall and receding, with no immediately appreciable effect, until the water creates a small channel through which it rushes with a constantly increasing current, eventually crushing the barrier and inundating the land. There were settlers in southwestern Pennsylvania shortly after 1750, but many of them abandoned their homes after Washington's capitulation at Fort Necessity. The withdrawal of the French after the Forbes campaign in 1758, the reclaiming of the Braddock Road by Alexander Finnie, the extension of it to Redstone by Colonel James Burd in the following year, and the availability of the Forbes Road induced the settlers to return to their abandoned homes and stimulated an influx of new settlers.[3]

The Monongahela country received a majority of these migrants, but Fort Pitt, at the forks of the Ohio, was a strategic spot that had a strong attraction for many of the earliest settlers. One report for the year 1760 indicates that aside from the garrison there were 200 huts in the little town, either completed or in the course of construction, and that the population was 149.[4] A report for the year 1761 placed the population, exclusive of the garrison, at 332.[5] Despite the efforts of Colonel Bouquet and colonial officials to prevent settlers from occupying land claimed by the Indians, the population increased steadily up to the year 1763. At that time, Pontiac's Conspiracy caused the unprotected pioneers to flee to Fort Ligonier or Fort Bedford, and once more to abandon their homes. But, with the collapse of the Indians' conspiracy at the Battle of Bushy Run on August 6, 1763, there was another wave of immigrants to the region, among whom were not only those who returned to their abandoned claims, but also a great number of new ones as well. During the next six years, regardless of the royal Proclamation of 1763, which forbade settlement west of the mountains, and despite the efforts of the imperial and colonial officials who attempted to enforce the provisions of the proclamation, there was a steady increase in population along the rivers and valleys and in the small villages of western Pennsylvania.

[3] James, "The First English-speaking Trans-Appalachian Frontier," in *Mississippi Valley Historical Review*, 17:55-71 (1930).
[4] *Pennsylvania Archives*, second series, 7:422.
[5] "Pittsburgh in 1761," in *Pennsylvania Magazine of History and Biography*, 6:347 (1882).

Much of the Monongahela Valley was occupied in the years 1765 and 1766, and a plan for the reconstruction of Pittsburgh was drawn up in 1764 and put into effect the next year. The Treaty of Fort Stanwix in 1768 eliminated the Indian claims to the southern part of the region, and in 1769 the Penns' agents opened an office for the sale of land in the recently purchased tract. Plots of land, three hundred acres in size, were offered for sale at approximately twenty cents per acre. That action was the signal for a veritable inundation of the land by new settlers. The French menace was removed at the end of the French and Indian wars by the Treaty of Paris in 1763; the Indian trouble was reduced; channels for immigration— the Braddock and Forbes roads—were opened; and reasonably cheap land was available. Within five years the population mounted to a total of probably fifty thousand individuals. In 1790, according to the first United States census, an aggregate of seventy-five thousand souls inhabited western Pennsylvania with a preponderant majority of them in the five counties then organized—Bedford, Westmoreland, Fayette, Allegheny, and Washington.[6] They were a group of people segregated in an American wilderness.

People from many lands bringing their particular customs, traditions, and ideals trekked across the mountains or followed the rivers to this isolated wilderness. At least a few representatives of nearly all nations and races settled in western Pennsylvania, where some played significant roles, and others left no visible results. First of all from the standpoint of numbers and probably first from the standpoints of respectability and significance were the English. Some of them came from their homeland bringing with them an aptitude for farming and sheep-raising. Others, like John Neville, who settled at Bower Hill just south of Pittsburgh, were born in Virginia or Maryland and transplanted something of the old tidewater South into the wilderness. A majority of the English people who

[6] United States Bureau of the Census, *Heads of Families . . . 1790, Pennsylvania*, 9-11.

came to the region entered by way of the Braddock Road and the Monongahela River and consequently settled in the Monongahela country, although in western Pennsylvania as elsewhere in the American colonies English people were found wherever settlements were made. It is probable that one-third of the population of the five early western counties was comprised of English people or those of English extraction and that the ratio was two-fifths or more in the three southwestern counties—Fayette, Washington, and Allegheny. Some of them, notably the Neville family, became affluent either because of large land holdings or by means of land traffic; others achieved economic prominence through commerce, as did the Wilkins family of Pittsburgh; and their economic leadership enhanced and was enhanced by their political leadership. While the economically favored Englishmen of the region tended to reflect the landed gentry of the homeland in political philosophy, the less fortunate reflected the traditional Englishman's jealousy of his individual rights.[7]

Of equal importance, numerically and in leadership, were those non-English immigrants from the British Isles: the Scotch-Irish, the Scotch, the Irish, and the Welsh. The Scotch, some of them educated in the University of Edinburgh; others, like Hugh Henry Brackenridge, the Pittsburgh lawyer, trained in American institutions of higher learning; and still a greater number with practically no education came to combat the wilderness with their thrift and hardiness. Many of them removed from the back country of Virginia or Maryland to the valleys of the Monongahela and Youghiogheny; others migrated from the inland counties of Pennsylvania across the mountains to the region of Fort Ligonier and Hannastown; and still others came directly from Philadelphia,

[7] The discussion of racial groups in this and the following paragraphs is based on James, "The First English-speaking Trans-Appalachian Frontier," in *Mississippi Valley Historical Review*, 17:55-71 (1930); American Council of Learned Societies, "Report ... on Linguistic and National Stocks," in American Historical Association, *Annual Report*, 1:193, 229, 251, 305 (1931); H. J. Ford, *Scotch-Irish*, 260-290; Buck, "Planting of Civilization," chap. 7.

their port of entry, with the result that they were equitably distributed throughout western Pennsylvania. Presbyterian, accustomed to a comparatively practical democracy in church government, doctrinaire, hardy, determined, and thrifty, they made ideal settlers and furnished many vigorous religious and political leaders.

The Scotch-Irish, descendants of Scotsmen transplanted to northern Ireland a century before, began to arrive in the American colonies in considerable numbers shortly after 1720. Like the English, they established settlements in all the colonies, but they proceeded generally to the frontiers, where they gravitated to the Shenandoah Valley and the back country of the South and particularly to the wilderness regions of Pennsylvania. Those for whom Philadelphia served as a port of entry moved on past the Quaker and German communities and settled along the rivers or went on up to the mountain ranges, turned to the right or left, and built homes in the fertile valleys. Those who entered through the port of Baltimore had several courses that they might pursue. Many of them went northward into Pennsylvania along the Susquehanna River and settled just beyond the Germans along the river or continued their journey to the mountains, where they entered the valleys and established settlements. Still others migrated westward from Baltimore to the Shenandoah Valley, thence to the Monongahela country by way of the Nemacolin Trail or Braddock Road and the road built by Colonel James Burd from a point on the Braddock Road near Gist's plantation to Redstone. Once arrived in western Pennsylvania, they took up land along the rivers and streams, and eventually constituted a cluster of Scotch-Irish settlements in southwestern Pennsylvania. Like their Scotch kinsmen, they were Presbyterians, doctrinaire, rugged, hardy, and industrious, but they were more spirited and audacious, and were possessed of a penchant for politics. Their political influence was vastly greater than their numbers would seem to warrant.

Among the non-English immigrants from the British Isles

to Pennsylvania were many Irish, Ulsterites, South Irish, and English-Irish, the latter tinctured with English blood and associations. They were drawn from the less economically favored classes of Ireland, and not a few of them came as indentured servants. Philadelphia and Baltimore were their chief ports of entry, just as in the case of the Scotch-Irish, and from those points they found their way into western Pennsylvania along the same routes as those used by the others. Regardless of their background and social conditions in Ireland, many of them became political leaders in the new country.

Finally, another group of the non-English element from the British Isles that made contributions to the ethnic structure of western Pennsylvania was that formed by the Welsh. Their native environment was similar to that of the English, but a greater percentage of them were familiar with trades and artisanship. They entered the frontier country by traveling directly overland from Philadelphia rather than by way of the Potomac, Braddock Road, and Monongahela River. Industrious, inoffensive, and quiet, they played a less prominent role in frontier politics than the English, the Scotch, or the Scotch-Irish.

The aggregate number of these non-English groups of people who came from the British Isles was probably as great as the total number of those of pure English stock. The political influence of the Scotch and Scotch-Irish apparently surpassed the collective strength of all other groups. Their dramatic instincts, their flair for politics, their adherence to an organized Presbyterian church that demanded trained leaders and afforded a place of congregation, their imagination and their boldness, all aided in giving them an incommensurate weight in early politics.

Another significant element in the ethnic composition of western Pennsylvania was the German. It was comprised, in the main, of Germans who had come westward from the eastern counties, second-generation Germans, who followed the

Forbes Road. They were farmers and were drawn to the fertile sections of land in Bedford, Westmoreland, and Fayette counties. Reliable, unimaginative, industrious, they became substantial settlers who were more interested in their land than in politics. The fact that they had to make a transition from their native language to the English, together with the fact that their mode of dress was considered peculiar, retarded their social integration, and this retardation in turn tended to minimize their political activities. Moreover, their numerous sects and churches prevented them from attaining a unity similar to that reached by the members of the Presbyterian church.

The adaptation of these ethnic groups to the pioneer life and to each other, their cultural contributions to the frontier, and the changes wrought by the wilderness environment upon their customs, institutions, and thoughts produced the resultant society of the period from 1773 to 1790. The people transposed some of their customs and institutions in their entirety to western Pennsylvania; they modified others to fit the new environment; and out of necessity they created new ones. The wilderness tended to change the immigrants, to make them hardier and less refined; it tended to democratize them; but it did not crush them.

There was a remarkable growth and expansion of settlement in western Pennsylvania during the years from 1773 to 1790. The population increased approximately fifty per cent, rising from fifty thousand to seventy-five thousand people. This increase was the result of two factors, natural reproduction and immigration. It is well known that pioneer families were generally large. Three reasons may be offered in explanation. First, birth control was practically unknown. Second, there was an abundance of available land and a dearth of laborers, with the result that the head of the family could utilize strong rugged sons to increase his labor supply and potential income. Third, pioneers located in isolated spots were lonely, and a large family gathered around a cheerful fireplace in the evening tended to dispel their loneliness.

Immigration during this period was equally significant in increasing the population and, in addition, it had a modifying effect upon the cultural and economic structure of society. Among those who came into the region were many intellectual leaders—preachers, lawyers, editors, and teachers; also, among the newcomers were many men who were to introduce a commercial atmosphere into the settlements. Moreover, hundreds of people passed through the region, some of whom stopped for a time on their way down the Ohio to western countries. Even though they were transients, they left their mark on the community, particularly upon Pittsburgh, where the purchase of supplies for their journey stimulated commerce. By 1790 the young agricultural society was disturbed by the development of a growing commercial element, which introduced a rivalry even in political controversies.

Pittsburgh, at the forks of the Ohio, was the first settlement in the region, in point of time, size, and significance. It grew slowly between 1764, when it was laid out, and 1790, despite the facts that it was the focal point for commerce and immigration and that a military garrison of some kind existed there at intervals throughout the period. Its growth was doubtless retarded by the difficulty entailed in procuring clear titles to the land, which was part of a tract reserved to the Penn family. Too, the danger of Indian raids checked its growth. From a settlement of a few log cabins and 149 people in 1760, Pittsburgh grew to a town of 376 inhabitants in 1790; at that time it had a score or more of stores, a weekly newspaper, a printing press, and an academy; two years earlier it had become the county seat of Allegheny County with a court and the proper political agencies. Hugh Henry Brackenridge, the young lawyer-journalist, in an effort to attract settlers described the town and region in most glowing terms in the columns of the *Pittsburgh Gazette*. A visitor in 1784 was less generous, however; he described the log houses as "paltry" and "dirty" and reported that the population was made up of Scots and Irishmen and that there were four lawyers, two physicians, and no clergymen. Another transient of the same year observed that the people were "inactive" and "indolent," although he saw some "well clothed gentlemen and ladies." Still another observer in 1785 reported that the people were engaged in commerce and tavern-keeping. Pittsburgh was not a prepossessing little town, but it was the commercial nerve center of the region then as truly as the great metropolis is today.[8]

Several other towns were founded during the era, many of which were hardly more than collections of cabins surrounding a store, a blacksmith shop, and a mill. Uniontown, in Fayette County, favorably situated on the Burd Road, was first settled about 1767 and became the county seat in 1784; Brownsville, at the mouth of Redstone Creek and at the site of Fort Burd was settled in 1769 and laid out as a town in 1785. In Washington County, the town of Washington was settled simultaneously with Brownsville and was made the county seat in 1781; it was reputed to have more industries in 1790 than Pittsburgh; Canonsburg on Chartiers Creek had a mill, a distillery, a store, and a tavern but few people at this time. Hannastown, county seat of Westmoreland County, had about thirty log houses in 1782 when it was destroyed by the Indians; it never regained its prominence, and Greensburg became the county seat in 1787. Bedford, in Bedford County, grew slowly and suffered a decrease in population during the decade 1763-73, probably because of the fear of Indians.[9]

The increase and expansion of the population, the Virginia-Pennsylvania controversy over the possession of the region, and the necessity of giving law, order, and protection to the settlers hastened the organization of new counties between 1773 and 1790. Westmoreland County was established in 1773 from that part of Bedford County west of Laurel Hill and south of the Ohio River. The territory included in the new

[8] Buck, "Planting of Civilization," chap. 7.
[9] Ellis, *Fayette County,* 279 ff., 424; Crumrine, *Washington County,* 476, 601-603; Boucher, *Old and New Westmoreland,* 1:401-418. For an explanation of the slow growth of Bedford, see Boucher, *Old and New Westmoreland,* 1:113.

county at that time was approximately the same as that included in the present counties of Westmoreland, Fayette, Greene, Washington, Cambria, the parts of Allegheny and Beaver counties below the Ohio River, and the southern parts of the present counties of Indiana and Armstrong. The Westmoreland County officials were unable to exercise a satisfactory jurisdiction from their seat at Hannastown, and in 1781 Washington County was organized for the territory west of the Monongahela and south of the Ohio. Two years later Fayette County was hewn out of Westmoreland, and a county seat was established at Uniontown. One more county, Allegheny, was organized in 1788. Parts of Washington and Westmoreland were joined to the territory west of the Allegheny River and north to Lake Erie and New York to form the latest county, of which Pittsburgh was the county seat. Western Pennsylvania thus included the counties of Bedford, Westmoreland, Washington, Fayette, and Allegheny. Bedford County, however, was more nearly a mountain county and not an integral part of western Pennsylvania except that the political origins of the later counties had existed there.

Virginia, claiming virtually the same territory as that included in the Pennsylvania county of Westmoreland in 1773, had organized three counties for the region in 1776. These counties, Yohogania, Monongalia, and Ohio, had courts and officials who functioned until 1780, but the Virginia jurisdiction ceased legally with the settlement of the boundary line in 1780. Thereafter the Virginia settlers in the region were gradually assimilated, but there were rumblings from many of them who preferred the Old Dominion.[10]

The economic, social, and cultural progress was slow but apparent in this segregated frontier region during this period. Families were practically self-sufficient. Utilizing the trees from the surrounding forest and later making their own bricks or quarrying stone from the adjacent hills, they built their own homes; they procured their food, with the exception of salt,

[10] Crumrine, *Washington County*, 158-222.

from the soil or from the forests; they made their own clothing; and in general they relied very little upon the outside world except for a few tools and their weapons. Their economic life was, for the most part, an individual, domestic one until they began producing a surplus of commodities that could be used in commerce. Under such conditions the possession of land was an important item, and, since many of the settlers were squatters, the legal title to the land ultimately became a prominent political issue. Except for a few settlers like John Neville who owned slaves the actual labor attached to farming was performed by the owner. He might be assisted by his sons, but he rarely made use of hired laborers on his farm. It was an era of relatively small-scale farming, an era of the ax, the hoe, and the primitive plow.[11]

Social life was limited and simple. Settlers had few opportunities to meet and mingle with their fellow men. Church services, funerals, weddings, sessions of court, militia musters, house or barn raisings, and housewarmings were the chief occasions for congregation. Rural churches were few, and transportation to and from them was frequently difficult; funerals and weddings were not daily occurrences; muster days were rare except in times of danger; and houses were raised but once. The family gathering about the fireplace in the evening was probably the most common and most important social gathering in the rural sections. It tended to foster an intellectual inbreeding and aided in developing a provincialism that was discernible in the politics of the period. The towns furnished greater opportunities for social intercourse but even there occasions for meeting were limited. The tavern was accessible to townsmen and travelers; sessions of court, town meetings, lodge meetings, and eventually literary and cultural societies provided meeting places; and business relations in the towns increased the contacts between men.

[11] For a discussion of this subject see Caley, "Child Life in Colonial Pennsylvania," in *Western Pennsylvania Historical Magazine*, 9:33-49, 104-121, 188-201, 256-275 (1926).

Nevertheless, social life at its best in western Pennsylvania was restricted and simple during the period from 1773 to 1790.

The cultural level, perforce, was generally low. The frontier had a tendency to retard if not actually to lower the culture introduced by the settlers. The people worked long and hard clearing the land, building homes, eking out a livelihood, and manufacturing their own household equipment and clothing. Tired and weary at the close of the day, they had little inclination, time, or literary equipment to improve their minds. Comparatively primitive conditions and the necessity of fighting the Indians dulled their finer sensibilities. Their children, the second generation, without the benefit of schools and with a restricted benefit of clergy, demonstrated evidences of intellectual decline. For a time the wilderness seemed to conquer those who came. The founding of churches, however, beginning in the decade 1770-80 and increasing during the next decade, introduced a social institution, and, because educated ministers were required, particularly in the Presbyterian churches, a cultural institution as well. The arrival of a number of university-trained clergymen and physicians provided an intellectual leadership, which by 1790 began to bolster up the waning culture of the first generation. Furthermore, the educated leaders realized the necessity for establishing schools in the region, and in 1787 under the sponsorship of Hugh Henry Brackenridge an academy was provided at Pittsburgh by the state legislature. The previous year John Scull had come across the mountains to found the *Pittsburgh Gazette,* the first trans-Appalachian newspaper.[12] Thereafter, the paper served not only as a source of information but also as an outlet for the expression of those who were inclined to write. Nevertheless, only the inception of a native culture existed in western Pennsylvania in 1790.

The political attitude of these western Pennsylvania farmers was determined by their background and environment. The fact that they were willing to leave established homes and mi-

[12] Andrews' *Pittsburgh's Post-Gazette* is a history of this paper and its successors.

grate to the wilderness was evidence of a dissatisfaction with their former life. Their discontent may have been only suggestive of a revolt against their former society, but their abandonment of the old home was indicative of a willingness to break with old traditions and old ideas. In a faint sense they had in them a germ of liberalism and were therefore susceptible to ideas that were produced by frontier influences. Whatever tendencies they had originally had toward democracy were accentuated by the wilderness environment, because the frontier has been the most effective of all agencies for democracy. There nobility, birth, wealth, and social position had less meaning than in older societies. One individual was potentially the equal of another because each one faced the same stark realities and because few individuals had a surplus of wealth to transmit to their sons. Social standing was less to be desired than dexterity in the use of the hoe, the ax, and the gun. Socially the pioneers were democratic and developed a practical rather than a philosophical democracy.

Furthermore, the frontier tended to create in the early settlers a spirit of independence and even of opposition. They found many adverse conditions; they fought the Indians; they struggled with the soil for a livelihood; they faced cold, hard winters; they fought diseases with inadequate medical facilities; and even the balance of trade was against them. The government failed to protect them sufficiently against the Indians or to aid them in their problems. Apparently every man's hand was against them. As a result they became independent, individualistic, and even antagonistic. They were independent in the sense that they were self-reliant and in the sense that they wanted no governmental interference in their activities. They opposed any form of restriction whether in the form of taxes, the regulation of commerce, or the fixing of their social customs. Opposition to an apparently oppressive government, in addition to their practical democratic attitude, served as a determinant for their political behavior.

From the beginning of the colony to the Revolution, the

Quakers had dominated Pennsylvania politics. A series of changes in the form of government between 1683 and 1696 modified the original form and provided for an elective assembly of twelve members and an elective council of eighteen. Each of the three original counties had equal weight in the election of the members to the assembly and to the council. Under this system of government the Quakers in Bucks, Chester, and Philadelphia counties gained a control over the colonial legislature that they held for almost a century and thus retarded the organization of new inland counties. In addition to this policy, the Quakers cultivated the friendship of the pacific, pious Germans who settled the land in the crescent surrounding Philadelphia to the north and west. The political alliance that they formed with the Germans enabled them to outweigh the more aggressive and politically minded Scotch and Scotch-Irish who had moved on past the German crescent to the frontier. During the quarter-century from 1750 to 1775, however, the vigor of the frontiersmen asserted itself, and, in the turbulence of the Revolution, the democratic elements of the inland counties, with the aid of the sympathetic unenfranchised population in Philadelphia, seized control of the colonial government and established a state constitution for the new commonwealth.[13]

[13] Selsam, *Pennsylvania Constitution of 1776*, 49-93.

REVOLUTIONARY POLITICS

CHAPTER TWO

WESTERN PENNSYLVANIA politics began during the early years of the American Revolution. Prior to the legislative act for the organization of Westmoreland County on February 26, 1773, there was little opportunity for the settlers of the West to express themselves in formal political action. The officers of the Pennsylvania county of Cumberland, organized in 1750, who had nominal jurisdiction over the region obviously could not administer effectively the laws for the territory west of Laurel Hill from their seat of justice in Carlisle. Even the organization of Bedford County with a county seat at Bedford in 1771 did not enable the Quaker colony to extend satisfactorily actual jurisdiction beyond the mountain ranges. Virginia made no efforts to bring law and order to the region except through military operations. The conflicts with the French required a succession of military commanders who governed and protected the people as well as they were able. Nor did the situation change at the close of the French and Indian War in 1763. A military post was maintained at Fort Pitt whose commandant was expected to restrict settlement west of the mountains in compliance with the provision of the Proclamation of 1763.

But problems of social conduct arose, and policies with regard to defense against the hostile Indians, possession of land, and means of facilitating commerce were necessary. The people sought cheap land and a clear title to it; they wanted protection against Indian raids; they desired a market for their products; they clamored for an equitable representation in the colonial assembly; and they opposed the eastern conservative class. These problems were first approached in an unofficial manner, in spontaneous and unauthorized meetings. The settlers who lived in a rough pioneer society, almost in a "state of nature," dealt out justice harshly, practically, and without any philosophical justification. They applied "tar and feathers" to some men and "hated" others out of the community; they banded together to repulse an Indian attack as they would to raise a house; and when they met at the mills or at the house raisings they grumbled about their unfortunate conditions and the indifference of their government. Yet when the long arm of the colonial government of Pennsylvania reached out to Hannastown in Westmoreland County, they were ready to take an active official part in the political affairs of the colony and to appeal to the assembly and council for a solution of their problems.

The new county had scarcely been organized before the American Revolution began. Within the same year two events occurred to arouse the feelings of the inhabitants of Westmoreland against the British government. First, the Virginia-Pennsylvania boundary dispute was brought to an acute stage by the aggressive action of Governor Dunmore of Virginia, who attempted to establish the Old Dominion colony's actual jurisdiction over southwestern Pennsylvania. Second, on December 16, 1773, the Boston patriots, as a demonstration of their hatred for parliamentary taxation and the mother country's domination, threw the British tea in the harbor. Each of these two events precipitated controversies, which raged concurrently, controversies that separately and jointly increased the anti-British animosity in western Pennsylvania and eventually developed there a patriotic element that bore a faint resemblance to a Whig party, despite the fact that there were many stanch Tories in Pittsburgh and its vicinity.

The Virginia-Pennsylvania boundary dispute, which began to boil in 1773, had simmered for over two decades. The governors of the crown colony of Virginia had asserted the claims of the Old Dominion colony to the territory west of Laurel Hill and the proprietaries of Pennsylvania had reiterated their claims to the same region. Neither claimant had made definite steps to extend jurisdiction over the disputed territory until enterprising Virginians made plans to effect settlements in the region and the French began to encroach upon the land in question. Virginia and, to a lesser extent, Pennsylvania aided in repulsing the French because of a desire to retain possession of the area and to acquire the revenue from the sale of the land.

Virginians probably settled first in southwestern Pennsylvania along the Monongahela River, but Pennsylvanians came almost simultaneously to the vicinity of Fort Ligonier, just west of the mountains. By the year 1765 two distinct settlements had been formed. The Virginians, who had procured titles to their land from the governor of Virginia, were dominant in the Monongahela and Youghiogheny valleys and in the region about Pittsburgh; and the Pennsylvanians, who acquired their land from the Penns, occupied territory about Fort Ligonier and Hannastown. Each group of settlers looked to their respective colonial governments to guarantee and protect their titles to the land. In addition to the general ethnic differences there now arose between these two settlements a political rift that was both local and inter-colonial. It existed concurrently with and was interwoven with the conflict between the democratic patriots of western Pennsylvania and the loyalists and conservatives of eastern Pennsylvania. Nor did it subside until the formation of Washington County in 1781 and of Fayette County in 1783, when the Virginians were enabled to enter into Pennsylvania political affairs as a unit and to conduct their own local affairs in the counties.

The conflict in civil jurisdiction, submerged during the French and Indian War, was renewed in 1763 when the king by a royal proclamation forbade his American subjects to settle west of the mountains. This step was taken ostensibly to prevent the hostility of the Indians, but the king's officers were empowered to enforce the provisions of the proclamation. Virginia belonged to the king, and the crown could have used an unfair advantage in restricting Pennsylvania settlers from entering the region and in fostering the cause of Virginia in the dispute. But as a matter of fact, the military commanders were unable to prevent effectively the influx of settlers either from Virginia or Pennsylvania. The organization of Westmoreland County on February 26, 1773, was a direct challenge to the Virginia governor.

Governor Dunmore of Virginia, an autocratic, harsh, provocative individual, precipitated the boundary dispute in 1773 by designating Dr. John Connolly as "Captain, Commandant of the Militia of Pittsburgh and its Dependencies" with instructions to uphold the jurisdiction of Virginia. Connolly, a half brother of General James Ewing, as well as a nephew of George Croghan, the Indian trader, and a son-in-law of Samuel Semple of Pittsburgh, was dictatorial and tactless in carrying out his instructions. He procured control of Fort Pitt in January of 1774, announced his intention of "moving to the House of Burgesses the Necessity of erecting a new County, to include Pittsburgh," and commanded "all Persons in the Dependency of Pittsburgh, to assembly themselves there as a Militia on the 25th Instant"; in other words, the Virginia program proposed the formation of a Virginia county to contest the jurisdiction of the Pennsylvania county of Westmoreland. Because of Connolly's high-handed action, Arthur St. Clair, magistrate of the Pennsylvania county, had him arrested and taken to Hannastown. Upon his promise to return to Hannastown for the April term of court, he was released and permitted to return to Pittsburgh.[1]

[1] For further details see Caley, "The Life and Adventures of Lieutenant-Colonel Connolly," in *Western Pennsylvania Historical Magazine*, 11:10-49, 76-111, 144-179, 225-259 (1928). See also Boucher, *Old and New Westmoreland*, 1:230-234; Beals, "Arthur St. Clair," 11-30; *Pennsylvania Colonial Records*, 10:141.

The political contest waxed warm during the ensuing weeks. Connolly, claiming that the territory was a part of the West Augusta district of Virginia, raised an armed force from the Virginia adherents. With these he appeared at Hannastown and interrupted the sitting of the April court of 1774. The Westmoreland magistrates remonstrated and were adamant; they insisted upon their right to act under the legislative authority of Pennsylvania and they proceeded to do so; upon which action three of them, Andrew McFarlane, Devereaux Smith, and Aeneas Mackay, were arrested by Connolly and sent to Virginia. The governor, however, released them and they returned to Westmoreland and again held court.

The Pennsylvania adherents began a series of public meetings to protest against the activities of Connolly and to petition their legislature for aid. One such meeting was held in Pittsburgh late in May. At that meeting St. Clair, Mackay, Croghan, and "some other of the Inhabitants of Pittsburgh" entered into an "association" for the defense of the county.[2] On June 5 a similar meeting was held at Hannastown, and about forty men marched to Turtle Creek to reënforce the post there.[3] Their ire was up and their instinct for self preservation asserted itself; they did not wait for the governor of Pennsylvania to take steps to protect them. They recognized Governor Penn's jurisdiction over the region but they were not satisfied with his hesitancy to act in the Virginia-Pennsylvania boundary dispute or with his failure to deal adequately with the Indians. To them Governor Dunmore represented the king, and their opposition to him was easily transposed into opposition to the crown. Consequently, they were ready to act in concert with the patriots of eastern Pennsylvania to effect a revolution while they carried on their political controversy on the smaller stage at home.

Connolly continued the struggle with the Pennsylvania settlers, and in June of 1775 he was again arrested and taken to Hannastown. But he was soon dismissed, as in the previous

[2] *Pennsylvania Archives,* first series, 4:504.   [3] *Ibid.,* 4:509.

year, after which he attempted to join Lord Dunmore, who had taken refuge on a British man-of-war. Captain John Neville of Virginia then was appointed commandant of Fort Pitt by the Revolutionary government of Virginia and took over his command on September 11, 1775. He retained his position until 1777, when he was transferred to the eastern theater of war.[4]

Virginia's subsequent attempts to exercise jurisdiction over the region consisted of political and legal tactics. Sessions of the Virginia courts of Augusta County were transferred to Pittsburgh on September 21, 1775, and were held there regularly until November 30, 1776. At that time the district was divided and three separate counties were established—Monongalia, Ohio, and Yohogania. This reorganization was intended to give Virginia a more effective control of the region. Yohogania County included most of the present counties of Allegheny and Washington.[5] Thus a local sectionalism within the region west of the mountains existed until the organization of Fayette County in 1783 under an act of the Pennsylvania legislature. This sectionalism was not sufficiently virulent, however, to lead to violence; nor did it permit the Tories to drive a wedge between the patriots of Westmoreland County and the Virginia counties; but it did lower the effectiveness of the western military campaigns. Apparently this sectionalism produced a situation in which two groups, maintaining separate legal units, worked together for a cause much greater than local ends.

When the oppressive Coercive Acts of 1774, England's answer to the Boston Tea Party of the previous year, persuaded the radical leaders in the seaboard cities that the time had come for action, committees of correspondence were formed, and Charles Thompson, a Whig leader of Philadelphia, forwarded a letter to the various counties in Pennsyl-

[4] Beals, "Arthur St. Clair," 28-30.
[5] Crumrine, "The Boundary Controversy between Pennsylvania and Virginia; 1748-1785," in Carnegie Museum of Pittsburgh, *Annals,* 1:505-524 (1901-02).

vania requesting the people to send representatives to a general meeting. In response, a "very respectable body of people" met in the log courthouse at Hannastown on July 11, 1774, to select delegates. Thus began political assemblages in western Pennsylvania.[6]

A "very respectable body" implied that a respectable number attended and that they were substantial, honest, and sincere even though dressed in homespun. Restless and grumbling about their own colonial government and that of the mother country as well, they straggled in from all directions, some walking, others on horseback, to express themselves in a formal meeting. Here and there among these squatters and debtors were men of education and outstanding ability, men who were to rise to leadership and fame, but in the main they were backwoodsmen. Their meeting in the log courthouse probably lacked the formality and dignity of similar meetings along the Atlantic seaboard but it was not lacking in purpose. They expressed simply their displeasure with the mother country and with their own legislature; and they designated two of their number to journey to Philadelphia to sit among such experienced leaders as Joseph Reed and Thomas Mifflin. Robert Hanna and James Cavet, justices of the peace, the one also a tavern-keeper and the other a county commissioner, were chosen delegates. It is very unlikely that these men did anything of significance in the Philadelphia convention. They probably did not arrive before the opening of the meeting since they had only four days in which to make the journey. They did appear before July 21, however, and signed their names to the instructions that were given to the assembly. Officially, at least, Westmoreland County was a party to the revolutionary movement. A committee of correspondence for the county was probably formed as was done in other counties at that time, but no records of it have been found.

In Pittsburgh on May 16, 1775, a meeting, comprised of the

[6] Lincoln, *Revolutionary Movement in Pennsylvania*, 173, 174; Boucher, *Old and New Westmoreland*, 1:263; Crumrine, *Washington County*, 180.

"inhabitants of that part of Augusta County that lies on the west side of the Laurel Hill," chose a committee of eighteen men for the district, including George Croghan, John Canon, John McCullough, John Gibson, Edward Cook, William Crawford, Samuel Semple, and John Neville, all men of prominence in the region. The committee in turn chose a "standing committee," which was empowered to call the general committee at any time it deemed necessary. Among the resolutions adopted was one that approved of New England "opposing the invaders of American rights and privileges to the utmost extreme" and another to raise fifteen pounds current money to defray the expenses of the delegates of their colony to the general congress.[7]

The following day a similar meeting was held in Hannastown, which adopted resolutions of a radical nature. The remonstrants declared that the Parliament of Great Britain had endeavored to reduce the inhabitants of Massachusetts Bay to a more wretched state of slavery than ever before existed in any state or country; that they would resist and oppose Parliament by every means that God had placed in their power; that they were still loyal to the king; that they would coöperate with a general plan of defense in the event that England should invade America; and that the people of the township should meet on Wednesday, July 24, to accede to an association and to choose officers. These meetings and resolutions, a year prior to the act of independence, suggest that western men, whether citizens of Virginia, as many Pittsburghers believed themselves to be, or of Pennsylvania, as the Hannastown group believed,[8] were not merely reflecting the sentiments of eastern patriots but were already prepared to oppose the crown in a Whig movement. As yet there was no well-defined party, nor was there a single movement in Westmoreland County.

The following year the Revolutionary opponents of the

[7] Craig, *Pittsburgh*, 114-120; Crumrine, *Washington County*, 180.
[8] Craig, *Pittsburgh*, 120-125.

crown decided upon a convention to consider the formation of a new government for Pennsylvania. This action was highly acceptable to the men of the western counties because the proposed reconstruction afforded the possibility of a more democratic government, one in which the western counties would be more equitably represented. Furthermore, all officials and magistrates in Pennsylvania had taken an oath to protect and support the crown, an oath which many of them now desired to terminate. The conference met in Carpenter's Hall in Philadelphia on June 18, 1776.[9]

Edward Cook and James Perry were Westmoreland's delegates in that body. The convention immediately determined to vote by counties, allowing one vote to each county and one for the city of Philadelphia. It next voted to accept the recommendation of the Continental Congress to the effect that in cases where "no government sufficient to the exigencies of their affairs" existed, assemblies and conventions should adopt "such government as shall in the opinion of the representatives of the people, best conduce to the happiness and safety of their constituents in particular, and America in general." It then resolved that the present government in the province was not competent and that a constitutional convention, in the authority of the people only, should meet to formulate a frame of government. Edward Cook served upon the committee that evolved a scheme of representation. Every man who had joined a county association in the colony, according to the committee's recommendation, was to enjoy the franchise, provided he were twenty-one years of age or older, had lived in the province one year or more, and had paid taxes prior to the date of the resolution. The last provision was rescinded for Westmoreland County, because when that county had been organized in 1773 it had been stipulated that the people should be exempted from taxation for three years. The convention set Monday, July 8, as the date for the election of delegates to the constitutional convention and July 15 as the time for the

[9] Pennsylvania Constitutional Convention, 1776, *Proceedings,* 35.

assembling of the delegates in the city of Philadelphia.[10]

The Westmoreland delegates and the Westmoreland people were enthusiastic about the constitutional convention, as were the people from all the newer counties, because each county and the city of Philadelphia were accorded equal representation. Immediately the western counties transferred any allegiance they may have had for the old conservative-controlled assembly to the convention because of the weight they would have in the deliberations of the latter body. The conservative assembly had overplayed its hand and the patriots, or democrats, were now in the saddle.[11]

Westmoreland County, for the purpose of the election of delegates, was divided into two districts: one for those people in the territory south of the Youghiogheny, who were to vote at Sparks's Fort; and one for all others, who were to vote at Hannastown. The eight men chosen by Westmoreland County to aid in making the first state constitution were prominent patriots in the region and democratic in their beliefs. Thomas Barr, a native Pennsylvanian, born in Lancaster County, had migrated to Derry Township, Westmoreland County, in 1770. He had already been active in forming companies to fight the Indians and was to serve as a justice of the peace and a member of the Pennsylvania Assembly. Edward Cook, a farmer, distiller, storekeeper, and slave owner who had lands on the Monongahela and Youghiogheny rivers, had sprung from English parents in the Cumberland Valley in Pennsylvania and had arrived in Westmoreland County in 1772. He was subsequently a frontier soldier, justice of the peace of Westmoreland and Washington counties, an associate judge in Fayette County, interested in establishing the Pittsburgh Academy in 1787, and an agent in terminating the Whiskey Insurrection. James Perry is less well known although, like Cook, he was a member of the provincial conference that met in Carpenter's Hall at Philadelphia on June 18,

---

[10] Pennsylvania Constitutional Convention, 1776, *Proceedings,* 37-41.
[11] Selsam, *Pennsylvania Constitution of 1776,* 134.

1776. Later he moved from his home near the cabin of John Fraser at the mouth of Turtle Creek to Kentucky.

John McClelland, like Thomas Barr, was born in Lancaster County from whence he came to that portion of Westmoreland that later fell within Fayette. Later he represented Westmoreland in the assembly and took part in the Whiskey Insurrection. Christopher Lobenger, born of German parents in Lancaster County, came to Mount Pleasant Township, Westmoreland, in 1772 and later served in the general assembly. John Carmichael had come from Cumberland County, settled near Redstone Creek, built a mill and distillery and later, in 1777, served in the assembly. John Moore, another product of Lancaster County, was a farmer and carpenter, a justice of the peace in 1777-85, president judge in 1785-90, and a senator from the district of Allegheny and Westmoreland for the year 1792. Colonel James Smith was an Indian fighter, ranger, associator, Revolutionary soldier, and later, in 1776 and 1777, a member of the assembly. These eight men, born in and conditioned by the social and political atmosphere of the newer counties, were essentially democratic and patriotic. With the exception of James Perry, who for some reason seems not to have attended the convention, they joined forces with their revolutionary friends from the eastern counties to produce what has been termed the most democratic constitution in the world.[12]

The constitution consisted of two parts, a bill of rights and a frame of government. The bill of rights advanced the doctrines of personal equality and inalienable rights, freedom of worship, government for the benefit of the governed, protection and security of the people, freedom of speech, and the rights of assemblage and petition. Under the new frame of government all property qualifications for the franchise were removed, and any "free man" having sufficient interest for and an attachment to the state might offer himself as a candidate for office. The supreme legislative power was vested in a single

[12] Sketches of these men are in Boucher, *Old and New Westmoreland*, 271-274.

house, the general assembly, which was elected annually and whose members might serve only four years in seven and only two years in succession. Representation was based upon the number of taxables. The executive consisted of a supreme executive council of twelve, whose president was a mere presiding officer and whose membership included one representative from each of the eleven counties and one from the city of Philadelphia. An unusual institution in American government, a body of censors, was to be elected every seventh year for a term of one year to "enquire whether the constitution has been preserved inviolate in every part; and whether the legislative and executive branches of the government have performed their duty, as guardians of the people, or assumed to themselves or exercised other or greater powers than they are entitled to by the constitution."[13] In it alone was vested the power to institute proceedings to amend the constitution.

Ninety-five of the ninety-six delegates were present at the signing of the constitution; twenty-three did not sign, and five of those twenty-three were from the western counties.[14] Apparently every member from Westmoreland County, except the absent James Perry, belonged to the ultra-democratic group and attached his name to the constitution. Not only were these men democratically inclined themselves, but they reflected the democracy of their constituents. Furthermore, their alliance with the eastern democrats to effect the constitution of 1776 was indicative of the attitude that they and their constituents would assume for many years to come. Exuberant and exultant in their triumph over the aristocratic element in the eastern counties, they determined to cling tenaciously to their new constitution which accorded them increased weight in the legislature and gave them a voice in the executive department.

Neither the people of Westmoreland County nor their friends just east of the mountains were content to rest after

[13] Pennsylvania Constitutional Convention, 1776, *Proceedings*, 64.
[14] Selsam, *Pennsylvania Constitution of 1776*, 164.

this political victory. They were still confronted by the danger of Indian raids, by the local sectionalism between the Virginia settlers in the Monongahela country and the Pennsylvania pioneers in the vicinity of Hannastown, by an unfavorable balance of trade with the eastern merchants, by a scarcity of money, and by poor means of transportation. Eastern merchants and bankers held the whip hand economically and financially, if not politically, and soon they were to gather the economic fruit of the Revolution and to oppose the ultra-democratic constitution that they had helped to make. Consequently, the western men continued their alliance with the democrats, now designated as Constitutionalists, and followed in the state legislature the vigorous leadership of George Bryan and Robert Whitehill in opposition to the aristocratic Anti-Constitutionalist group led by James Wilson and Robert Morris.[15] This alliance enabled the democratic element to dominate the assembly for a decade, although their control was seriously challenged in 1780 and 1781.

During the years of the Revolution, the Indian depredations raised grave apprehensions in Westmoreland County. There was not a single year from 1774 to 1783 that petitions and supplications were not made to the assembly and the executive council for aid against the Indians. The minutes of the executive council bear ample evidence of the pressing nature of the problem.[16] But it must be remembered that those were years of warfare for Philadelphia and that it was more urgent to drive General Howe from eastern Pennsylvania than it was to repel the Indians in the partially settled region of western Pennsylvania. Regardless of the inability of the government to aid them, the harassed citizens west of the mountains remained loyal, but they were developing an independence that smacked of sectionalism.

Their dissatisfaction was increased by the long-drawn-out controversy over the boundary dispute with Virginia. The

[15] Konkle, *George Bryan*, 189 ff.
[16] *Pennsylvania Colonial Records*, 11:261, 262; 12:246; 13:83; 14:185.

final definition of the boundary in 1780 and the organization of Washington County in the following year, however, paved the way for the elimination of the sectional struggle in western Pennsylvania. The new county included the territory west of the Monongahela River, the region in which the Virginia partisans had been strongest. But the expectation that this arrangement would permit those who had been rivals of Westmoreland to enter Pennsylvania politics harmoniously and as a unit was not realized immediately.[17]

Washington County was established on March 28, 1781, and a few days later, on April 2, Thomas Scott was named its prothonotary, James Marshel was commissioned as its lieutenant, and John Canon and Daniel Leet were designated as its sublieutenants. Subsequently, on June 16, elections were held for the purpose of choosing "two fit persons for justices of the peace for each township." From the names submitted the supreme executive council appointed one justice for each township. Before the council could act, however, a letter signed by Isaac Israel, John Canon, John McDowell, and others prominent on the frontier protested the election on the grounds that many men had been absent from home engaged in the expedition of George Rogers Clark in the West. But the end of the local question was in sight, and it mattered little whether Virginia or Pennsylvania advocates were selected for the offices, because in either group the majority were democrats and pioneers. Furthermore, the addition of the assemblymen and councilor from the new county was particularly desirable to the eastern leaders in 1781.[18]

The Constitutionalists, successful in 1776 in the formation of the constitution, consolidated their gains during the years from 1776 to 1779. Their leadership was not unchallenged, however. Joseph Reed, George Bryan, Robert Whitehill, and their friends found it necessary to use various means and de-

[17] Crumrine, "The Boundary Controversy between Pennsylvania and Virginia; 1748-1785," in Carnegie Museum of Pittsburgh, *Annals*, 1:523, 524 (1901-02).
[18] Crumrine, *Washington County*, 223-232.

vices to hold control of the assembly and to cultivate the western men to offset the onslaughts of James Wilson, Robert Morris, and George Clymer. The democrats were aided by the fact that the Tories were deprived of the franchise and by the fact that the presence of the British army in Philadelphia during 1777-78 increased the patriotic fervor of the western men. Moreover, the leadership of George Bryan as vice president of the council was a vital force in their domination. In the early part of 1779 the assembly decisively defeated an effort on the part of the conservatives to call a constitutional convention by a vote of forty-seven to seven. And on October 12 of the same year an election was held in which an overwhelming victory for the Constitutionalists resulted. Even Robert Morris and George Clymer were displaced. It was the peak of democratic strength, and the party rode hard during the next few months; on November 24, 1779, by a vote of forty to seven it passed a divesting act to vest the property of the proprietaries in the commonwealth of Pennsylvania. The Act for the Gradual Emancipation of Slaves was passed on March 1, 1780, by a vote of thirty-four to twenty-one; and while the Westmoreland assemblymen voted almost invariably with the Constitutionalists, curiously enough they opposed this act.[19]

At the time of the Constitutionalists' greatest strength and activity, however, events were transpiring that were to weaken them. For one thing, their leader, George Bryan, was appointed to the state supreme court on April 5, 1780, and was thus removed from the immediate field of politics. Secondly, in the spring of 1780, Wilson, Morris, and their friends attempted to establish a bank to facilitate the supplying of funds to the army. This movement was so popular that it reached fruition on July 17 in the formation, under a state charter, of the Bank of Pennsylvania, which enjoyed such success that by October it met with widespread approval. As a result, Wilson and his friends were strengthened and the Constitutionalists weakened. The following year, 1781, the bank was trans-

[19] Konkle, *George Bryan,* 171, 172, 199, 213-215.

formed into a national bank, the Bank of North America, chartered by Congress. Robert Morris was placed in the position of financier-general, a position in which he could put the Bank of North America to great political use.

Emboldened by their increasing popularity, the Anti-Constitutionalists made an attack on George Bryan of the supreme court by reducing his salary to three hundred pounds. Furthermore, the emission of three hundred thousand pounds of state currency the following year diminished the value of the old currency, and George Bryan, receiving a fixed salary, was placed in a difficult position. His western friends favored cheap currency because the pioneers had debts to pay, whereas he desired a currency with a fixed value. The Anti-Constitutionalists had embarrassed the Constitutionalists again. The national spirit, increased by the fall of Charleston in 1780 and evidenced in the movement to establish the Bank of North America, surged higher with the glad news of the surrender of Cornwallis at Yorktown. The Constitutionalists were hard pressed.[20] Thenceforward to 1783 the Anti-Constitutionalists, followers of Wilson and Morris, continued their attacks upon the judiciary in an effort to weaken Bryan's prestige and power; they constantly supported the national bank; and they hoped that their policies would enable them to gain control of the council of censors, scheduled to meet in 1783. They had high anticipations of dominating that body, of uprooting the constitution, and of producing a new, conservative one more pliable to the interests and desires of the aristocratic society in the eastern counties. The outlook was not without promise for them although the representatives of the western counties were steadfast in their support of the existing plan of government.

Despite the efforts of the Anti-Constitutionalists, one additional democratic county was erected in time to return a stanch defender of the constitution of 1776 to the council of censors. Fayette County was established by an act of assem-

[20] Konkle, *George Bryan*, 232, 233.

bly of September 26, 1783. The boundary, as defined by the act, separated the territory of Westmoreland County between the Monongahela and Youghiogheny rivers and a straight line joining these rivers drawn due east from the mouth of Speers Run on the Monongahela. That part of the present county that lies east of the Youghiogheny was not included until the following year. The addition of this territory to Fayette County proved to be most fortunate as a political step because it made John Smilie, a democrat with political experience, who had just arrived and taken up his residence on the north side of the Youghiogheny, a resident of Fayette County rather than of Westmoreland. Thereafter he could coöperate with William Findley of Westmoreland County in the legislature and in political councils without having to contest the elections with him. Two strong westerners were always available instead of one, even on the supreme executive council.

From 1781 to 1783 the settlers had sought a separate county because of the inconvenience encountered in transacting their legal business in Hannastown. Now they were in a position to send a member to the assembly, one to the supreme executive council, and a belated member to the council of censors. John Smilie, for many years to come a pillar of democracy, first in the county, then in the state, and later in the nation, was their choice, first for the council of censors and later, from 1784 to 1785, for the assembly. Isaac Meason was their first choice, in 1783, for the supreme executive council.[21] The organization of this county also tended to placate the Virginia partisans who lived in that region, thus putting an end to the local struggle that had existed for many years and solidifying the political strength of the western democrats.

At the close of the American Revolution, then, western Pennsylvania consisted of three counties: Westmoreland, Washington, and Fayette. The people, nearly all pioneer farmers, had joined in the American Revolution and had rid themselves of the Tories. Psychologically, they had developed

[21] Ellis, *Fayette County*, 129-132, 154, 155.

a singleness of thought and purpose resulting in a unity of political action that gave them a faint resemblance to the Whig party of the Revolution. But because of the Revolutionary psychology and because of their environment and their local problems, they became more radical democrats than their friends east of the mountains. Revolutionary writers and philosophers had created a fervor for liberty, independence, and self-government and had utilized the rights-of-man theory to justify the Revolution. That doctrine was wholly acceptable to the western farmer and seemed to be an interpretation of his natural condition. The Revolution, as the democratic Pennsylvanians observed it, appeared to be not only a struggle against the unjust domination of England over the colonies, but also a struggle against domination of the colony by the conservative classes of Pennsylvania. In both controversies the democratic elements were triumphantly conscious of success.

The close of the Revolution brought a certain release to the men of the back counties, who were free to proceed with their plans without the charge of being unpatriotic. They were no longer required to submerge their interests in a general cause. These interests were determined by local and environmental conditions. They wanted cheap paper money because they were in debt; they opposed the Bank of North America because their economically disadvantageous position caused them to fear the domination of a financial power; they desired protection against the Indians; and they opposed taxation ostensibly because they received little benefit from the government but really because they had an innate objection to taxation; and they wanted cheap land.

BACK-COUNTRY DEMOCRACY ORGANIZES

CHAPTER THREE

AT the close of the Revolution the people of western Pennsylvania occupied a strategic position that permitted them to advance measures in the legislature to solve their problems. The wisest course in the achievement of their program lay in a continued allegiance with the democrats of the eastern counties and the consolidation of their own strength. They were able to make great strides in such consolidation because this back-country democracy was blessed with vigorous, able, young political leaders who were alert and ready and because the formation of Washington and Fayette counties increased the number of local officeholders who could be used as a nucleus for democratic organization.

The leaders of this back-country democracy make an impressive array as they pass in review. Many of them were Revolutionary soldiers, some of them were officers, and nearly all had a belligerent contempt for Alexander Hamilton's aristocratic "Society of Cincinnati." A majority of them were land owners and farmers, and some were even prominent landholders, although none of them were speculators such as Robert Morris and George Washington. The charge could not be made that although they represented the people they were "not of the people." Their interests were the same as those of their constituents.

Old Westmoreland's coterie of leaders stands out in bold relief. William Findley, John Baird, and William Todd, two Scotch-Irishmen and an Irishman, formed a triumvirate that was all powerful in the politics of that county for a decade following the war. All farmers, all democrats, all fighters, all neighbors (they lived to the southeast of Greensburg and within a few miles of each other), they were popular with their own people and they gave their county an incredible weight in the state government.

William Findley was destined to become the political dean of the three, both in length of service and in political significance. Grandson of a native Scotchman, he was born in Ulster, Ireland, in 1741. After receiving an adequate although informal education, he emigrated to Pennsylvania in 1763 with the intention of becoming a farmer. Indian depredations along the frontier deterred him from his original purpose, and he taught school for several years in what is now Franklin County, then a part of Cumberland. His military activities in the Revolution were obscured by his political activities, which included continuous service on the county committee of safety. In 1782 he moved to Westmoreland County, where he took up land near the present site of Youngstown. For almost forty years, until his death in 1821, he commuted to and from his home and Philadelphia, Harrisburg, and Washington, dividing his time between his large family and his continuous political duties. Here is one politician who the historian can believe was really sincere when he declined to run for reëlection to Congress in 1799 with the assertion that he preferred to spend the winter with his family. But his friends virtually commandeered him for the state senate because the prestige of his name would aid in the election of Thomas McKean as governor and in the triumph of Jefferson's party in the state.

His popularity was a source of great irritation to his political rivals, especially to the witty, literary Pittsburgh lawyer, Hugh Henry Brackenridge, who never understood the reasons for Findley's success. A weaver and farmer, reputedly unlearned, with no marked ability for speaking, Findley outmaneuvered the scholarly lawyer in nearly all their contests and, in the ratifying convention, bested even James Wilson on a point of history. The explanation of his strength rests upon many factors. As his writings attest, he was not the "clodhopper" that his enemies portrayed him to be. He was "of his people," a fact that endeared him to the Westmoreland pioneers; he fought for the interests of his region; he was earnest in his democracy. A large, beardless man with a florid complexion, tasteful in garb, and wearing a large white beaver hat, he visited the mills, the stills, and the sessions of court to converse upon current political questions. He had a winning way with people, and he was a quiet but effective campaigner.[1]

One of Findley's closest neighbors and stanchest associates was William Todd, an Irishman, who had first settled in Bedford County in 1765 but had removed to Westmoreland County before the close of the Revolution. He was a man of promise even before he went to Westmoreland to settle upon the land that he had obtained by warrant. He had already served as one of the judges of election, as county commissioner, and as justice of the peace in Bedford County. He represented Westmoreland, subsequently, in the assembly and in both the ratifying convention and the convention of 1790; he served as an associate judge in his county; and he closed his political career in the state senate.[2]

John Baird, a Scotch-Irishman, "a man of mark west of the Alleghenies," lived on his farm only a few miles to the southwest of Findley and Todd. Born about 1740 in the part of Lancaster County that was later included in Dauphin, he came across the mountains about 1770 and took up land in what afterwards became Huntingdon Township. Before 1771 he had served in his county as an overseer of the poor, as county commissioner, and as justice of the peace. During the Revolution he devoted himself to recruiting militiamen. In later years he served as a member of the supreme executive council, a member of the Pennsylvania State House of Representa-

---

[1] For a full account of Findley's part in state politics see C. Schramm, "William Findley in Pennsylvania Politics."
[2] McMaster and Stone, *Pennsylvania and the Federal Constitution*, 754.

tives, and as an associate judge of Westmoreland County.[3]

While the collective strength of these three neighbors gave them a preponderance of influence in the county, it did not represent the entire political weight of Westmoreland. To the south of them, near Laurelville, lived Christopher Lobenger, Pennsylvania Dutchman, who had already served on the Revolutionary committee of correspondence and in the constitutional convention of 1776 and was to serve in the Pennsylvania House of Representatives. Only a few miles northeast of Greensburg were two more colleagues, Thomas Barr and John Moore. Both of them had migrated from Lancaster County to Westmoreland before the Revolution; both of them had served in the constitutional convention of 1776; and both of them were to hold the offices of justice of the peace and after 1790 associate judge of Westmoreland County. Lobenger, Barr, and Moore were proper company politically and congenial friends for Findley, Todd, and Baird, and all contributed to the rise of back-country democracy.

The Pittsburgh area of Westmoreland in 1783 did not lack able men but it furnished less positive leadership than did the Hannastown section. The men in the western part of the county had fitted into the Virginia organization before 1780 and naturally required a few years to find their niches in the Quaker state. Moreover, Pittsburgh's early settlers were removed from their county seat some thirty miles and thus handicapped politically. Furthermore, they were divided between agricultural and commercial pursuits and were traders and professional soldiers rather than politicians. George Croghan, Samuel Semple, and John Gibson were prominent men in trade and border warfare but they were not politicians in the strict sense.[4] And finally, the two most promising politicians at the forks of the Ohio in 1783, John Neville and Hugh

[3] McMaster and Stone, *Pennsylvania and the Federal Constitution*, 714, 715.
[4] A complete account of Croghan's activities is in Volwiler, *George Croghan;* for material on Semple (also known as Sample), see Dahlinger, *Pittsburgh,* 78; and on Gibson, see Gibson, "General John Gibson," in *Western Pennsylvania Historical Magazine,* 5:298-310 (1922).

Henry Brackenridge, were temperamentally and environmentally unfitted to assume democratic leadership in the region.

General John Neville, the more prominent one of the two, already enjoyed the prestige of a long military career. As a young Virginian of twenty-three he had served in the Braddock expedition; he had participated in the Dunmore expedition of 1774; and he had fought in the Virginia ranks during the Revolution, first as commandant at Fort Pitt and later as a colonel of the fourth regiment, which entitled him to become a charter member of the Virginia Society of Cincinnati. After the Revolution he began the development of an estate in the Chartiers Valley upon land that he had acquired some years earlier. Like the Virginian he was, he built a mansion, "Bower Hill," some seven miles southwest of Pittsburgh, stocked his acres with slaves, and engaged in politics. He sat in the supreme executive council, the ratifying convention, and the assembly, and served as the inspector of revenue for the fourth district of Pennsylvania, which included the western counties. Birth and experience coöperated to make him an aristocrat even in a frontier environment, and since some of his neighbors opposed aristocracy he never quite gained complete domination of the district in which he lived.[5]

Hugh Henry Brackenridge, an adroit, sarcastic Pittsburgh lawyer, was a democrat but a difficult one for his friends. His parents had brought him, a five-year-old boy, from Scotland to York County, Pennsylvania, in 1753. There the transplanted Scotch boy grew to young manhood, conditioned by the relatively simple environment of his adopted home. He attended Princeton College, where he was a classmate of Philip Freneau, James Madison, and William Bradford—worthy classmates for any student. After he was graduated in 1772 he taught school, served as a chaplain during the Revolution, edited a magazine for a year, studied law under "the celebrated Samuel Chase of Annapolis and was admitted to the bar in Philadelphia in 1780." The following year he went to

[5] For a more complete account see Felton, "General John Neville."

Pittsburgh to pursue his career and fortune. Henceforth his activities baffled his contemporaries. Philosophically he was a democrat, yet his cultural training caused him to have a contempt for the unlettered democracy of the West. A satirical literary ability, which he utilized unstintingly in writing essays and poetry for the *Pittsburgh Gazette,* frequently got him into difficulties because the people misunderstood him. To them and to many history students he appeared to be an unpredictable sophist; at one time he was a thorn in the side of democracy; at another he pricked the Federalists; and he finally found a haven in the ranks of McKean and Jefferson when the former appointed him to the bench of the Supreme Court of Pennsylvania in 1799 in return for services rendered to the party. Yet western Pennsylvania democrats never fully trusted him nor did he ever deeply appreciate them.[6]

Democracy was well represented by Fayette County men in 1783. There the leader was John Smilie, an Irishman, a farmer and a friend of Findley. He migrated from his homeland as a young man and arrived in Lancaster County before the Revolution. He began his political career in 1775, at thirty-three years of age, as a vigorous democrat and patriot and closed it almost forty years later, a venerable Democratic congressman, at the age of seventy-one. Smilie served in the Carpenter's Hall conference of 1775 and again in 1776; he sat in the assembly for Lancaster County in 1778 and 1779; he moved to Westmoreland County in 1781 and two years later served that county in the council of censors until Fayette County was organized, after which he represented the new county in the same body. For thirty years thereafter he served in the assembly, the supreme executive council, the ratifying convention of 1787, the constitutional convention of 1789-90, the upper house of the new state legislature, and the United States Congress and finally died in harness in 1813. Like Findley, he met his constituents on equal terms, talked

---

[6] The best account of Brackenridge's activities is in Newlin, *Hugh Henry Brackenridge.*

with them about crops, Indians, and politics and held their confidence.[7]

Smilie was buttressed by a number of able men in his county. Prominent among them was Edward Cook, who lived on his large estate in the extreme northern part, near the Monongahela River. In addition to serving as a member of the committee of conference that met at Carpenter's Hall on June 18, 1776, he commanded a battalion on the frontier in 1781 and was county lieutenant for the years of 1782 and 1783; he served as a justice of the peace in both Westmoreland and Fayette counties; and after the constitution of 1790 was put into effect, he became an associate judge of Fayette County. Cook was a prominent lay figure in the Presbyterian church and was deeply interested in education; as a trustee, he lent his influence and time to the Pittsburgh Academy. His last notable public work was rendered during the Whiskey Insurrection of 1794 when he labored to bring the uprising to a close.

Smilie's most able colleague in 1784 was probably Nathaniel Breading, a scion of Irish ancestors, whose parents had removed to Pennsylvania in about 1728. Breading received a classical education and taught school for a few years before the Revolution but engaged in actual military activities during the years 1777 and 1778. He moved to Lucerne Township, Fayette County, in 1784 and almost immediately was made a justice of the peace and in the following year one of the judges of the court of common pleas. After aiding in the running of the boundary lines between Pennsylvania and Virginia, he served as a member of the supreme executive council; he was a member of the Pennsylvania convention to ratify the federal Constitution; and in 1791 he became an associate judge in his county, in which position he participated in the Whiskey Insurrection by using his legal prerogatives in an effort to preserve law and order.[8]

There were other men in this county who contributed to the

[7] United States Congress, *Biographical Directory*, p. 1533.
[8] Ellis, *Fayette County*, 650.

development of back-country democracy throughout the next fifteen years, but their names had not appeared in conventions before 1784, and the ablest of them, Albert Gallatin, had not yet become a resident of Pennsylvania.[9] Thomas Clare, who lived at the mouth of Georges Creek; Ephraim Douglass, a farmer and neighbor of Gallatin and a tax collector; and James Finley, a prominent preacher who was to become a member of the Pennsylvania House of Representatives in 1794, were all active in politics although Finley was the only one to hold an office of significance.[10] The Fayette County men headed by Smilie and Breading presented almost if not quite as capable leadership as did the Westmoreland County democrats. The addition of the young Genevan, Albert Gallatin, in 1788 made the Fayette County representation very strong.

Washington County's leaders at the close of the Revolution were as able as those of the neighboring counties, but they were not so completely in accord in their political ideas. They were all interested in the development of western Pennsylvania and stood together as a rule upon such issues as protection against the Indians, navigation of the Mississippi, and the clearing of the land titles, but they disagreed on the question of a strong central government. John Neville, of the Westmoreland group, who owned land that extended into Washington County belonged to the well-to-do aristocratic class which was antipathetic to back-country democracy. He represented Washington County in the ratifying convention of 1787 and was one of only two western Pennsylvanians to sign the document of ratification.

Thomas Scott, who was born in Lancaster County in 1739 and had settled with his family on Dunlaps Creek near the Monongahela in 1770, was the only other western man who signed the ratification of the constitution. He had served as a justice of the peace for Westmoreland County in 1774, in the

[9] H. Adams, *Life of Albert Gallatin*, 3, 7, 10, 16, 26, 46, 60, 62.
[10] *Ibid.*, 62; Crumrine, *Washington County*, 225-230; Ellis, *Fayette County*, 234.

assembly in 1776, and on the supreme executive council from 1777 to 1780 as a Westmoreland member. When Washington County was organized in 1781, he was appointed prothonotary in the new county, a position that he held until 1789. The previous year he had been elected to Congress on a general ticket that was comprised of Federalists; he was western Pennsylvania's first congressman.[11]

Of similar political sentiment was the celebrated preacher, John McMillan, frequently referred to as the high priest of Presbyterianism in the region. He never held a political office but he did not lose an opportunity to comment upon public questions to members of his congregation. Upon occasions he closed his regular religious services and before his congregation could disperse, plunged immediately into a discussion of politics. Undoubtedly he had great influence with his parishioners and probably with ministers of other congregations because he urged other preachers to follow the same course with their flocks. The exact weight that these clerics had in politics in the region is difficult to estimate but it was not negligible.[12]

Despite the influence of Neville, Scott, McMillan, and others, Washington County had men of democratic inclinations in 1783. James Marshel, born in Lancaster County in 1753, settled in Cross Creek Township before the Revolution. He served as a captain of the militia and as a justice of the peace in Westmoreland County. When the county of Washington was organized he was commissioned as one of its presiding judges; he acted as sheriff from 1784 to 1787; he was a delegate to the ratifying convention in 1787; he served as a member of the assembly from 1789 to 1790; and he was deeply involved in the Whiskey Insurrection as one of the rebels.[13]

But in Washington County, as in Westmoreland and

[11] United States Congress, *Biographical Directory*, p. 1502.
[12] Crumrine, *Washington County*, 871; *Centenary Memorial of ... Presbyterianism in Western Pennsylvania*, 11-34.
[13] Crumrine, *Washington County*, 728.

Fayette counties, it is probable that the most pungent leadership was furnished by a group of three men. David Bradford, John McDowell, and James Allison, brothers-in-law, who settled originally in the Chartiers Valley, were among a group of approximately twenty families that came to Pennsylvania in 1773 and 1774. David Bradford was born in Maryland and was the son of James Bradford, who was reputedly an immigrant from Ireland. He was admitted to the bar of Washington County and in 1783 was appointed deputy attorney-general for the county. He may well be described as a violent and rash democrat for the part he took in the Whiskey Insurrection, but he was a fiery leader and popular in his own county, which elected him to the assembly in 1792. James Allison, married to one of Bradford's sisters, came to western Pennsylvania in 1774 and settled on Chartiers Creek. He served as a justice of the peace in the county for many years, took a prominent part in the Whiskey Insurrection, and served in the state house of representatives from 1798 to 1802. John McDowell, born in Ireland, married to another of Bradford's sisters, likewise arrived in 1773 and settled on Chartiers Creek. The most prominent of the three brothers-in-law, he served as a justice of the peace in Yohogania County, as a commissioner of Washington County in 1781, in the council of censors in 1783-84, and in the state house of representatives from 1798 to 1802 and closed his career as an associate judge of the county from 1802 to 1809. These three men, closely related and living near each other, had ample opportunity to effect a family machine that was very powerful in Washington County.[14]

A few miles to the east of Chartiers Creek, David Redick, an Irishman, took up land. He had married the daughter of Jonathan Hoge, brother of David Hoge, Sr., who later came to Washington. Redick was admitted to the bar of Washington County in 1782, was a member of the supreme executive council from 1786 to 1788, was appointed prothonotary of the

[14] Crumrine, *Washington County*, 204, 707, 869, 870.

county in 1791, and, naturally, was deep in the Whiskey Insurrection. He was less radical than Bradford and realized the necessity of acquiescing to the demands of the federal government. He and Findley were chosen to confer with Washington in 1794 in an unsuccessful effort to prevent the march of the army into western Pennsylvania. Even though he was a stanch democrat and was deeply interested in western people he acquiesced in the acceptance of the constitution more readily than Findley, Smilie, or Gallatin.[15]

There were other political leaders of less prominence in the county, as well as a group of younger men, who were later to become famous. James Edgar, one of the early settlers, served in the ratifying convention of 1787. John Canon, probably a Virginian, the founder of Canonsburg, was a prominent local leader although he did not aspire to political offices outside the county. James Ross, a young lawyer admitted to the bar in 1784, was merely getting acquainted in the county. Alexander Addison, like Ross, a protégé of John McMillan, probably did not arrive in the county until 1785. These younger men, however, were not democrats and were destined eventually to hand over their county to the Federalists. But for the time being Washington County's democrats held the county in the ranks of back-country democracy.[16]

The organization of newer counties and the creation thereby of local offices enhanced and integrated the leadership and significance of these western men. Officeholders, then as now, formed the skeleton of a political organization, and even in frontier counties there were many offices to be filled. Some local officers were elected by their peers, some were appointed by the supreme executive council, and others were nominated by their constituents and then chosen by the council. The justices of the peace, at least one for each township in the three counties of Westmoreland, Washington, and Fayette, were

[15] Crumrine, *Washington County*, 479.
[16] Material on Edgar, Canon, and Addison is in Crumrine, *Washington County*, 736 226, 485. For material on Ross, see Brownson, *James Ross*.

WILLIAM FINDLEY

*From a portrait in the possession of the Historical Society of Pennsylvania, by
Albert Rosenthal, after Charles Wilson Peale*

nominated by the electors, who chose two, from whom the council selected one. The justices, as a whole, were men of integrity. Some of them were men of intelligence and legal training but many were tavern-keepers, farmers, or craftsmen and untrained in law. Virtually every one of them, however, was imbued with back-country democracy, and his log cabin court room served as a meeting place in which he might expound his political theories or at least denounce aristocracy.

The justices of the peace established the early courts, to which many people came, either to observe the trials or to visit. The court day was an occasion for a social gathering at which politics was a pertinent topic of conversation. At a time when a convocation was not readily obtainable, the congregation of individuals in and about the court room or those who lolled about the courtyard furnished an audience for a politician, and the people, returning to their homes, served as vehicles to disseminate information. This agency for spreading political propaganda was undoubtedly slow but it was effective, because, as a rule, the candidate met his constituents under favorable circumstances. They came to the court meetings in a holiday mood, brought their food with them, warmed themselves with home-distilled whiskey which they did not want taxed, and were in a receptive mood. On a few occasions when they attended court meetings in a turbulent mood, they were even more receptive to subtle, or not so subtle attacks on any movement antagonistic to their interests. In days of extreme agitation, they flocked naturally to the courthouse, even when court was not in session, to pass resolutions and adopt remonstrances. Furthermore, they failed to understand why any of them were required to stand trial in any other court than their own local one, and it was a source of resentment that justice in federal courts was not carried to them instead of their being carried to it across the mountains and at their own expense. Justices of the peace and court days remained effective agencies for political campaigning, and the local administration of justice remained a subject for campaigns for more than two decades after the Revolution.[17]

The elective officers, however—the coroner, sheriff and, later, the three county commissioners—had more influence in shaping political policies. Of particular significance were the commissioners, who were the business managers of the county, and the sheriff, who enforced the laws and conducted the sheriff's sales of land upon which installments and taxes had not been paid. Since land problems and taxation were pressing questions in the newer counties, the sheriff's office was an important one and its occupant a significant figure. A sheriff whose sympathies rested with those landowners who wanted lax administration of enforced sales was certain to have a strong following in his county. Since there was only one sheriff for each county, his weight as a political figure was great.

During these early years the militia officers, lieutenants, and sublieutenants of the counties were appointed by the supreme executive council and were less significant politically than at a later date. Even so, the fact that they were in charge of muster days (ideal occasions for political propaganda) and of the defense of the counties made them men of weight. About the turn of the century they became increasingly important because they were elective officers and in some instances the election of brigade officers assumed the proportions of a regular legislative election. They, with the other local officials—the coroner, prothonotary, commissioner, and sheriff—formed a skeleton for organization and leadership in the counties.[18]

The county's representatives in the state legislature and on the supreme executive council completed the list of officials. The members of the assembly were elected yearly and were eligible to serve not more than two years in succession nor more than four in seven.[19] That provision in itself precluded a machine of the modern type. The western men stood to-

[17] Pennsylvania Constitutional Convention, 1776, *Proceedings,* 62. For the steps in the organization of the courts see Crumrine, *Washington County,* 228-231.
[18] Pennsylvania Constitutional Convention, 1776, *Proceedings,* 62; Crumrine, *Washington County,* 224.
[19] Pennsylvania Constitutional Convention, 1776, *Proceedings,* 57, 58.

gether stanchly, however, and formed a determined democratic block in the assembly. In addition, they served as a link between eastern democrats and their own people and as such played a prominent part in the political development of the western counties. Each county had a representative on the supreme executive council, which in 1783 was composed of thirteen members and in 1784 of fifteen.[20] It was a somewhat unwieldy executive but there was rarely a full attendance, and under such circumstances the relative weight of any one member became greater. A strong western man of the experience of William Findley or John Smilie thereby had an incommensurate influence in the council. The appointive power of the council further increased the individual member's political significance in his own county, a fact that explains to a great extent the development of a strong rugged democracy in western Pennsylvania and the role that Findley and Smilie had in that development.

There were factors that served as deterrents to the organization of a party west of the mountains in 1783, factors that retarded but did not prevent the rise of a strong political movement. The lack of communication, the absence of newspapers, poor transportation, inadequate postal facilities, and a paucity of social gatherings lowered the efficiency of political organization. The increase in the number of churches during the seventies and eighties, the increasing number and popularity of taverns, the court meetings and militia muster rolls served to offset these disadvantages to some extent, and despite the retarding factors a vigorous vocal democracy grew in the back counties. Their leaders were able and quick to utilize any opportunity to weld and organize democratic sentiment. The year 1783 presented favorable opportunities.

In state politics at the close of the Revolution the battle was fierce along three fronts. The Wilsonian, conservative, Anti-Constitutional group had high hopes that were riding on the rising tide of sentiment for the national bank. These men

[20] Pennsylvania Constitutional Convention, 1776, *Proceedings*, 60.

planned to capture the assembly, the supreme executive council, and the council of censors, which, according to the constitution of 1776, was to convene in the latter part of that year. Control of the assembly and of the council would permit Wilson and Robert Morris to consummate their bank plans, and control of the council of censors would enable them to revise the ultrademocratic constitution of 1776. Success for them in all these plans would mean the complete collapse of the radical group—Bryan, Whitehill, Findley, and Smilie. The democrats, on the other hand, hoped to capture the assembly, council, and council of censors first, then demolish the national bank's state charter and thus crush the Wilsonian program before it was completed.[21]

The contest was heated and close. Because the western counties held fast for democracy, Philadelphia was the center of action. The conservative party was successful in the eastern counties, however, and captured the assembly.[22] In the midst of the excitement in Philadelphia, four conservatives were chosen for the council of censors. The city of Philadelphia sent Samuel Miles and Thomas Fitzsimons, and the county returned Frederick Muhlenberg and Arthur St. Clair.[23] As the council of censors assembled, it appeared that the Wilsonian group was to predominate there because in the first vote their advantage was twelve to ten.[24] The democratic group then girded their loins and found a way of saving the constitution that had granted the western counties a disproportionately large representation in the government.

Westmoreland and Washington counties sent a solid phalanx of loyal Constitutionalists to the meeting of the censors. From Westmoreland went William Findley and John Smilie, and from Washington went James Edgar and John McDowell. These four men joined forces with John Whitehill of Lancaster County, Joseph Hart and Samuel Smith of Bucks

[21] Konkle, *George Bryan*, 251.   [22] *Ibid.*, 258.
[23] Pennsylvania Constitutional Convention, 1776, *Proceedings*, 67.
[24] Konkle, *George Bryan*, 259.

County, Simon Dreisback of Northampton County, and Baltzer Gehr of Berks County, and, under the leadership of Whitehill, Findley, and Smilie, constituted an unbreakable bloc during the first session of the censors, which was held from November 10, 1783, to January 24, 1784.[25] It will be recalled that this council of censors was authorized by section 47 of the frame of government in the constitution of 1776. "In order that the freedom of this commonwealth may be preserved inviolate for ever," reads that section, "there shall be chosen, by ballot, by the freemen in each city and county respectively, on the second Tuesday in October," in 1783 and in every seventh year thereafter, a council of censors. A majority of the councilors was to constitute a quorum in every case, except on the calling of a convention "in which two-thirds of the whole number elected shall agree."[26] The whole number in November of 1783 was twenty-six, two from each of the twelve counties and two from the city of Philadelphia.[27] Eighteen favorable votes, therefore, were necessary to revise the constitution.

There was no quorum available until Wednesday, November 13. The body organized with Frederick Muhlenberg, president; Thomas Fitzsimons, chairman of the rules committee; and Judge Samuel Miles as chairman of the committee to confer with the executive council. On November 19 the actual work began, and on that day two incidents of note occurred. First, a committee including Fitzsimons, Anthony Wayne, Smilie, William Irvine, and James Read was constituted to "enquire and report, whether the constitution has been preserved inviolate in every part." Second, two petitions signed by "sundry" inhabitants of the city and county of Philadelphia were presented, which set forth that the laws and the constitution and the freedom of voting had been violated in the last election and asked that the facts be heard and the election be declared null and void. This petition drew the first significant vote of the session, on December 31, in which the

[25] Pennsylvania Constitutional Convention, 1776, *Proceedings*, 69.
[26] *Ibid.*, 64.   [27] *Ibid.*, 67.

request was denied by a vote of fourteen to seven, with Muhlenberg and the other members whose seats were contested voting with the majority. Smilie and Findley were among the dissenting seven and contended that of the 1620 votes cast 230 seemed to be "stuffed" and 340 illegally cast, altogether enough votes to change the results (a contention that has a strangely familiar and modern ring). The Philadelphia contingent kept their seats for the time being, however, although new depositions were presented under the management of Samuel Bryan, son of George Bryan.[28]

The committee "to enquire" about the constitution reported on January 2, 1784, "that some articles of the constitution of this commonwealth, are materially defective, and absolutely require alteration and amendment." The vote in favor of the report and for revision of the constitution was twelve to ten, with the western stalwarts voting solidly in the negative. The following day a committee was appointed to report those articles that were materially defective and to recommend alterations. The work of reporting the articles began on January 19, and votes were taken upon individual sections with a constant twelve-to-nine vote favorable to revisions. The majority advised that there should be a bicameral legislature to provide a check upon the possibility of a current majority of one house pushing through a popular but unwise measure; reported that the supreme executive council constituted a material defect because a number of men could not act with sufficient decision in an emergency, because a group of men in a council so selected could not be held directly responsible by the people, and because the election of the president by a joint meeting of the assembly and executive council enabled the dominant majority of the legislature to dominate the executive branch of the government; and advised that the term of seven years for the judges of the supreme court weakened their positions and made them sub-

[28] Pennsylvania Constitutional Convention, 1776, *Proceedings*, 68; Konkle, *George Bryan*, 258.

BACK-COUNTRY DEMOCRACY ORGANIZES

servient to the executive council. These reports all looked toward a conservative check upon a democratic government.

In addition to a single executive for the commonwealth, the committee proposed that a legislative council, established upon proportionate representation, serve as an upper house in the bicameral legislature. This suggestion was a dart that touched the hearts of the back-country democrats. Thus far each county, regardless of the number of taxables, had one representative on the executive council.[29] According to Muhlenberg's statement, the four counties, Bedford, Westmoreland, Washington, and the recently established county of Fayette, had an aggregate of fifteen hundred taxables and four seats in the supreme executive council of thirteen, whereas the remainder of the state had eight thousand taxables and only seven representatives on the council.[30] The proposed legislative council would allot a total of only four representatives to the four counties west of the mountains and twenty-three to the eastern counties. The change from the ratio of four to seven to the ratio of four to twenty-three would mean that the weight of the western democrats would be practically annihilated. Furthermore, it was proposed that the first western members of the legislative council should be elected for one year only and thereafter for three, while the eastern representatives were to be elected for three years. The star of the Wilson-Morris party was in the ascendancy, and the leaders hoped to overthrow western Pennsylvania democracy within the year.

Whitehill, Findley, and Smilie were too astute to be outdone. They resorted to an undemocratic trick to preserve their democratic constitution. They insisted that when the members first voted upon the report on the constitution that the twelve-to-ten vote was really a defeat because section 47 of the frame of government stipulated that a two-thirds majority

[29] Pennsylvania Constitutional Convention, 1776, *Proceedings*, 68-77.
[30] Harding, "Party Struggles over the First Pennsylvania Constitution," in American Historical Association, *Annual Report*, 388 (1894).

was necessary to call a constitutional convention. Furthermore, they contended that every subsequent vote on the specific articles was unconstitutional and irrelevant. Upon this ground the nine took their stand and at no time in the voting would they yield. They summarized their reasons for dissenting and signed their names to an article of dissension in which they reiterated that the delegates understood that their first vote upon the report on the constitution was equivalent to one upon the question of the calling of a convention; that a constitution should not be changed lightly; and that the present constitution was produced in harmony and had aided in winning the Revolution. Their arguments, except for the first, which had to do with the two-thirds rule, were merely political verbiage. The equal representation that had been given them as a bribe for their aid in the Revolution was now dear to them and they intended to hold it, and the delegates from western Pennsylvania were responsible for holding the line during the first session. A little bloc of four led by Findley and Smilie and supported by Whitehill drew to themselves five additional men from different geographical sections to thwart the majority. Many times since in American history, but never more effectively or ironically, have minority blocs in the name of democracy frustrated the desires of the majority. The conservatives by the same monotonous vote, twelve to nine, attached their reasons for assenting, after which the council adjourned until June 1. Meanwhile the political wheel was turning.[31]

In the interim between the first and second sessions of the council of censors, the contest between the two groups was no less grim in the legislature. The attitude of the majority in the first session of the council had indicated to the democrats that the Anti-Constitutionalists expected to gain control of the state legislature to further insure the Wilsonian program of nationalism and the continuation of the Bank of North America with its state charter. To offset these expectations

[31] Pennsylvania Constitutional Convention, 1776, *Proceedings*, 77-80.

the Constitutionalists on January 19, 1784, revealed plans for a new Bank of Pennsylvania. The national bank group attempted to thwart this plan by issuing additional stocks to individuals who would effectively support their financial institution. The Constitutionalists in a counter-offensive made formal application to the assembly for a charter on February 10. But after hearings on March 2 and 3 in which the national bank adherents fought the new bank, the appeal for a charter was withdrawn. In this movement for a new state bank Whitehill, Findley, and Smilie were in the vanguard.[32]

The Constitutionalists were more successful, however, in their efforts to acquire control of the council of censors before its second session. Judge Miles, delegate from the city of Philadelphia, had been accused of dishonesty by the assembly and though he was acquitted he was sufficiently embarrassed to necessitate his withdrawal from the council. George Bryan was elected to replace him on June 8 and took his seat on June 24. Thereafter the contests in both the assembly and council became very bitter and ran concurrently. In the assembly the question of the status of the University of Pennsylvania held the center of the stage. The democrats feared that the Wilsonian republicans would succeed in restoring to the College of Philadelphia the property that had been confiscated and transferred to the University of Pennsylvania. The assembly had taken the property of the college in 1779, ostensibly because its charter required the trustees to take an oath of allegiance to the king of England. The provision for such an oath was odious to the patriots during the Revolution. Furthermore, some of the trustees had strong Tory leanings and were conservatives. A revision of the test oaths by the assembly would obviate the chief complaint raised against the trustees in 1779 and enable them to press their claim for a restoration of the property. After many bitter skirmishes a vote upon the revisions of the test oaths disclosed an even division, twenty-five to twenty-five, and when Speaker Gray

[32] Konkle, *George Bryan*, 264.

cast his vote with the Anti-Constitutionalists, nineteen members rushed out of the body, thereby destroying a quorum. The democrats also feared that the conservatives might attempt to restore the proprietary estates, another move that would point toward an aristocracy.[33]

Their fears were groundless, however, because the council of censors, with the addition of George Bryan and of James Potter of Northumberland County, who replaced the deceased James Hunter on June 7, executed an about-face. The committee to report on whether or not the constitution had been violated underwent a revision. To the original five, which had included only Smilie for the Constitutionalists, Findley and Richard McAllister had been added on January 20, 1784. On June 24 Bryan of Philadelphia and James Moore of Chester County were placed on the committee, and later, on July 7 and 14 respectively, James Potter and James M'Lene were added.

The first test in the council came, on July 2, 1784, upon the question of a delinquent county commissioner who failed to send in tax information, and the Constitutionalists had a fifteen-to-five, or a three-fourths majority. Fitzsimons, St. Clair, Wayne, Hartley, and Read of the original twelve Anti-Constitutionalists were adamant. Thereafter, the democrats rode hard through the remaining work of the session. On July 21 a resolution headed by Bryan and Smilie called for the original manuscript of the constitution of 1776. The enlarged committee began its deliberation upon the document. The council took time out on August 13 to agree by a vote of thirteen to eleven to investigate all branches of the government but on August 16 returned to a consideration of the committee's report of the constitution, at which time the new report was substituted for the report of the first session by a vote of fourteen to nine. The committee found that the printer had made nineteen errors in publishing the document.

But errors in printing were inconsequential in comparsion

[33] Konkle, *George Bryan*, 260, 267.

to the errors found in the administering of the government between 1781 and 1784. The majority of fourteen councilmen marched through the acts of the assembly from 1781 to 1784, pointing out unconstitutional steps. Some one must have kept a day-by-day account of the unconstitutional acts during that period in anticipation of such an opportunity, so minute in detail were they. Of great political significance was the condemnation of the incorporation of the Bank of North America on April 1, 1782, an act by which the assembly had acknowledged the right of Congress to incorporate, a right which the majority of the council claimed did not exist under the constitution.[34] Also the efforts of the minority to have declared unconstitutional the act of 1779, which confiscated the property of the College of Philadelphia, was defeated by the democrats with the explanation that they considered "these governments within the government of the state, holding common estates of large value, and exercising the power of making bye-laws, as against the spirit and the policy of democracy, and only to be endured in order to obtain advantages which may greatly counterbalance the inconveniencies and dangers which accompany them."[35] The democrats, Bryan, Whitehill, Findley, and Smilie, had presented an invincible front to aristocratic policies and had served notice of their intentions with regard to bank measures should they gain control in the forthcoming assembly.

On September 25, almost a year after the council of censors organized, it adjourned. But the democrats had thwarted every move of the conservatives, and the delegates from among the back-country democrats had played no small role. In the first session, with the majority against them and without the leadership of the redoubtable Bryan, the four western men, stout under the leadership of Findley and Smilie, had drawn enough strength from the remainder of the state to pre-

---

[34] Konkle, *George Bryan*, 260, 261; Pennsylvania Constitutional Convention, 1776, *Proceedings*, 83-117.
[35] Pennsylvania Constitutional Convention, 1776, *Proceedings*, 122.

vent a two-thirds majority. For their sturdiness they drew upon themselves the enmity of F. A. Muhlenberg, who complained in a letter to his brother about the delegates from the back counties of Bedford, Westmoreland, Washington, and Fayette, who with no more than fifteen hundred taxables had as much weight as the remainder of the state's delegates, who represented eight thousand taxables. In the second session they had carried all opposition before them and temporarily seemed to have the Wilsonian republicans beaten. Needless to say, back-country democracy was satisfied with its sons.

Furthermore, the western people were to live with high hopes for at least another year, because the October elections of 1784 sent men of the democratic faith from the three western counties to the assembly and to the supreme executive council. William Findley and William Todd were Westmoreland's representatives; John Smilie went from the newly established Fayette County; and Matthew Ritchie from Washington County completed the western group in the assembly. They were among friends because the assembly on November 12 showed a majority of forty-three to fifteen in favor of the constitution and of the censors' report. The whole republican program seemed destined to destruction, particularly the plans for the Bank of North America.[36]

The chief battle seemed to turn about the question of whether the state currency should be supported by the state or by the bank. The democrats and, of course, a great majority of western men preferred that the state should establish the currency in order that they who were debtors might have cheap money with which to wipe out their debts. The national bank by refusing to recognize currency or by discounting it could precipitate a depreciation of the value of that form of money. Since the bank had been incorporated by the state of Pennsylvania, a repeal of the charter would cripple the bank because there was a question as to whether Congress could issue such a charter.

[36] Konkle, *George Bryan*, 270.

The bank opponents opened the fight on April 4, 1785, when the repeal was reported. They were jubilant and triumphant over the victory in the council of censors, and, with a preponderant majority in the assembly, their fight was easy —too easy; for in the end they overplayed their hand. Petitions from all over the state came into the assembly further encouraging its members to repeal the bank's charter, and on September 13, 1785, they mustered a vote of forty-seven to twelve for its death. Smilie and Findley, particularly the former, were in the thick of the fight gleefully brandishing their swords. But as frequently happens when a powerful victor crushes a weaker foe, public opinion quickly reversed itself; and in the October elections of 1785 there was a reaction that almost swept away the majority of the anti-bank men. They had not anticipated the effect that a repeal of the charter would have upon public credit. The western counties, however, with very little dissent stood behind their representatives. The pioneer farmers were anti-bank, anti-tax men and back-country democrats.[37]

Again Findley, Todd, and Smilie returned to the assembly to lead the fight on the bank. This time the radicals really needed them. Wilson's candidate for speaker was defeated by only a narrow margin, thirty-three to twenty-nine. Mifflin was barely elected over Clymer. Samuel Bryan was chosen clerk of the assembly by a vote of thirty-three to thirty. The contest for the vice presidency was also warmly contested. That office took on added importance that year because Franklin, president of the council, was an old man who was not expected to attend the meetings regularly. Consequently, many duties of the president would fall upon the vice president. The friends of Wilson attempted a trick to arrange for a quick call of a joint meeting before all the western men could arrive, but the plan leaked out, and on the same evening it was reported that two or three of the "western skunks" had appeared in Philadelphia. The result was an acquiescence on the part of the

[37] Konkle, *George Bryan*, 271, 273, 274.

conservatives in the choice of Captain Owen Biddle for the vice presidency of the council.[38]

The western men, however, had lost even in victory. The tide was turning in favor of a stronger national government and particularly to the granting of the purse strings to Congress. By July 11, 1785, eleven of the thirteen states had reported favorably for the Wilson resolution of April 18, 1783, which authorized the delegates to agree to give Congress the power of the purse. The effect of the national movement encouraged the conservatives in Pennsylvania, and throughout the session of 1785-86 they fought valiantly to rescind the bank repeal. John Smilie was the western champion in this session. He spoke often and vigorously. On March 23, 1786, the repeal of the bank charter was taken up, and on April 1, by a vote of forty-one to twenty-eight, the bank lost. Although the western men had gained this victory, the national movement was proving too strong for them. The western counties were still proud of their leaders and still retained Findley, Todd, and Smilie in 1786-87, but the conservatives east of the mountains outweighed them in the assembly and they became only a determined minority.[39]

The bank question had received more attention than other issues; the bank had been hated with gusto and had been defeated. The opposers of the bank had supported measures looking to the improvement of roads in the West; they had favored a land policy that would provide a moratorium; and they favored, at least morally, the opening of the Mississippi River to western commerce. For more than a decade, however, western representatives were to assume the role of a protesting minority. The essential nature of back-country democracy did not change; rather, in the position of oppositionists, the western people probably became more virulent democrats than they had been during the years of the Revolution and immediately after.

[38] Konkle, *George Bryan*, 274, 278.   [39] *Ibid.*, 279-281.

BACK-COUNTRY DEMOCRACY IN OPPOSITION

CHAPTER FOUR

THE political pendulum that had swung so far in the direction of liberty, equality, and independence during the American Revolution was definitely swinging backward by 1786 and within a decade had reached the opposite extremity of the arc as represented by the political ideals and the highly organized Federalist party of Alexander Hamilton. By 1786 Samuel Adams and other Revolutionary leaders in Massachusetts had become so conservative that they opposed Daniel Shays and his impoverished, cheap-money friends and suppressed them in the famous "Shays's Rebellion." In the same year the delegates from five states who met in convention at Annapolis ostensibly to consider a revision of the Articles of Confederation to stabilize commerce reached a conclusion that a convention should be called the following year to revise the articles sufficiently to stabilize the central government. Everywhere along the seaboard the backwash of the Revolution had set in; nationalism and conservatism were on the rise. The leadership for this movement was furnished by the same social classes that had been prominent in pre-Revolutionary days—the merchants, the financiers, planters, and professional men. There were few if any small farmers, laborers, or backwoodsmen among the leaders or even in the ranks of the revisionists.

In the Quaker state the conservatives under the leadership of James Wilson and Robert Morris, Revolutionary luminaries, gained control of the government in 1786 and for a decade marched forward triumphantly with their program. While they overcame the minority opposition of the back-country democrats during that interval, however, they did not destroy it nor allay it. In fact the western men, unsuccessful at every turn, only became more desperate, more exasperated with each successive defeat.

The earliest indication that there was to be a rift in the unbroken radical ranks of western Pennsylvania occurred with the appearance of the first issue of the *Pittsburgh Gazette* on July 29, 1786. John Scull, a young man with mildly Federalist inclinations at that time, founded and edited this "first newspaper west of the Mountains." He printed many articles from democratic pens in his paper and professed to be nonpartisan in political matters, but the small weekly journal became a significant Federalist instrument in Pittsburgh, the future citadel of western Federalism. Already the little town was becoming ambitious; already its commercial activities were producing economic and political conflicts with the agricultural interests in Westmoreland, Washington, and Fayette counties, and a movement was taking form to establish a new county in which Pittsburgh would play a prominent part. Therefore a newspaper to serve as a sounding board for the ambitious men in the town and to herald to the rest of the world the admirable agricultural and commercial advantages of the region was indispensable. The columns of the paper were available not only for that purpose, but also as a vehicle of expression for the literary-minded citizens, particularly those who were interested in writing political treatises. Hugh Henry Brackenridge, because he was of a literary turn of mind, because he was ambitious for Pittsburgh, and because he had political aspirations, aided the young editor to secure a printing press and to establish his paper.[1]

The second challenge to the supremacy of back-country democracy came from the efforts of this same unpredictable

[1] See Andrews, *Pittsburgh's Post-Gazette*, 1; Brackenridge's writings in the *Gazette* are collected in H. H. Brackenridge, *Gazette Publications*.

politician, H. H. Brackenridge, who, on September 9, 1786, through the medium of the *Pittsburgh Gazette,* announced his candidacy for a seat in the assembly. He suggested to the public that the dominant issues were the settling of the land patents; the encouragement of Pittsburgh—"that it be made a borough, that it have a seat of justice, that it have a school endowed in it"; and the navigation of the Mississippi. On September 30, under the pseudonym of "Angus MacMore," he criticized the actions of the western assemblymen on the ground that they neglected western interests. In his condemnation he said, "I would wish to see a great deal less said, and more done. The vanity of talking appears to be visible in many of them. There are two or three of them that are up and down every minute like the elbow of a man playing on the fiddle." He further asserted, "All last year was taken up about the bank. The devil take them and the bank both. The concerns of the country are neglected on account of this bank, when it might have stood another year, till we had time to consider the consequences of the institution." Bold words and apparently impolitic, yet it must be remembered that they were spoken by an eastern scholar who had migrated to the West and who knew that the more his adopted city grew in size and importance the more progress he could make in his profession of the law.

Brackenridge's campaign was successful, and he joined William Findley and James Barr to represent Westmoreland County in the state assembly. Their western colleagues in this assembly were Theophilus Philips and John Gilchrist, of Fayette County, and James Allison, John Flenniken, and James McDowell, of Washington County.[2] John Baird, John Smilie, and David Redick, of Westmoreland, Fayette, and Washington counties, respectively, were the West's contingent to the supreme executive council.[3] Brackenridge was destined

[2] *Pittsburgh Gazette,* November 15, 1786; December 6, 1786.
[3] McMaster and Stone, *Pennsylvania and the Federal Constitution,* 714; Ellis, *Fayette County,* 155; Crumrine, *Washington County,* 479.

to be an independent and therefore a misfit in this group of men. Elected for the primary purpose of procuring the establishment of Allegheny County, he pressed that issue hard but soon forgot some of his campaign pledges. His colleagues and constituents, however, did not forget.

The first session of the eleventh assembly, which opened on October 25, 1786, was a particularly significant one for Pennsylvania. Benjamin Franklin was president of the council. The Anti-Constitutionalists were in the majority in the assembly and were anxious to undo as much as possible of the legislation enacted by the radicals during the previous decade. The land problem, which was staring them in the face and which was to continue to be a pressing problem for many years to come, the regranting of the charter of the Bank of North America, the founding of Allegheny County, and the question of the federal Constitution, all demanded consideration.

The land question was raised on November 13 by a petition from 553 people of Washington County who stated their grievances with respect to the state excise on spirituous liquor, to disadvantageous land laws, to defects in the laying and collection of taxes, and to the extravagant fees of land surveyors. A separate petition, signed by 280 citizens of the same county, for an alleviation of their difficulties in completing the titles to their land was also presented.[4] This problem had sorely distressed the settlers in western Pennsylvania for many years. Land procured before 1776 was obtained by warrant and surveyed, and the patent was recorded in the land office at Philadelphia. The purchase was seldom completed at the time the warrant was procured; the settlers agreed to pay the remaining debt and interest at later dates, but few reduced the principal and many allowed the interest to fall in arrears. They probably hoped that the Penn family would be unable to collect its debts after the Revolution; they certainly had an insufficient amount of money to meet payments; and they found

---

[4] Pennsylvania General Assembly, *Minutes of the First Session of the Eleventh General Assembly*, 32.

the trip to the land office in Philadelphia an inconvenience.

The Divesting Act of 1779 depriving the Penns of the ownership of all lands except stipulated tracts was a partial fulfillment of the settlers' anticipations. Their hopes that the state would not require them to liquidate their debts were futile, however, because an act of 1781 specified that the patents were to be cleared by April 10, 1787. Thereafter all land upon which the titles were not cleared was to be designated by the land agent to the county commissioner, who was obligated to sell the land for the purpose of procuring the arrearages to the state. Furthermore, those settlers who had squatted upon land and improved it without taking out patents would lose possession of their land.

Franklin sent a communication to the assembly on November 15 in which he reviewed the land situation, referring to the law of 1781, observing that few titles would be completed by April 10, 1787, and indicating that many patents had not been taken for land occupied by settlers. He asserted that the final day for settlement was near and that one of two courses should be pursued: either to continue the indulgence to settlers and extend the time for settlement or to make easier the payment of the money. The latter policy he thought might be accomplished by permitting the settlers to dispose of a part of their obligations by submitting to the land office the depreciated bills of credit, paper money, which had been issued in 1781.[5] This policy appealed to the western representatives as a whole, and Brackenridge, prior to his election, had expressed himself as favoring it. But when the measure came up in the assembly he placed himself in opposition to the proposal. He defended his stand in the columns of the *Pittsburgh Gazette* of February 3, 1787, with logic that, however good it may appear now, was not then sufficiently clear or simple to appeal to his constituents.

Brackenridge reasoned that the measure if adopted would be injurious to the western people; it would create a

[5] *Pittsburgh Gazette,* November 22, 1786.

demand for the depreciated state certificates; the price of the certificate would increase in value; the people of western counties would find it extremely difficult to procure the money to purchase the certificates to pay for the patents on their land; the policy would lead eventually to speculation on the part of those who had available money; only the speculators would benefit thereby; and the unfortunate farmers would have to pay ten or fifteen shillings for certificates that they could at the present obtain for two shillings and sixpence the pound. These arguments, probably sincere with Brackenridge, have the ring of sophistry about them even now and surely were unconvincing to his constituents. They believed him a traitor to their interests and felt that his ear had been caught by the smooth voice of Robert Morris. They may well have been correct, because it is evident that a man of Brackenridge's culture and background could find more in common with eastern assemblymen than with his simple uneducated constituents. His colleagues from the western counties were outraged by his apparent desertion on the land issue and, though he labored diligently for other interests of his people, broke with him.

Brackenridge fostered and furthered a bill for the establishment of Allegheny County and on November 30, 1786, became a member of the committee to bring in such a bill. He served upon a committee, established on November 17, to draw up a plan for the sale of reserved land opposite Pittsburgh, in which he made an unsuccessful effort to set aside some of it as an endowment for the Pittsburgh Academy but failed because of the efforts of Findley. On December 7 he was placed upon a committee to prepare a bill providing that titles to improve land should be issued only to actual settlers; on December 12 he was included on a committee to report on petitions for improving roads to the West; and on the same day his bill for incorporating a "religious Christian Society" in Pittsburgh was introduced.[6]

[6] Pennsylvania General Assembly, *Minutes of the First Session of the Eleventh General Assembly*, 42, 57, 68, 72, 75.

But on the following day, December 13, Brackenridge crossed the Rubicon when he joined the eastern bank group that was anxious to restore the charter of the bank.[7] This was contrary to his campaign promises and to the desires of his people. Shortly thereafter he laid himself open to deadly shafts of criticism. He and a number of western men, including William Findley, David Redick, and John Smilie, met at the home of Chief Justice McKean, where a discussion on the bank occurred. Redick asserted that it was believed "that Mr. Morris had it in view to make an advantage of the bank to himself and a few friends, rather than to serve the public." Brackenridge hotly replied, that "the people were fools; if they would let Mr. Morris alone, he would make Pennsylvania a great people, but they would not suffer him to do it." John Smilie entered the verbal justing and declared that he did not think anyone had the right to make such a statement. Brackenridge reputedly "dropped his brows" and closed his mouth. But the damage had been done and his colleagues pressed their advantage. A few minutes later Redick asked Brackenridge if he did not think the western Pennsylvanians would be disgruntled because he had opposed receiving the certificates in clearing the land titles. Brackenridge made a bad situation worse by saying that he would satisfy his constituents with a statement in the *Pittsburgh Gazette*.[8] If he thought his people at home were simple rustic fools and his colleagues lacking in resources he was soon to be disillusioned.

Brackenridge's facile pen did attempt to undo the political damage caused by his loose tongue and by his unpopular votes on the acceptance of state certificates and on the bank, but to no avail.[9] A correspondent signing himself "A Farmer" in the *Gazette* for January 20, 1787, accused him of selling "the good will of his country for a dinner of some stockholders fat beef" and added, "Must I quit my title to a most excellent tract of

---

[7] Pennsylvania General Assembly, *Minutes of the First Session of the Eleventh General Assembly*, 76.
[8] *Pittsburgh Gazette*, April 21, 1787.   [9] *Ibid.*, January 16, 1787.

land; after my pains of having it surveyed, riding to Philadelphia, entering my survey, with the addition of a considerable expence, and no small fatigue of body? What must my feelings be at such a prospect? Nay, the very horse I rode, poor Jack... were he alive, would groan to hear I had lost both my labour and my purse, and all to satisfy the voracious maw of some greesy broker."

William Findley, less learned but more direct, entered the journalistic war with a review of Brackenridge's legislative and forensic ventures of the preceding months. Findley would not let the people forget that they had been dubbed fools and that an effort had been made to hoodwink them. If backcountry democracy was outweighed in the state legislature by the conservative vote of the eastern counties, it was waging an exultant battle on Brackenridge in its own territory. To the democrats Brackenridge epitomized conservatism and treachery, and Findley was to capitalize upon Brackenridge's claim of erudition.

The second session of the eleventh assembly sat from February 20 to March 29, 1787, and furthered the business taken up during the first session. Brackenridge, with the indifferent acquiescence of western members, struggled to have the assembly express an opinion upon the proposed Spanish treaty, which would open the Mississippi to western commerce, a commerce very essential to western Pennsylvanians. He summarized his trials and tribulations in the files of the *Pittsburgh Gazette:*

It was difficult to obtain leave, because ... a number of eastern members, especially of the mercantile interest, were in favor of admitting the Spanish proposition, and they are much disgusted with the behavior of the greater part of our western members in what has respected trade. This gives them a prejudice against the country in general. They say that we come down like Huns, Goths and Vandals upon them, and join with those who tear up charters, and the most sacred engagements of government.[10]

[10] *Pittsburgh Gazette,* April 28, 1787.

He reasoned with these "eastern members," and they, because he seemed "liberal," gave him an opportunity to introduce his resolutions and to discuss them, but warned him that he need not expect support for his resolutions. Once he had the floor, he made an impassioned plea for justice for the West:

It is laid down by some merchants with whom I have conversed, that a trade with the western country would be more profitable than a trade with Spain. This country will be the Germany of America; *officina gentium,* the great birth place of nations, where millions yet unborn shall exist: it will be the Russia of America in point of the trade which will be carried on. Iron, lumber, hemp, hides, fur and other things will be carried hence by the merchants of these very towns on the sea coast, and like the towns in Holland and England by the Russian trade, they will be enriched and [ag]grandized. Not until the population of the western country is extended will even Philadelphia become a great city. I have seen this during the war; the traders coming from this city, planting themselves on our rivers with merchandise and stores, and collecting the produce of the country, descending by the Ohio river, and vending their cargoes at New-Orleans, or in foreign markets—returned again to this city, and laid out the money which they had acquired.... Since the decline of trade, even at this time, the whole country languishes: the wheat of last year lies in the barn: there is no object to prompt industry—we are sinking to the pastoral and bordering on the barbaric state.

Brackenridge feared the arousal of a separative, frontier movement and continued, "Is it of no service to preserve the affections of this infant country? Make peace with the young lion; an injury in distress is not easily forgotten—favors to the unprotected are more gratefully remembered. The western country may long be preserved by the maternal embrace of the eastern part of the continent." But he could not enlist the aid of the West. Back-country democracy—"the young lion"—had not enough strength to make its claws felt. A few years later, however, the "young lion" of the western counties was to join forces with a "young lion" of the eastern counties to sweep the Federalists from power in the state.[11]

Brackenridge's heroic efforts were not unnoticed by some individuals at home and others in Philadelphia. A discussion of his conduct was resumed in the *Pittsburgh Gazette* between the second and third sessions of the eleventh assembly. "A Farmer" avowed that no member of any country had ever been "possessed with greater zeal to serve his constituents," and that he remained independent in order to take advantage of any opportunity to serve his country that might arise. In the same issue of the *Gazette* a Philadelphian stated that Brackenridge's speeches on the bank and on the Mississippi question showed him to be an enlightened legislator. "They were admired by good judges," he said, "and thought to be equal to any of the speeches of Pitt and Fox in the house of commons in England."[12] The farmers who feared that they would be dispossessed of their improved land were not easily won by rhetorical arguments, however, and the erudite lawyer decided to attempt once more to justify himself to his people through the medium of the *Gazette*. Consequently he published an article "To the Inhabitants of the Western Country" beginning on April 21, 1787, and continuing through seven weekly installments. He essayed to show that he had been loyal to the interests of the western counties and that his change of front on the question of the state certificates was the result of an honest change of opinion after his election. In his explanation he expressed the theory that a legislator should be representative in fact, with the privilege of forming his own judgments and not merely a delegate relaying the ideas of his constituents. He added that the policies in the state should be formulated with regard to the exigencies of the whole state rather than of a part of the state. Brackenridge was not a provincial back-country democrat; he had a more cosmopolitan background, and he probably never became indoctrinated with the frontier spirit of provincial democracy.

Findley and Smilie had shown less interest than had Brack-

[11] *Pittsburgh Gazette*, May 5, 1787.   [12] *Ibid.*, April 14, 1787.

enridge in the land-title bill and the Mississippi question, and they had opposed the road bill. But they knew their people. They opposed what their friends believed to be a monster—the bank; they favored the use of the depreciated certificates, which eastern bankers did not want; and they went among their people in a friendly, companionable way.

The remaining session of the eleventh assembly was a significant one; on March 17 the bank charter was revived by vote of the assembly.[13] Brackenridge alone of the western representatives cast an affirmative vote, which was one of a majority of thirty-five to twenty-eight. He alone of the western men favored the building of a road from Philadelphia to Chester. And he was alone among the western representatives in the movement to provide for a state convention to ratify the federal Constitution.

The affairs of the state of Pennsylvania were closely interwoven with the movement that resulted in the calling of the federal Constitutional Convention in 1787. The aristocratic, conservative class of the Atlantic seaboard, the same element that in Pennsylvania had tried to condemn the state constitution of 1776 in the council of censors in 1783-84 and had failed, sponsored the nationalist movement, which eventually led to the replacing of the Articles of Confederation by a new constitution. James Wilson, Robert Morris, and Frederick Muhlenberg were the prime movers in the national movement in the state. They wanted a stronger government to protect commerce, which would necessitate a national army and a central government empowered to levy taxes. Those advantages had not seemed possible to them under the government provided by the Articles of Confederation. Furthermore, while from 1785 to 1787 their party had control of the state assembly and while they had restored the charter of the bank, their certainty of controlling their opponents west of the mountains was not assured. Collecting taxes was an unpopular activity; ejecting farmers from their improved lands was a dangerous

[13] Konkle, *George Bryan*, 299.

step for those politically ambitious; and the protection of the western settlers against Indian depredations was a huge task for a state government. A turn of the political wheel might give Findley, Smilie, and Whitehill another opportunity to have their way in the state legislature; hence a strong central government would be advantageous not only to the economic welfare but also to the political fortunes of the eastern commercialists. The conservatives were ready and anxious to join Madison, Hamilton, and others in the formation of a federal constitution.

Not a single member from western Pennsylvania participated in the deliberations of the federal Constitutional Convention. Nor was there a single one to represent the western point of view with any degree of vigor. The western people were primarily responsible for their own plight in this matter, however, because it was the bitter fight that Smilie and Findley waged against the bank charter that led to conservative domination of the state assembly. Findley, however, declared that he could have served among the "Constitutional fathers" but that he had declined because there was no provision for paying the expenses of the members and since he was so far removed from Philadelphia, the scene of action.[14] He nevertheless received two votes in the election of delegates, a matter that was embarrassing to him at a later time when his opponents pointed out that those two votes represented his influence.

The Constitutional Convention sat behind closed doors in Philadelphia for four months during the summer of 1787, from May to September 17. The delegates met in the chamber usually occupied by the General Assembly of Pennsylvania, which convened for the time being in a room immediately above. Naturally, information of the completion of the Constitution was transmitted at once to the members of the assembly and on September 17, the date of its adoption, a copy of the document was unofficially submitted to them. On the same

[14] McMaster and Stone, *Pennsylvania and the Federal Constitution*, 115.

day a copy, duly signed by thirty-nine members of the convention, some resolutions, and a letter, all signed by Washington, were ordered to be forwarded to Congress, which in turn was to transmit them to the states. Unofficially and informally, the state assemblymen began discussing the proposed constitution at their boarding places and in the taverns. The Philadelphia newspapers printed the document, and its first appearance created a favorable reaction in Philadelphia circles. But the western assemblymen, save Brackenridge, voiced surprise and opposition.

One week after the completion of the Constitution the assembly took official note of its existence when Findley moved that the "House would direct one thousand copies in English and five hundred copies in German, of the Constitution . . . to be printed and distributed among the citizens of Pennsylvania." Brackenridge insisted upon an amendment to provide for "a proper person to translate the Plan into the German language."[15] This was the last time, however, that these two men were to coöperate on the consideration of the ratification of the Constitution.

The Federalists, who favored the ratification of the Constitution, were anxious to profit by the wave of sentiment favorable to it before the opponents, the Anti-Federalists, had an opportunity to build up an opposition. Federalist leaders, who were already thoroughly familiar with the document and satisfied with its provisions, had an advantage in that they could plunge into the steps necessary to complete its ratification. Consequently they wanted the assembly to call a ratifying convention before the adjournment of the legislature, which was set for Saturday, September 29. Such a procedure would give western farmers less time in which to become acquainted with those features of the new plan that were unsatisfactory to them.

Although the assembly had not yet received an official copy of the new document from the old Congress, nevertheless on

[15] Pennsylvania General Assembly, *Proceedings and Debates,* 85.

the morning of Friday, September 28, the day before adjournment, George Clymer opened the question of providing for a ratifying convention. Findley and Whitehill, leading the opposition to the new Constitution, attempted to frustrate the passage of the motion made by Clymer. Whitehill urged that it be postponed until the assembly could have time to consider such an important subject. To the arguments of Fitzsimons and Clymer that the measure was too important to delay, Findley replied that its importance was the very reason that it should be treated with deliberation. Brackenridge, the only western man who favored the measure, then spoke in its behalf. Whitehill objected again, on the ground that the assembly had not received an official report from Congress, but the objections were useless because the conservative majority by a vote of forty-three to nineteen agreed to the resolution to call a convention. The date for the convention, however, was not determined in the morning session.[16]

When the assembly reconvened at four o'clock in the afternoon only forty-four members, two less than a quorum, appeared. Gerardus Wynkoop observed that the absentees were chiefly those who had opposed the measure in the morning session and moved that the sergeant at arms be dispatched to fetch them, a measure that was duly ordered. Upon the return of the sergeant, he was immediately examined at the bar of the house as follows:

Mr. Speaker. Well Sergeant, have you seen the absent members? *Sergeant.* Yes, Sir, I saw R. Whitehill, Kennedy, Mitchell, Piper, Powell, Dale, Findley, Bar, Wright, M'Dowel, Flenniken, Allison, Gilchrist, M'Calmont, R. Clarke, Antis and Miley.

Mr. Speaker. What did you say to them? *Sergeant.* I told the gentlemen that the Speaker and the house had sent for them, and says they, There is no house.

Mr. Speaker. Did you let them know they were desired to attend? *Sergeant.* Yes, Sir, but they told me they could not attend this afternoon, for they had not made up their minds yet.

[16] McMaster and Stone, *Pennsylvania and the Federal Constitution,* 27-60.

Mr. D. Clymer. How is that? *Sergeant.* They had not made up their minds this afternoon to wait on you.

Mr. Speaker. Who told you this? *Sergeant.* Mr. Whitehill told me the first.

Mr. Speaker. Where did you see them? *Sergeant.* At a house in Sixth street; Major Boyd's, I think.

D. Clymer. You say Mr. Whitehill told you first there was no house; who told you afterward? *Sergeant.* Mr. Clarke said they must go *electioneering* now.

D. Clymer. I would be glad to know what conversation there was among them, and who was there? *Sergeant.* There was a member of council with them, Mr. M'Laine, and he asked me, Who sent you?

Mr. Speaker. Was there no other person in the room? *Sergeant.* Yes, I saw Mr. Smiley there.

D. Clymer. Was there no private citizens? *Sergeant.* No, Sir.

D. Clymer. There was none then but MEN IN PUBLIC OFFICES? *Sergeant.* No.

D. Clymer. Well; and pray what did the honorable Mr. Smiley say? *Sergeant.* He said nothing.

D. Clymer. Could all the persons in the room hear Mr. M'Laine's question? *Sergeant.* Yes, Sir.

D. Clymer. And did they seem pretty unanimous in their determination not to come? that is, did it appear so to you? *Sergeant.* Yes, Sir, as I understood it, nearly.

D. Clymer. Did you hear of any one willing to come? *Sergeant.* No, Sir.   [*D. Clymer.*] Sergeant, you may retire.

For the moment the conservatives were baffled. Their radical colleagues had apparently outwitted them. The speaker, at a loss as to what to do, recapitulated the unfinished business and "wished to know what the members would choose to do." Wynkoop wanted to know if there was a way by which they could compel the absentees to attend. "If there is not, then *God be merciful to us!!!*" he moaned.[17]

Meanwhile, the nineteen recalcitrant members discussed ways and means of thwarting the majority on the morrow,

[17] McMaster and Stone, *Pennsylvania and the Federal Constitution*, 60-62.

and chuckled among themselves at the discomfiture of their adversaries. Evidently they "made up their minds" not to attend the following day, because when the Speaker took the chair at nine o'clock the following morning, again only forty-four members answered the roll call. Clymer, however, presented to the chair the resolutions of Congress and an official copy of the Constitution. Now the legislature could proceed in a regular way if a quorum could be obtained. Perhaps the information that the official copy had been received would fetch the absent ones. Consequently the sergeant at arms and the clerk of the house were directed to find them and request their attendance. The two officers first located James M'Calmont of Franklin County and Jacob Miley of Dauphin County, who when shown the resolution of Congress "stoutly said they would not go." But citizens who were close at hand broke into their lodgings, seized them, dragged them not gently "through the streets to the State House, and thrust them into the assembly room, with clothes torn and faces white with rage." Thus was the quorum completed.

The assembly minutes merely say "in a few minutes Mr. James M'Calmont and Mr. Jacob Miley entered the house." M'Calmont shortly afterward complained that he had been brought by force to the assembly and asked to be dismissed, but his request was refused. When informed that absentees would be fined five shillings if their absence prevented a quorum, he reached into his pocket, pulled out some silver and said, "Well, sir, here is your 5s. to let me go." Amid laughter, the Speaker refused the money and the debate went on. As the vote was about to be taken, M'Calmont made a dash for the door, and when some one shouted, "Stop him," he was detained. Upon Brackenridge's motion, the assembly designated the first Tuesday in November (only a month away) for the election of delegates to the ratifying convention. It was ironical that the only man west of the mountains then present in the assembly should suggest the time for election.[18]

[18] McMaster and Stone, *Pennsylvania and the Federal Constitution*, 4, 5, 65, 70, 71.

But what of the western men who tried unsuccessfully to delay the call for the convention? They were busy preparing an address to the people in which they enumerated ten objections to the new plan of government. The plan was offensive because it was too expensive; it provided for a government of three branches; it would minimize state governments; taxation was vested in Congress; liberty of the press was not assured; trial by jury was abolished in civil cases; the federal judiciary would destroy the judiciary of the state; there was no provision for a rotation in offices; there was no bill of rights; and there was the possibility of a standing army. The address, which in a negative way expressed their political philosophy, was signed by sixteen of the nineteen members, and among the signers were the names of every member of the assembly from the western part of Pennsylvania except Brackenridge.

While these members were laboring over their address the house was examining the clerk who had gone with the sergeant at arms to find them. After relating that M'Calmont and Miley were found at Major Boyd's house and had refused to come, the clerk continued,

Before I got from that door I saw Col. Piper and some other member, who I do not recollect, at a great distance. I went after them to the corner of Arch and Sixth streets. I saw Mr. Barr and Mr. Findley, Col. Piper and some other member, going toward Market tsreet [sic]. *Mr. Findley looked round and saw me, as I supposed, for he mended his pace.* I followed Mr. Piper and Mr. Barr, who kept on to Market street, and soon turned the corner— before I got there. *I lost sight of Mr. Findley, who I supposed had got into some house.*

The clerk stated that he had been successful in locating some members but that they had refused to attend the assembly. Whitehill he found but could not approach. Evidently the maid at Whitehill's lodging place was not forewarned by that assemblyman, because the clerk declared that, "*she informed me that Mr. Whitehill was upstairs; she went up, and staid some time, when she returned and told me he was not at home.*"[19]

This amusing and undignified game of hide and seek that these assemblymen played with the sergeant and clerk was not foolish, although it was futile. The opponents of the Constitution were utilizing the only visible means that remained to them to prevent the unseemly haste of the Federalists in calling a ratifying convention. Their actions in opposing the new Constitution may have been inadvisable, but they were correct in interpreting the sentiments of their constituents, who, as future events were to prove, were not displeased with the efforts of their representatives to frustrate the ratification of the Constitution.

The assembly adjourned on September 29, after determining that there should be a state convention to consider the ratification of the Constitution, that the election of delegates should occur on the first Tuesday in November, and that the convention should meet in Philadelphia. The representatives of western Pennsylvania hurried home to continue the controversy among their people. In Pittsburgh, Brackenridge, without the aid of his Federalist friends in the assembly, pitted himself against his Anti-Federalist colleagues in an interesting and merry, if losing battle.

He dipped his pen in satire and began. First of all, he set himself to the task of demolishing the nineteen dissenting members and particularly of attacking the address of the sixteen that criticized the new Constitution and the manner in which its friends had pushed it forward. The Anti-Federalists, in an address to the people, had lamented that Pennsylvania's delegates had belonged to only one party and had been uniformly "opposed to that constitution for which you have on every occasion manifested your attachment." In reply, Brackenridge asked, "How long will the cry of *constitution* be made use of by designing men to sanction bad measures, or prevent good?" This argument, which has been used on many occasions since by men who wanted to change a constitution, is

[19] McMaster and Stone, *Pennsylvania and the Federal Constitution*, 67-69.

evidently one of long standing. "It is true," Brackenridge continued, "the delegates were 'all citizens of Philadelphia,' and all of them of 'one political party,' but surely they were all men of understanding, and against whose characters in private life, nothing can be shewn. Why not consider the work and let the men alone?"

The intransigent assembly members had charged that the delegates had not been "calculated to represent the landed interest of Pennsylvania." Brackenridge asserted that "all these delegates have land in the state," and that they understood the "landed interest, if that can be supposed distinct from any other interest, as well as any men in the state; some of them, have more land than all the sixteen remonstrants put together; one of them has more land even in Washington county, than the representatives of that county have there or any where else." What Brackenridge neglected to say was that some of Pennsylvania's landed delegates to the federal convention were land speculators and not actual settlers. But the settlers in western Pennsylvania did not miss the point. The "landed interest" of the speculator was not the same thing as the "landed interest" of the settler. The speculators were dispossessing too many settlers of improved land. Brackenridge impoliticly continued to speak down to his constituents. He declared that if the Constitution failed of ratification because of sectional prejudice and lack of familiarity with its provisions that he could only say, "O Israel thou art destroyed for the lack of knowledge."[20]

Another method employed by Brackenridge in his effort to defeat his western colleagues was the use of Hudibrastic verse. He intended thereby to ridicule Findley and his friends for hiding in the basements and garrets to avoid being hauled into the assembly. With his best irony he wrote:

> AWAY from me all jests and slurrs,
> On Pennsylvania senators,
> Save those alone the worthless few,

[20] *Pittsburgh Gazette,* October 21, 27, 1787.

> Who from the senate house withdrew
> When was proposed new government,
> For as if demon had been sent
> To strike them with phrenetic fury,
> They ran off headlong hurry scurry:
> Some ran to cellars, or absconded
> In kitchens, and were there impounded.
> 'Mongst these there was a western wight,
> Who took the fore way in the flight;
> He got a garrett by his clambering,
> And lay all day in his mind hammering
> Escape from danger and alarms
> Of furious, fiery sergeant at arms,
> Aided by tumultuous rabble,
> Who from the galley slipt cable
> To take and bring him to the house,
> While here he lay entrenched like mouse.

He continued in an effort to make ridiculous the arguments of the objectors. He put the following words into Findley's mouth:

> Now at this critical non plus,
> Our wight arose and argued thus:
> Though constitution's almost done,
> There's still some picking in the bone,
> A new occasion gives new use,
> And let's the prejudices loose,
> No writing can be understood,
> Or read at once by the multitude,
> And in obscurity there's fear;
> So, we can get a foot-hold here,
> Say that this novel government,
> Is form'd by them with an intent,
> To eat up the offices of the state,
> And make each one of themselves great.
> That under this outrageous system
> No man alive will dare say peas t' them,
> That soldiers arm'd with battle axes,
> Henceforward will collect the taxes;

> That the convention in great fury,
> Have taken away the trial by jury;
> That liberty of press is gone,
> We shall be hang'd each mothers son;
> Say Lord knows what, as comes in head,
> Pretences for a scare crow made.[21]

If "truth is stranger than fiction," poetry may nevertheless contain hidden truth. Soldiers "arm'd with battle axes" did come to "collect the taxes" within a half a dozen years, and the trial by jury was taken away. Findley and his associates did not appear so ridiculous then.

Brackenridge further attempted to disparage Findley and thereby injure the Anti-Federalists' cause, by referring scornfully to the fact that Findley was a weaver. It was a mistake. The people whom Findley represented were suspicious of aristocracy and the intelligentsia, and when Brackenridge's clever satire appeared it only served to increase the strength of Findley with the pioneer farmers. The witty lawyer was ridiculing one of their own kind. Findley was a martyred hero as he walked among his democratic friends. Not only did the satire tend to strengthen Findley but it tended to obscure the more significant issue, the ratification of the Constitution.

While Findley was electioneering against the federal Constitution, his colleagues were constantly talking among their friends, pointing out that a new federal government as proposed by the Constitution would increase taxes, deprive the state government of its powers, and provide for a national standing army to enforce its acts. Their campaigning was eminently successful, and the great majority of western Pennsylvania farmers opposed the ratification of the Constitution.

Brackenridge had offered himself as a delegate to the ratifying convention, but he was made to realize that his fervor for the Constitution was not appreciated by his people, because, despite his efforts in the previous session of the assembly and his literary contributions to the *Gazette,* he was not successful.

[21] *Pittsburgh Gazette,* November 3, 1787.

The elections were held on November 6, and when the returns were in it was found that Westmoreland County had chosen William Findley, John Baird, and William Todd, Democrats all, unwavering in their opposition to the new plan of government. Fayette County sent Nathaniel Breading and John Smilie to join Findley and the Westmoreland delegation. Washington County sent a split delegation: James Marshel and James Edgar, Anti-Federalists; and John Neville and Thomas Scott, Federalists.[22] The latter two represented the manufacturing and commercial interests, which were in the ascendancy, particularly in the towns of Pittsburgh and Washington.

Brackenridge's defeat gave him time to practice law and to write additional verses. With unbecoming bitterness he once more lampooned the Westmoreland "weaver" in verses entitled, "On the Popularity of —— [sic]." After asking why a man with a mind no bigger than that of a fly should be thought the savior of his country, he continued:

> What though he wished to damn the motion,
> *Of opening passage to the ocean*
> By Mississippi; and what's more,
> *Of making roads, to our own door;*
> And voted with a stubborn will,
> Against the *Pittsburgh County* bill.
> What though constituents be disgrac'd
> *By flying from his post* in haste,
> And taking shelter in a garret,
> Like vile rat catcher, or gray ferret;
> This circumstance has done him good,
> With th' injudicious multitude;
> They wish to justify their choice
> In sending such a thing to the house,
> And so the more, he runs a stern,
> They hold him up with new concern,
> A kind of partnership in shame,
> But binds the faster him and them.

[22] McMaster and Stone, *Pennsylvania and the Federal Constitution*, 213.

In another section of the verses he again belittled Findley:

> But why aloft did Traddle rise,
> As if he wanted wasps or flies?
> A cellar was the proper place,
> To hide himself in his disgrace;
> There he could weave; and while at work,
> Be thought a Paddy just from Cork;
> For who would ask, let who would come,
> *What senator is that at the loom?*[23]

Brackenridge could describe back-country democracy but he could not understand it. Nor was he ever to be the recipient of the confidence or the votes of these western people as were the less brilliant but more reliable Findley and Smilie.

Brackenridge's bitterness about his defeat would have been alleviated, however, had he known immediately about the treatment received by some of his successful opponents during the night of the election. In Philadelphia the Federalists were victorious by an overwhelming majority, and as part of a triumphant celebration a number of the citizens sought out leading Anti-Federalists and humiliated them. A mob went to the house of Major Boyd, the lodging place of John Smilie, John Baird, Abraham Smith, James M'Calmont, James McLean, John Piper, and William Findley, all assemblymen and all Anti-Federalists, broke the door, hurled stones through the windows, and reviled the inmates with odious names. The outraged assemblymen complained to the supreme executive council, which through its president, Benjamin Franklin, offered a reward for the apprehension and punishment of the reveling trouble makers. There were no arrests. The demonstration seems not to have broken the determination of western Pennsylvania's delegates, however, for they met in convention prepared to oppose ratification in every possible way.[24]

The convention came to order on November 21, 1787, with

---

[23] *Pittsburgh Gazette*, December 1, 1787; Newlin, *Hugh Henry Brackenridge*, 96-98.
[24] McMaster and Stone, *Pennsylvania and the Federal Constitution*, 13.

sixty of the sixty-nine delegates present. Throughout the voting the Federalists had virtually a two-to-one majority. Never were there more than forty-six votes cast by the Federalists and never less than twenty-three by the Anti-Federalists. The first vote showed a forty-four to twenty-four division. The brunt of the struggle therefore rested upon the Anti-Federalists, who were led by the familiar trio, Whitehill, Findley, and Smilie. The defense of the Constitution was led by James Wilson and Thomas McKean, with Wilson assuming the greater responsibility because he had served as a member of the Constitutional Convention and was more familiar with the provisions of the document. But in spite of Wilson's superior knowledge of the document and of his amazing legal ability he was not much more than a match for his ablest adversaries, who on occasions embarrassed him to no little extent. Findley had said that the deliberations in the council of censors had been a great political education for Wilson. Whitehill and Smilie had been in that same school and had also served in the assembly with Findley. In addition, Smilie was at present a member of the executive council. These men fought the Federalists every step of the way. It is to be regretted that complete records of the debate were not kept, because a heated battle, even when far less significant than this controversy, is always interesting.

Thomas McKean opened the question of ratification in offering the resolution, "That this Convention do adopt and ratify the Constitution of Federal Government as agreed upon by the Federal Convention at Philadelphia on the 17th day of September, 1787." Wilson, "as the only member of this respectable body, who had the honor of a seat in the late Federal Convention," then entered into a long explanation of the nature of the proposed federal government and the reasons that had prompted the "Constitutional fathers" to choose that particular form. He reported that there were three forms of government from which the convention might have chosen, "monarchical, aristocratical, and democratical." Each had its advantages and disadvantages. Again, he said that America could choose any of the following plans of governmental organization: "She may dissolve the individual sovereignty of the States, and become one consolidated empire; she may be divided into thirteen separate, independent and unconnected commonwealths; she may be erected into two or more confederacies; or, lastly, she may become one comprehensive Federal Republic." The form of empire was not feasible, he thought, because the territory would be too vast to administer the laws and rival empires would foster jealousies. The concensus of opinion among the constitutional fathers was that the states should adopt the policy, "Unite or Die"; hence the decision of that body for a "Federal Republic." Wilson justified then the decision in favor of a federal rather than a consolidated government:

Another, and perhaps the most important obstacle to the proceedings of the Federal Convention, arose in drawing the line between national and the individual governments of the states.

On this point a general principle readily occurred, that whatever object was confined in its nature and operation to a particular State, ought to be subject to the separate government of the States; but whatever in its nature and operation extended beyond a particular State, ought to be comprehended within the federal jurisdiction. The great difficulty, therefore, was the application of this general principle, for it was found impracticable to enumerate and distinguish the various objects to which it extended; and as the mathematics only are capable of demonstration, it ought not to be thought extraordinary that the convention could not develop a subject involved in such endless perplexity. If, however, the proposed constitution should be adopted, I trust that in the theory there will be found such harmony, and in the practice such mutual confidence between the national and individual governments, that every sentiment of jealousy and apprehension will be effectively destroyed.[25]

Wilson's expressed hope for harmony between the federal government and the state governments was probably not very

[25] McMaster and Stone, *Pennsylvania and the Federal Constitution*, 218-225.

sanguine; even while he spoke, western Pennsylvanians were impatient to answer him. Smilie of Fayette County immediately opposed McKean's resolution and counseled against haste in the ratification. Thenceforth Smilie, Findley, and Whitehill fought the ratification of the Constitution at every turn.[26] These men were democratic, modest landowners, representatives of a pioneer agricultural society in which the farmers had improved their lands but only a few had paid for them, and representatives of a debtor class, who objected to taxation. They led a gallant fight for a local democracy as opposed to a strong federal republic. In addition, there may have been the feeling among them that a change in government might deprive them of their political leadership in the state. And furthermore they realized that the adoption of the federal Constitution would necessitate the modification of their state constitution of 1776 because it was not consonant with the proposed federal plan.

These men contended that the new Constitution would create a consolidation and not a confederation of states. Did not the preamble say, "We the people" and not, "We the states"? It was a pact between individuals forming a society and not between states forming a government. They reasoned further that states would be reduced to mere corporations because the votes in Congress would be cast by individuals and not by states; because the taxing power of the federal government would destroy state sovereignties, as two independent and sovereign taxing powers could not exist in the same community; because Congress could regulate elections; because the judiciary was coextensive with the legislative power; because congressmen were to be paid out of the national, and not out of the state treasury; because there were no annual elections and no bill of rights. This plan was alarming to sectional Democrats.

An additional objection was found in the fact that the Constitution failed to provide for trial by jury in civil cases. On

[26] McMaster and Stone, *Pennsylvania and the Federal Constitution*, 231.

BACK-COUNTRY DEMOCRACY IN OPPOSITION 89

December 8 Findley observed that when trial by jury in Sweden fell into disuse tyranny prevailed. Wilson and McKean thought he was in error upon the fact and "called warmly" for his authority to verify the fact that Sweden had enjoyed trial by jury. Findley, reputedly unlearned, could not remember his authority but thought perhaps he could produce it. Accordingly the following Monday afternoon he carried to the convention a copy of *Modern Universal History* and the third volume of Blackstone's *Commentaries*, which definitely established his point. He read the passage and concluded witheringly:

I am not accustomed, Mr. President, to have my word disputed in public bodies, upon the statement of fact; but in this convention it has already occured more than once. It is now evident however, that I was contradicted on this subject improperly and unjustly, by the learned Chief Justice and Counsellor from the city. That the account given in the Universal History should escape the recollection or observation of the best informed man, is not extraordinary, but this I will observe, that if my son had been at the study of the law for six months, and was not acquainted with the passage in Blackstone, I should be justified in whipping him. But the contradiction coming from the quarter known to this Convention, I am at a loss whether to ascribe it to the want of veracity, or the ignorance of the learned members.

The following morning Wilson admitted that he had not believed Findley correct in his assertion that trials by jury had existed in Sweden. He did not pretend to remember everything. But he added:

Those whose stock of knowledge is limited to a few items, may easily remember and refer to them; but many things may be overlooked and forgotten in a magazine of literature. It may therefore with propriety be said by my honorable colleague, as it was formerly said by Sir John Maynard to a petulant student, who reproached him with an ignorance of a trifling point, "Young man, I have forgotten more law than ever you learned."[27]

[27] McMaster and Stone, *Pennsylvania and the Federal Constitution*, 300, 359-361.

The opponents of ratification contended that they had found defects, and certainly they had found arguments, but they could not find enough votes to stem the tide; on December 12 by a vote of forty-six to twenty-three the state convention of Pennsylvania ratified the federal Constitution. Thomas Scott and John Neville were the only western Pennsylvanians who favored the new plan of government. Both were delegates from Washington County, and they comprised just half of that county's delegation. Their two colleagues from the same county, James Marshel and James Edgar, voted with the entire delegation from Westmoreland and Fayette counties against ratification and refused to attach their names to the ratifying document. The vote for western Pennsylvania stood seven to two against the Constitution and probably was representative of the sentiment of the region. The townspeople of Pittsburgh and Washington, in Washington County, were assuming an attitude that was more conservative than that of their agricultural neighbors. The two towns were fast becoming Federalist islands in a sea of democracy.

The battle was not yet won by the Federalists, because nine states were required to ratify, and there was evidence of stout opposition in many states. It was not until the following June that New Hampshire assured the formation of the new government by its ratification. The months from December, 1787, to June, 1788, were busy ones for both Federalists and Anti-Federalists. The delegates in the minority in the Pennsylvania convention lost no time in publishing the reasons for their dissent. On December 18 there appeared in the *Pennsylvania Packet* a long address that is, in effect, an exposition of their political philosophy.

The Anti-Federalist minority objected to the haste with which the ratification was obtained and to the secret session of the federal convention and asserted they had offered to the state convention the following suggestions for changing the Constitution: that the right of conscience should be held inviolable; that in controversies respecting property and in suits between man and man, trial by jury should prevail; that in capital and criminal prosecutions a man should have the right to demand the cause and nature of his accusation; that excessive bail should not be required; that warrants unsupported by evidence should not be granted; that freedom of speech should be guaranteed; that state legislatures should not be restrained from enacting laws imposing taxes, except on imports and exports; that the states should control the elections of congressmen and that the number of congressmen should be increased; that the states should control their individual militias and that the militias should leave the state only with the state's consent; that the three branches of the government should function separately and that a constitutional council should be appointed to advise the president; that treaties should not be valid if in contravention to the Constitution of the United States or the constitutions of the individual states; and that the judiciary power of the United States should be limited to cases affecting ambassadors and other public ministers; to cases of admiralty and maritime jurisdiction; to controversies in which the United States was one of the adversaries; to controversies between states, between a state and citizens of different states, between citizens claiming land under grants from different states, and between a state or citizens thereof and a foreign state.

The minority delegates claimed that such an extensive area as that of the United States could not be governed except by a despotic power. They criticized the Constitution because the powers of the federal government established thereby would annihilate the powers of the state and because whereas the powers of Congress over the purse and sword would be unlimited, the states would be divested of every means of defense. Their address was signed by all the minority delegates except those of Washington County, James Marshel and James Edgar. The full delegations from Westmoreland and Fayette counties attached their names and thus committed themselves to a democratic philosophy of government, one that favored a weak central government with great powers reserved to the states and home rule by the people within the states.

This address of the dissenters acquired added significance in view of the developments in western Pennsylvania within the next six years. The people were to face a change in their own state constitution, an unpopular excise tax on spirituous liquors, a regional protest against that tax, and an actual federal army sent to suppress the violent resistance of a backcountry democracy. One need not agree with the principles of government expressed in the articles of dissent to appreciate the prescience of the so-called unlearned delegates from the western part of the state. Nor was their prescience greater than their determination and courage, for they returned to their homes and continued the fight during the ensuing year. Even in June when they learned that nine states had ratified the Constitution and definitely established the "Federal Republic," they did not cease their efforts; and they sent delegates to the Harrisburg Convention of November 8, 1788, which met for the purpose of proposing amendments to the new Constitution.

Apparently all western Pennsylvania was a rostrum upon which the merits and faults of the new Constitution were debated. Wherever they congregated, men were discussing the new government. They argued at the ferries, the mills, the taverns, the distilleries, before and after church services on Sunday, and even among their own family circles. Unfortunately, these individual man-to-man debates were not reported or preserved verbatim. From them the historian might obtain the real political philosophy of the plain people. Those arguments and observations that found their way into the files of the *Pittsburgh Gazette* were preserved, however, and from them a partial account of the controversies may be reconstructed.

Near the end of January, 1788, the more articulate men began their literary battle in earnest. The "Address and Reasons of the Dissent of the Minority of the State of Pennsylvania to the Constituents" began in the January 26 issue and continued through three issues to February 9. "Hudibras," probably Hugh Henry Brackenridge, was ready for the fray. The half-column essay on January 26 began:

Being in your town the ... other day, I found a number of people huddled together at a public corner, attending to one who, from the loudness of his voice, appeared to be zealously affected with his subject. I drew near, and found he was entertaining his audence [sic] with what he called tricks, sometimes defects, and at other times faults, in the constitution now before the public for their consideration.

Hudibras was astonished that a government formed by Washington and Franklin could have tricks, faults, and defects. "O! Washington," he exclaimed, "why didst thou not practise thy tricks upon us when it was year after year, in thy power, and when thou couldst easily have availed thyself of all the gold and honors a British monarch could bestow?" Hudibras could not understand why Washington should now practice tricks when he had not done so before. It was not the last time that Washington's name and influence were to be utilized in combating political opponents. Two weeks later "Hampden" in a long article opposed the Constitution on the grounds that the Convention had surpassed its authority and that the House of Representatives was too small. Furthermore, he doubted the loyalty and patriotism of some of the active lawyers among the majority members of the Constitutional Convention.

The controversy wandered frequently from the merits of the Constitution to questions of the integrity of the individuals. The Brackenridge-Findley duel broke forth again in the February 23 issue of the *Gazette*. The Pittsburgh lawyer offered proof of the fallaciousness of four statements attributed to Findley and concluded with the assertion that there were many other such statements that could be refuted but that he doubted that the value of such procedure would be worth the paper required. He signed his name. Findley, choosing to rely upon his successes in the various elections, apparently made no reply.

It is very likely that Brackenridge was the author of a column, "Cursory Remarks on the Federal Constitution," printed in the *Gazette* on March 1, because "Findley the Weaver" was once more mentioned. It was a facetious argument for the Constitution, yet almost 150 years later his remarks do not seem entirely ridiculous. The author feared and opposed the Constitution because it contained no provision with regard to the sex of the president. "Is it provided that he shall be of the male gender?" he asked. He continued, in mock alarm, "What shall we think, if in progress of time we should come to have an old *woman* at the head of our affairs? But what security have we that he shall be a *white man?* . . . is there any security that he shall be a *freeman?*" He concluded that phase of the article with the question, "Shall we in affairs of a civil nature, leave a door open to bastards, eunuchs, and the devil knows what?"

Some critics had asserted that the Senate was too aristocratic; and the author of the "Cursory Remarks" wittily supplemented their argument: "There is not a word said with regard to the ancestry of any of them [*the senators*]; whether they should be altogether Irish or only Scotch Irish. . . . they may overturn all authority, and make the shilelah the supreme law of the land." He likewise burlesqued the idea that there should be a larger number of representatives in the lower house. "The house of representatives is so large that it never can be built. They may begin it, but it never can be finished. Ten miles square! Babylon itself, unless the suburbs are taken into view, was not of greater extent."

Then the author of these remarks turned to the Bill of Rights as a more significant subject and stated: "The want of a *bill of rights* is the great evil. There was no occasion for a bill of *wrongs;* for there will be *wrongs* enough. But oh! a *bill of rights.* What is the nature of a *bill of rights? It is a schedule or inventory of those powers which the Congress do not possess.* ... When it is specified what powers are given, why not also what powers are not given. ... The *rights of conscience* are swept away," he lamented. "The Confession of Faith, the Shorter Catechism, and the Pilgrims Progress are to go. ... The *liberty of the press;* that is gone ... Not so much as the advertisement for a stray horse, or a runaway negro, can be put in any of the Gazettes. ... The *trial by jury*, that is knocked in the head, and all that worthy class of men, the lawyers, who live by haranguing and bending the juries, are demolished." He asked whether there was anything in the Constitution with regard to having a beard or measuring a pair of breeches. Finally, he reported that a neighbor of his who had been talking with Findley "says, that under this constitution all weavers are to be put to death." Many ideas that were lampooned in the eighteenth century have assumed a serious aspect in the twentieth century.

During this period David Redick's integrity had been questioned. The rumor spread that he had written to the "northern insurgents" (Daniel Shays's followers in Massachusetts) asking them to oppose the Constitution. Redick wrote an open letter to the *Gazette* denying that he had a desire to create a civil war and reminding the readers that Shays's Rebellion of 1786 had been put down some time before the meeting of the Constitutional Convention. He was not, however, so stanch in his opposition to the new Constitution as was Findley. Redick reported that "from the movement in which it [Constitution] was adopted by the state convention, I have used my influence to reconcile the minds of its disapprovers to it. He was unusual in that respect. Simultaneously with Redick's comments, "Sommers" of Greensburg published an appeal "To the People" entreating them to oppose the Constitution by calling on the assembly as a last resort, an appeal that bore no immediate fruit.[28]

Then began a month of sermons, probably written by the ir-

[28] *Pittsburgh Gazette,* March 15, 1788.

repressible and versatile Brackenridge who had acted as chaplain in the American army during the Revolution. The first appeared in the *Gazette* for March 22. The text (Isaiah 3:12) read as follows, "Oh, my people, they which lead thee cause thee to err, and destroy the way of thy paths." A few men who had temporary influence, it continued, had misled the people, but it had always been so. The opposition to the Constitution was the result of the teaching of the leaders, who had caused the people to err. The second sermon appeared the following week with the text,"My people are destroyed for lack of knowledge (Hosea 4:12)." Again the preacher condemned the men who represented western Pennsylvania and opposed the Constitution. The third, with another appropriate text, "Say ye not a confederacy, to all to whom this people shall say a confederacy (Isaiah 8:12)," appeared on April 5 and Brackenridge proceeded to show that the foes of the Constitution had misused the term "confederacy." Finally, he closed his series of sermons with a modern title, "We all roar like Bears." He compared the Anti-Federalist orators to bears. "The councillor of F—e [*Smilie?*], who lately stood upon his hind feet and roared for the space of three hours, to a multitude at U—n town, may be denominated a full grown bear, those are only cubs who have taken the tone from him, and with the same ursine disposition, have less strength of lungs."[29]

The Anti-Federalists in western Pennsylvania continued to roar to no avail. While the pioneer farmers remained adamant in their opposition to the Constitution, states along the seaboard were ratifying one by one, and Brackenridge and the Federalists in Pittsburgh and Washington were exulting. The final blow was struck when New Hampshire ratified on June 21, 1788. The federal republic was assured, and Findley, Smilie, and their followers could hope for nothing more than procuring amendments to the Constitution.

In Pittsburgh the supporters of the Constitution and of federal government celebrated, but a little prematurely. On

[29] *Pittsburgh Gazette,* March 22, 29; April 5, 12, 1788.

Friday, June 20, the day before New Hampshire ratified, the rumor flashed through the streets that Virginia had ratified the Constitution, thereby becoming the ninth state to do so. The following evening, almost at the same time that the New Hampshire legislature was taking the decisive step, a host, reputedly consisting of fifteen hundred people of the city and neighboring county, repaired to Grant's Hill to celebrate. It was a joyful occasion, particularly so to Brackenridge, who was enjoying complete vindication and a real triumph over his western Pennsylvania adversaries. There on Grant's Hill, "a beautiful rising mount to the east of the city," he addressed the people whose hearts and hopes were with the new government:

Oh my compatriots: . . . A union of nine states has taken place, and you are now citizens of a new empire: an empire, not the effect of chance, not hewn out by the sword; but formed by the skill of sages, and the design of wise men. Who is there who does not spring in height, and find himself taller by the circumstance? For you have acquired superior strength; you are become a great people.

After a discussion of the relationship of states to the federal government in which he compared the states to heavenly globes moving in a fixed orbit and never approaching too close or going too far from the center, he paid his respects to the Anti-Federalists:

But who are those fell monsters who growl . . . They are the opponents of the new system. O, ignorance, where is thy cave? . . . O, frogs of the marsh, local demagogues, insidious declamers, your pond is about to be dried up. No more amongst the weeds, and in the muddy fluid, shall you lift your hoarse voice. The marsh is drained, the dome aspires, and the bright tinges of the rising day, gild its summits.

But to the men of Pittsburgh who had supported the new government he averred that the hills, mountains and streams, even the Ohio, would approve their approbation. He closed with the hope that future generations would preserve the Constitution and show themselves worthy of it. The close of the speech was the signal for three rousing cheers and the throwing of hats into the air. Nine piles of wood representing the nine states that had ratified were lighted. Four piles were left "uninflamed," but the pile representing New Hampshire caught fire. Then the pile for Rhode Island, covered with tar and feathers, ignited, and subsequently those of New York and North Carolina began to burn. Thus as the people danced around, the wind blowing sparks from the nine piles lighted the "uninflamed piles."[30] It was not an unportentous ceremony, because the ratification movement in the nine states undoubtedly influenced the four tardy ones to join hands in establishing the republic.

So ended the ratification struggle in western Pennsylvania. Townspeople of Pittsburgh and Washington, with scattered support throughout the region, were the sole bearers of the torch for the new government. At home they were in the minority, but in the Union they were a part of the successful party. The pioneer farmers and democrats had behaved as had their friends in other states. They were by background and nature opposed to a strong government, and they had been provincial but bitter and sincere in their opposition. When they realized that they could no longer thwart the new government, they laid plans to effect amendments to the Constitution and they aided in procuring the Bill of Rights, which represents a compromise between the Federalists and the Anti-Federalists.

In western Pennsylvania steps were taken to further amendments shortly after the final ratification was secured. A meeting was held in Greensburg on August 5 to establish a county committee of correspondence for the purpose of stimulating a general sentiment for the Bill of Rights.[31] Similar meetings were probably held in other towns, because as early as August 18 a Uniontown meeting selected and certified Albert Gallatin and John Smilie as delegates to the Harrisburg Convention, which was held on September 3 for the purpose

[30] *Pittsburgh Gazette,* June 28, 1788.   [31] *Ibid.,* August 9, 1788.

of considering amendments. The seriousness of the people can be sensed by the fact that the certificate was signed by Nathaniel Breading, former member of the supreme executive council; James Finley, later an assemblyman; and Daniel Canon, Zadock Springer, and Joseph Torrence, also a future member of the assembly.[32] James Marshel was sent to the convention from Washington County, but for some reason no delegate from Westmoreland County appeared. It was a small delegation but the choice of men was fortunate. It contained Albert Gallatin, who was engaging in his first public act in a career that was to be prominent for over a generation. Here was a man at whom the Federalists could not sneer because of the lack of background or education.

The notes that Gallatin kept and the reports of the resolutions of the Harrisburg Convention indicate that the Anti-Federalists were not reconciled to the Constitution as first adopted. The activities of the convention consisted of expressing the desire for a confederation stronger than had existed under the Articles of Confederation but not so strong as provided for in the new Constitution. The delegates sought a new convention to revise the Constitution and drew up resolutions that contained some twelve proposals, among them the following: the powers of Congress should be expressly limited; the number of representatives should be apportioned one to twenty thousand people; senators should be liable to recall; Congress should not regulate the election of congressmen; there should be no standing army in times of peace except by vote of a two-thirds majority; states should be permitted to organize militias that would not be subject to martial law; and Congress should establish no courts other than the Supreme Court, except for admiralty jurisdiction.[33]

Apparently the work of this convention was of little significance other than to indicate the tenacity of the Anti-Federal-

[32] Gallatin Papers, vol. 4.
[33] *Ibid.*, For a brief account of the Harrisburg Convention see P. L. Ford, *Harrisburg Convention*.

ists, because no official action resulted. While the Bill of Rights was incorporated, there is no evidence to warrant the assertion that the first ten amendments to the Constitution developed out of this meeting or that Albert Gallatin was the author of them, because similar complaints and suggestions were registered in other states, in some cases even before the ratification of the Constitution. It is even probable that the democratic minority in the Harrisburg Convention had little expectation of accomplishing anything tangible in frustrating the new federal government. It was more likely that they were merely fighting on that front to prevent an attack by the conservatives on another front, namely, the Pennsylvania state constitution of 1776. It was evident that the existing state constitution and the state government under it would have to be modified to establish a working relationship with the new federal government, but the people of western Pennsylvania were still attached to their ultra-democratic constitution and were just as aggressive, though less successful, in defending it in 1789 and 1790 as they had been in the meeting of the council of censors in 1783-84.

THE CHALLENGE OF FEDERALISM

CHAPTER FIVE

THE inception of the movement for a new state constitution began in eastern Pennsylvania in the summer of 1788. The revision of the constitution had been desired as early as 1781, and a strong effort to accomplish a change had been made in the council of censors in 1783-84. The conservative majority had never reached a two-thirds level, however, and as has already been indicated the movement was defeated by a stubborn minority. Now in 1788, the conservative republicans, who had effected the ratification of the federal Constitution and were dominant in the state legislature and council, sought ways and means of calling a constitutional convention. The problem was not easy even with their complete control of the state government, because the constitution provided that a vote of the council of censors in which two-thirds of the members concurred was the only method by which a convention might be called. The council, according to the constitution, would not meet again until 1790, and the followers of Wilson were impatient. Furthermore, the council, comprised of two members from each county, would in all probability contain a minority sufficient to block the calling of a convention in 1790, just as it had done in 1783-84. Hence the necessity of achieving the end in a different, if unconstitutional manner. But it was desirable to cloak the movement with a semblance of legality. The assembly was employed as the agency, and the political philosophy of "inalienable rights of men" and "government for common benefit" was utilized as the justification for the actions of the Republicans.

Consequently, on March 20, 1789, Gerardus Wynkoop offered a motion in the assembly to provide for the calling of a convention. Four days later the motion was read a second time with amendments specifying that the election of delegates should occur at the same time and at the same places as the election for representatives to the assembly. The vote was carried by a majority of forty-one to seventeen. Listed among the majority was one western Pennsylvanian, John McDowell, of Allegheny County. Six of the seventeen who opposed the motion were representatives of Westmoreland, Fayette, and Washington counties.[1] Numerically the minority members were helpless, but those who lived west of the mountains were not hopeless. They were quick to emphasize the unconstitutionality of the act and to oppose western participation in a state convention.

Letters were exchanged between the democratic leaders of the four western counties in an endeavor to find a way to oppose a convention. Gallatin appears to have been the most active participant in the resulting effort to have the four counties withold delegates from the convention. On October 7 he wrote to Alexander Addison of Washington, who was a candidate, asked him to withdraw, and pointed out to him that the convention had been called in an irregular manner.[2] Addison was in favor of the ratification of the constitution, however, and did not accede to Gallatin's wish. To James Marshel, Gallatin wrote urging that no delegates be sent from Washington County and enclosed resolutions adopted by the people of Fayette County to the effect that that county would not elect delegates. Marshel replied on October 9: "am happy to find that the good people in your County are not disposed to Elect members for the proposed Convention. I

[1] Pennsylvania Constitutional Convention, 1776, *Proceedings,* 129, 130; William Findley's activity in the Constitutional Convention is told in detail in C. Schramm, "William Findley in Pennsylvania Politics." [2] Gallatin Papers, vol. 15.

THE CHALLENGE OF FEDERALISM 103

heartily agree with you that the Measure is Unconstitutional, Unnecessary and highly Improper and that the most prudent step for us at present is the measure proposed by the people of your County." He offered the opinion that the people of his county would adopt the resolution not to send delegates, promised to distribute copies of the resolution, and congratulated Gallatin upon a "well worded" resolution.

On the same day David Redick of Allegheny County wrote to Gallatin expressing joy that there were "a few friends to liberty every here and there through the continent, the misfortune is, they are scattered thinly and want the immediate means of communication, whilst the friends of Aristocracy are more active, more strongly braced up." He regretted that the action had not come three months earlier, because there was now insufficient time for deliberation, but he was willing to coöperate. John Flenniken of Fayette County, who had seen one of Gallatin's letters, wrote to him on October 11 concurring in the idea that the proposed calling of the convention was unconstitutional.[3]

There was insufficient time for effective organization, however, and all these efforts came to naught. The elections were held as designated, and delegates were chosen. The four western counties sent a full delegation of eight. Westmoreland chose William Findley, as usual, and William Todd; Fayette selected the familiar John Smilie and Albert Gallatin, despite the latter's efforts to prevent western Pennsylvania's participation in the convention; Washington sent Alexander Addison, a rising Federalist, and John Hoge, new to that county but familiar with politics; and Allegheny sent the Anti-Federalist, David Redick, and a promising, brilliant young Federalist, James Ross, whose presence was to be felt for a generation in state and national politics.[4]

It was a worthy delegation; every man was able, and Findley, Smilie, Ross, and Gallatin were outstanding—the

[3] Gallatin Papers, vol. 4.
[4] Pennsylvania Constitutional Convention, 1776, *Proceedings*, 138.

latter two were brilliant. Furthermore, it was a representative delegation. Addison and Ross were stanch Federalists reflecting, or perhaps determining, the political ideas of their professional and mercantile constituents. The remaining six were Anti-Federalists and democratic, true to the wishes of the agricultural constituency that opposed the revision of the constitution of 1776. Probably the six-to-two ratio was representative of the inclinations of the people in the western counties. Those delegates who were opposed to the modification of the constitution realized that the majority of the members of the convention favored revision, and as a result the minority determined to salvage as much of the political philosophy and governmental machinery from the old constitution as they could, rather than to oppose the formation of a new one.

The men from the western counties found themselves among familiar faces when the convention met in Philadelphia on November 24, 1789. James Wilson, Thomas McKean, Thomas Mifflin, Robert Whitehill, and many other eminent and experienced leaders were present. Practically every member who sat in that body had served either in the general assembly, the supreme executive council, or the council of censors. Some of them had served in all three, and Judge Wilson had been, in addition, a member of the federal Constitutional Convention of 1787. It was an impressive array of men, but the delegates from the western counties were not out of their depth. In fact, there was a complaint from the citizens of Philadelphia to the effect that the region west of the Susquehanna had an inordinate amount of influence in the convention. This influence was due to their individual and collective abilities and to the manner in which the deliberations were conducted.

The convention organized on November 25, with Thomas Mifflin as president. A discussion of rules for transacting the business of the convention led to the decision to follow the practice of considering measures in a committee of the whole in order to permit greater liberty of debate and discussion. Order was less strict in the committee of the whole than it was in the convention. In the convention no member was permitted to speak more than twice except by special permission, but in the committee of the whole each member could speak upon a question as often as he desired, and some members did address the group as many as eight or ten times. After unrestricted discussion in the committee of the whole, the questions were then presented to the convention for ratification.

Chief Justice McKean was chosen to be chairman of the committee of the whole and by a unanimous vote was accorded the privilege of offering resolutions, voting upon measures, and discussing measures under deliberation.[5] Once measures were referred by the committee of the whole to the convention and adopted in the convention, they were then referred to a select committee of nine members who were instructed to form and prepare a draft for the proposed constitution. The committee of nine was chosen by vote, and on December 11 the names of the members of this committee were announced. William Findley was the only member who received the unanimous vote of the convention and as a result was named chairman of the committee, which also included Edward Hand, Henry Miller, James Wilson, William Irvine, William Lewis, James Ross, Charles Smith, and Alexander Addison.[6] There is little wonder that eastern Pennsylvanians were disappointed at the personnel of this committee, but they need not have entertained any fears, because James Ross and Alexander Addison, two members from the extreme western counties, were Federalists.

William Findley wielded great influence in the deliberations even though his sympathies and votes were with the minority. The conservative revisionists had enough strength

[5] Pennsylvania Constitutional Convention, 1776, *Proceedings*, 137-153; William Findley, "Fraud Detected," in *Farmers' Register* (Greensburg), September 28, 1799.   [6] Pennsylvania Constitutional Convention, 1776, *Proceedings*, 154.

to effect any modifications that they desired but they were anxious to accomplish a revised constitution without irritating or alienating the friends of the old constitution. Judge Wilson, looked upon as the ablest statesman in the assemblage, assumed the lead in the attack on the constitution of 1776, but Findley took him aside and with some well-chosen words pointed out that the convention was comprised of many of the ablest men of the state, who were, nevertheless, "greatly influenced by the old party Jealousies." He suggested to Wilson that declamatory attacks on the old constitution would only increase the breach, that many members of the convention were "attached to Penn's Constitution" because the colony had prospered under it and because it had carried them through the war. These men, Findley said, were to be instructed rather than irritated.[7]

Wilson approved Findley's plan for conciliating the factions among the delegates and sought Findley's advice as to the manner in which the business ought to be conducted. It was Findley's opinion that the general resolutions regarding amendment to the constitution ought to be laid on the table as subjects for discussion but that in debate the old constitution must be treated with a "delicacy approaching reverence." Wilson agreed, asked Findley to bring forward the resolutions, and promised that he would support them. Findley preferred what he called a preparatory discourse with resolutions to follow from the floor. As a result, he delivered a long opening address in which he reviewed the "perfections and defects of Penn's government" and the constitution of 1776. He pointed out that even though the present constitution might be good in theory, many deviations had been made from it, great differences of opinion had always existed about it, and the voluntary election of the present convention was such a testimony of lack of confidence in it that it was inconsistent to think that it would be possible to restore its efficiency without important

[7] Findley, "An Autobiographical Letter," in *Pennsylvania Magazine of History and Biography,* 5:445 (1881).

THE CHALLENGE OF FEDERALISM 107

alterations. Findley himself believed that this speech was the most effective towards harmonizing the factions of any he had ever made.[8] An impartial view would lead to the conclusion that it had at least a great influence in shaping the conduct and deliberations of the convention. The minority members acceded to modifications that they did not want, but they also secured concessions that the majority were reluctant to make and probably would not have made except for this spirit of conciliation.

Because Judge Wilson had prepared a draft of a constitution, Findley and others insisted that he take the lead in the committee of the whole in offering resolutions for the new frame of government.[9] The convention accepted Wilson's resolutions on the general principles of government and on the alterations necessary to accomplish the revisions. His resolutions suggested that the legislature should consist of more than one branch, that the executive powers should be vested in a single person with a qualified negative on the legislature, that the judges should hold their positions for life or during good behavior and should receive fixed salaries, and that a bill of rights should be accurately defined.[10]

The delegates from western Pennsylvania were of the same mind on a majority of the principles adopted. Ross and Addison, of course, favored a more conservative form of government and were more heartily in accord with the proposed alterations made by Wilson than were their colleagues. Ross indicated his attitude by proposing that the lower house of the legislature elect the members of the upper house. Gallatin led the opposition to this proposal and urged that state senators be chosen by popular vote, and he was successful in having his idea accepted. He and his friends were not so fortunate in other points, however. Gallatin's notes indicate that he favored a larger representation in the house, greater liberty

---

[8] William Findley, "Fraud Detected," in *Farmers' Register* (Greensburg), September 28, 1799. [9] C. Schramm, "William Findley in Pennsylvania Politics," 52.
[10] Pennsylvania Constitutional Convention, 1776, *Proceedings,* 166-175.

with the press, extension of the franchise, and greater equity in law.[11] Findley wished to add an advisory council to the executive department for the purpose of restricting the powers of the governor, but failed. He also preferred a three-fifths rather than a two-thirds vote in the legislature to override a governor's veto, but again he was unsuccessful. He did succeed, however, in securing the appointment of a secretary of the commonwealth to countersign all the governor's commissions and orders drawn upon the treasury department for "appropriated monies" and to keep the records of the supreme executive council at the call of both houses. Furthermore, Findley was instrumental in procuring a provision for establishing at least one school in each county with the state paying part of the salary of the master, thereby enabling the poor to be educated gratis; in addition, he secured a provision to further the promotion of the arts and sciences in one or more universities by state aid.[12]

A second committee, which included Findley as chairman and Wilson, Hand, and Ross, was instructed to prepare a schedule for putting the government into operation. They reported on February 24 that all laws in force at the time of the amending of the constitution and not inconsistent with the changes should remain as if no alteration had been made; that all officers appointed by the executive department should continue in office until September 1, 1791, except in cases of expiration of term or the death or resignation of the officer, when no reappointment would be made; that justice should be administered in the counties until September 1, 1790, by the same justices in the same courts and in the same manner as before; that the president of the supreme executive council and the council should continue to exercise their authority until the third Tuesday in December, 1790; that the same

---

[11] Gallatin Papers, vol. 15. These papers contain Gallatin's notes for speeches on popular election of senators, right of suffrage, liberty of press, place of courts and equity in law, and estimates on representation.
[12] C. Schramm, "William Findley in Pennsylvania Politics," 57-60.

number of representatives should be elected until a census of the taxpayers could be made; that the election of senators should be made in the same manner and by the same regulations as applied to the representatives; that the election of the governor should be conducted in the same manner as that of the representatives; and that the election returns be made to the president of the supreme executive council and immediately directed to the Speaker of the senate.[13]

Two days later, on February 26, the first session of the convention was adjourned until August 9, 1790. It was ordered upon a motion by Wilson, seconded by Findley, that the constitution as agreed upon by the convention be published "for the consideration of the good people of Pennsylvania."[14]

The second session of the convention met as scheduled, and again the delegates and the committee of the whole studied the proposed constitution by section without making any significant changes. One serious objection to the proposed plan of government was voiced through a memorial from the Society of Friends on August 21, 1790. The members of this society objected to the section that "proposed that those who conscientiously scruple to bear arms shall pay an equivalent for personal service," because to support a war was contrary to their religious scruples. Their request was rejected, however, by a vote of thirty-nine to twenty-three. The constitution was brought before the members of the convention on September 2, adopted, and "engrossed." The engrossed copy was then delivered to the master of rolls to be recorded, and the convention was adjourned.[15]

The government of Pennsylvania under this plan paralleled the federal government in many respects. The former plural executive was supplanted by a single executive elected for a term of three years. The legislature consisted of two houses: the lower, designated as the house of representatives, whose members were elected annually; and the upper, called the

[13] Pennsylvania Constitutional Convention, 1776, *Proceedings*, 236.
[14] *Ibid.*, 246.   [15] *Ibid.*, 274, 294-308.

senate, whose members were elected for a period of four years. The franchise was extended to all free, white, male citizens. A supreme court was also established. Obviously the new constitution was a compromise that the delegates from western Pennsylvania could subscribe to, because every one of them attached his name to the document.

The compromise, nevertheless, was a disappointment to the democratic elements in western Pennsylvania. They had failed to retain their old constitution that had given them so much weight in the state government just as they had failed in the legislature in 1786 and on the bank question, the navigation of the Mississippi, and in the ratifying convention of 1787. They were not ready for an open revolt, however, because the new form of government was sufficiently democratic to allow them to protect their interests, provided they could maintain a political solidarity in their own region and make an effective alliance with like-minded leaders in the eastern counties. Despite their able leaders, the outlook for western democrats was dubious because a conservative class was developing among them, and a much stronger national government was arising. One more humiliation, which was to be the climax of all their defeats, was approaching.

During the last decade of the eighteenth century the politics and problems of the United States, of the state of Pennsylvania, and of western Pennsylvania had many similarities. National tasks included the organization of a new government to deal with finance, land problems, commerce (both foreign and domestic), industrial development, Indian problems, and foreign affairs. Differences of opinion arose as the to best solution of these problems and to the policies of the government in solving them, with the result that two well-disciplined national parties, the Federalists and the Democratic Republicans, emerged. In Pennsylvania the tasks included the formation of a new state government to deal with problems of finance, land titles, commerce, the development of industry, Indian attacks, and, indirectly, foreign affairs. State political organizations paralleling those on the national stage arose. Naturally the people of western Pennsylvania, an integral part of the state, and, in a smaller way, of the United States, were interested in the same questions that confronted both national and state governments, and on this smaller stage, parties of federalistic and democratic tendencies became more clearly crystallized.

The democrats in the region were eager and ready for organization. In addition to the group of experienced leaders there was a group of rising young men who were to add new blood and greater pungency to the democratic cause, the most notable of whom was the "young giant," Albert Gallatin. Gallatin's previous training and experience prepared him admirably for his long political career. He was born in Geneva, Switzerland, in 1761 of an old and aristocratic but not noble family. Five of his ancestors had served as chief magistrates of that little self-governing city. His grandmother knew Voltaire well, and when she called upon the great thinker the young lad occasionally accompanied her and sat upon his knee, wondering at his wit and wisdom. Gallatin's academic education was completed at the college at Geneva, where he fraternized with a group of young men who, while not radical, understood and sympathized with the philosophy of Rousseau and the Physiocrats. After his graduation in 1779 his grandmother urged him to enter the army and upon receiving his reply that he would not serve a tyrant, she gave him a cuff on the ear, which probably did much toward hastening his journey to America. The young remonstrant landed at Cape Ann on July 14, 1780, taught the French language at Harvard, took an insignificant part in the Revolution, and in 1783 met Savary de Valcoulon, who had claims against the state of Virginia and who established a partnership with Gallatin for the purpose of procuring a hundred and twenty thousand acres of land. Gallatin's share was one-fourth of the estate, and was to be paid for by his superintendence of the project.[16]

[16] The material on Gallatin's early life in this and the following paragraphs, which

Thereafter Gallatin spent the years from 1783 to 1789 as an agent, interpreter, and partner of Savary. The winters he passed in Richmond, Virginia, where he increased both his experience and his circle of friends. The summers he utilized in purchasing, surveying, and clearing land, in storekeeping, and in making intermittent journeys to New York and Philadelphia. He soon concluded that land in Fayette County, Pennsylvania, was more valuable and that Indian raids were less likely to occur there than in Monongalia County, Virginia, with the result that he made an effort to establish a base of operations as near as possible to the Pennsylvania line. For that purpose he selected the farm of Thomas Clare, situated upon the Monongahela River and Georges Creek about four miles north of the Virginia line, and in 1785 he leased a house and five acres from Clare, upon which he established a store. Two years later he purchased from Clare 450 acres, to which he transferred the store and where he built his home, Friendship Hill. Grounded in European culture and education, acquainted with the tradition-smashing Voltaire, conversant with the philosophical democracy of Rousseau, he was now established on an American frontier where his theoretical democracy was to be tested by practical application.

From a humble and inconspicuous beginning in western Pennsylvania, Gallatin came up through the years to eminence and power, first in his adopted state, next in national affairs, and finally in international affairs—a man who played prominent roles in the affairs of many nations and on two continents. His success was the result of many factors. He himself believed that his ability to conduct legislative affairs in committees was the secret of his rise to prominence. Certainly he worked methodically and with assiduity; he understood problems of finance as did no other man of his time in the

---

is based on H. Adams, *Life of Albert Gallatin,* 1-84, and on the Gallatin Papers, vol. 15, has appeared in but slightly different form in Ferguson, "Albert Gallatin, Western Pennsylvania Politician," in *Western Pennsylvania Historical Magazine,* 16:183-195 (1933).

HUGH HENRY BRACKENRIDGE
From the contemporary drawing by Robert Smith

THE CHALLENGE OF FEDERALISM 113

United States except Alexander Hamilton; he was just as methodical in collecting and tabulating election statistics as he was in the making of his financial reports; and he conducted his correspondence with local and national politicians with the same care. In addition, he was tactful, cosmopolitan, and pleasant. He could match the intellectual ability of any man in the state, and his entrance into politics gave the Democrats an intellectual prestige that they had not enjoyed before. The fact that Gallatin was a farmer brought him the confidence of his neighbors. He was a valuable addition to the Democratic party in western Pennsylvania and was a fit associate in every respect for Findley and Smilie.

There were other prominent names among the Democrats, though none so outstanding as Gallatin. John Baptiste Charles Lucas, born in Normandy in 1758, trained in the Honfleur and Paris law schools, and graduated from the law department of the University of Caen in 1782, came to America and settled on a farm near Pittsburgh about 1785, where he lived for twenty years. During his sojourn in the region he served six years in the state senate, some nine years as a judge of the common pleas court, and two years in the lower house of Congress. It was he who drew down the wrath of Judge Addison in the incident that eventually brought about Addison's impeachment. Samuel Ewalt, first sheriff of Allegheny County, who lived on a farm (now a part of the Treesdale Farms) a few miles north of Pittsburgh;[17] Michael Rugh, a neighbor of Findley in Westmoreland County;[18] and John and William Hoge, whose father David had owned the land upon which the the town of Washington stood, were only a few of the young Democrats who were on the highway to prominence.[19] Every ounce of their strength was needed, because a powerful opposition was arising.

John Neville from his home, Bower Hill, which overlooked the Chartiers Valley, guided the political fortunes of the

---
[17] For material on Ewalt and Lucas, see Dahlinger, *Pittsburgh*, 41, 47, 48.
[18] *Pittsburgh Gazette*, November 1, 1794. [19] Crumrine, *Washington County*, 479.

Neville family, which was the focal point of early Federalism in the western region. His economic eminence and his political prestige, gained in the supreme executive council and in the ratifying convention, made him a man of power. But his own power was enhanced by that of several influential men who were connected with the family. His son, Presley Neville, was nearly, if not quite, as able as the father. The younger Neville had a summer home just at the foot of the hill within hailing distance of Bower Hill, as well as a town home in Pittsburgh. He was a gentleman but indifferent to work or to study, apparently unwilling to apply himself to the study of law under the direction of Brackenridge for a period of longer than six months. He was a man of great influence in the community, however. He dispensed hospitality lavishly, served in the legislature, in the prothonotary office, and as brigade inspector for the militia of Allegheny County. He was also a surveyor and land speculator.[20]

Abraham Kirkpatrick, a brother-in-law of John Neville and a major in the Revolution, added his weight and influence to that of the "Neville Connection." A son-in-law of John Neville, Isaac Craig, who was an Irish immigrant, was another influential member of the family. Craig was stationed at Fort Pitt in 1780 and became deputy quartermaster-general in the West in 1791, a position that required him to do much purchasing and to control many men. John Woods, son of George Woods who came to western Pennsylvania as a land agent for the Penn family, became the attorney for the Nevilles and very naturally became intimate, socially and politically, with this powerful "Connection."[21] All these men were men of better than average ability, all were active in the economic life of the community, and all were well-to-do, with political sympathies akin to those of Hamilton. John and Presley Neville received the confidence and favors of the Federalist party in both the state and national government.

[20] Felton, "General John Neville," 31-59; Hogg, "Presley Neville," 16-25.
[21] Dahlinger, *Pittsburgh*, 131, 132.

Supporting the members of the "Neville Connection" and in some respects leading them were other men of similar political faith. James Ross of Washington and, after 1795, of Pittsburgh, destined to become the West's most conspicuous Federalist leader, was just rising to full stature in 1790. A Scotch-Irishman, born in York County in 1762 and educated at Princeton, he removed to western Pennsylvania and taught in John McMillan's school. He studied law intermittently with his teaching and was admitted to the bar in Washington County in 1784. His magnificent personality and ability soon won for him recognition in the legal field, and his marriage to the daughter of George Woods brought social prestige. His experience in the convention of 1789-90 fitted him for a political career, which was blighted only by the overwhelming force of Jeffersonian Democracy.[22]

Another stalwart of this group was the hard-headed Scotchman of Washington, Alexander Addison. Educated at Aberdeen University, Scotland, he arrived in Washington County in 1785, where he studied law under David Redick and was admitted to the bar. Six years later he was made president judge of the fifth judicial district of Pennsylvania, eloquent testimony of his ability. He was a rabid Federalist and a devotee of law and order; he rigidly opposed the Whiskey Insurrection and exerted his influence to suppress it. Nevertheless, his very vigor and aggressiveness may have been liabilities rather than assets to his party, because of the enmities that they created. He permitted his violent partisanship to color his behavior on the bench, and he condemned not only criminal offenders but political opponents. When in 1803 he harshly overruled an associate judge, the Democrat, John B. C. Lucas, he was tried and impeached by the state legislature. During the ten years from 1790 to 1800, however, he was a bulwark of Federalism in the region and when he overruled Lucas he was only following the Federalist practice initiated by the national administration of using the court to retard

[22] For a short account of the career of James Ross, see Brownson, *James Ross,* 1-52.

the measures and advances of the opposing political party.[23]

There were many lieutenants for growing Federalism, some old, some new. Thomas Scott, who had been Neville's only colleague to ratify the Constitution; John McMillan, whose fame and power as a preacher were increasing; Thomas Stokely, "Land Jobber," who had lived in Washington since 1782 but entered politics only in the decade of the nineties; James O'Hara, a prominent merchant and industrialist of Pittsburgh;[24] John Wilkins, another thrifty and enterprising business man of Pittsburgh;[25] and James Finley, the Presbyterian preacher from Fayette County, were the more conspicuous advocates of Hamilton's doctrines. Well-to-do business and professional men, with an occasional gentleman farmer, they had economic and intellectual affiliations with the commercial and economic classes of the Atlantic seaboard. They had wealth, ability, social prestige, and the advantage of a newspaper, the *Pittsburgh Gazette,* which was mildly Federalist; but they could not appeal to the agricultural class, which was as yet more numerous and contributed more votes than the urban classes.

It would be inaccurate to imply that these leaders, either Democratic or Federalist, were members of highly organized or regimented parties in 1790, because there was as yet no national party in the modern sense. There was no group of people with a permanent political organization or a well-developed program. There were those who had definite ideas upon the forms and purposes of government and upon the advantages that they sought from the government, but there was no well-oiled political machine to put through those measures or to subjugate personalities to the machine. For many years to come in western Pennsylvania, a man with a strong personality and a following—a Gallatin, or a Ross, or a

---

[23] Crumrine, *Bench and Bar of Washington County,* 39-46. See also T. Lloyd, *Trial of Alexander Addison.*
[24] A good account of James O'Hara is in E. C. Schramm, "General James O'Hara."
[25] Dahlinger, *Pittsburgh,* 117.

THE CHALLENGE OF FEDERALISM   117

John Hoge—could demolish loosely formed parties. Nevertheless, the arrows were pointing toward the Federalism of Hamilton and the Democracy, or Republicanism, of Jefferson, even in the chaotic political realm of this young western society, and parties were soon to emerge.

The election of 1790 showed that the friends of democracy were still preponderant west of the mountains even though they were among a minority in the state as a whole. John Neville and James Finley were the only Federalist members returned to the state house, while five Democrats, Findley, Baird, Ritchie, Minor, and Gallatin, were returned. A full quota of Democrats was sent to the senate—Richard Butler for the district comprised of Westmoreland and Allegheny, John Smilie and John Hoge from the district of Fayette and Washington.[26] While complete election statistics are not available to indicate the exact ratio of the two party groups, it is probable that the ratio of five Democrats to two Federalists in the house was indicative of the relative strength of the parties in the region. The fact that Thomas Scott had been elected to Congress in 1789 by the Federalists does not obviate this conclusion, because he was elected upon a general state ticket of eight congressmen. Federalists east of the mountains really determined the result, and his election may have been contrary to the desires of a majority of his constituents.[27]

The successful candidates to the state legislature from the West were unusually prominent in the session of 1790-91. Findley in the house and Smilie in the senate apparently assumed the leadership in the routine work of organizing their respective bodies. Because they were experienced parliamentarians and realized the necessity of orderly procedure in the conduct of business, they suggested practices and proposed committees that became fixtures in the parliamentary ma-

[26] Pennsylvania, *House Journal,* 1790-91, p. 3, 4; Pennsylvania, *Senate Journal,* 1790-91, p. 4.
[27] *Pennsylvania Packet,* (Philadelphia), December 20, 1788; *Pittsburgh Gazette,* December 24, 1788.

chinery of the two houses. Each in his own body made motions for committees—committees on claims against the state, on finance, on taxation, on land, and on transportation; and each offered suggestions upon the relationship of the two houses pertaining to the procedure in joint session and adjournment. Western Pennsylvania was most fortunate in having two men of such political and parliamentary experience. Not only did they suggest the committees but they also served upon a majority of them and wielded an inordinate amount of influence.[28]

Despite the activity of these two men, Albert Gallatin equaled them, perhaps surpassed them, in service during the first session of the newly formed legislature. In writing of his own activities in the legislature he said,"I acquired an extraordinary influence in that body (the Pennsylvania House of Representatives),—the more remarkable, as I was always in a *party* minority."[29] His statement was no exaggeration, for among his papers is a small committee book, similar to a carefully kept schedule or diary, which indicates that in that first session he served upon twenty-seven committees and that he made all the reports and drew all the bills for them.[30] A perusal of the *House Journal* for 1791-92 reveals that he served upon more than thirty-five committees, but some of them were relatively insignificant and he evidently disregarded them in his account. The preparation of the report for the committee on ways and means in his first session served as his passport into politics. It was a masterpiece of precision, clear, straightforward and concise. It is a well-known fact that it is possible for one or two assiduous men to dominate a committee and determine its policies; and Gallatin's ability and his willingness to contend with the prosaic routine of committee work made him indispensable and gave him great influence.[31]

The activities of Gallatin, Findley, and Smilie in regard to

---

[28] Pennsylvania, *House Journal,* 1790-91, p. 6, 7, 10, 18, 26, 29, 32, 40, 54, 55; Pennsylvania, *Senate Journal,* 1790-91, p. 107, 108.
[29] H. Adams, *Life of Albert Gallatin,* 83, 84.   [30] Gallatin Papers, vol. 15.
[31] Pennsylvania, *House Journal,* 1790-91, *passim.*

THE CHALLENGE OF FEDERALISM   119

legislative procedure did not deter them or their western colleagues from taking an active part in all legislation affecting their constituents. The perennial questions of the protection of the frontier against Indian raids, of the repeal of the excise upon distilled liquor, both state and federal, of surveying and improving roads and canals to facilitate westward transportation, of the clearing of land titles, and of making public lands more available to settlers, all arose, and upon these issues the men unanimously reflected the sentiment of their constituents. Even John Neville supported Gallatin's resolutions against the excise offered on January 22, 1791, to the effect, "that every species of taxation, which shall operate, directly or indirectly, as a duty on articles exported from any state, is unconstitutional." Neville, however, refused to sign the list of reasons given opposing the excise. The senate refused by a vote of nine to eight to concur with Gallatin's resolutions: Butler and Hoge voted nay, thereby aligning themselves with the Federalists rather than with their western friends. James Finley, Gallatin's own colleague from Fayette County, was the sole western man to oppose a bill entitled, "An Act to repeal so much of every act or acts of Assembly ... as relates to the collection of excise duties," which Gallatin introduced on April 9.[32] Finley's attitude was probably the result of the fact that he was a Federalist at heart and that he was a political and personal rival of Gallatin.

During the ensuing three years the Federalists ranks increased, though many of the Democrats were reëlected to offices—either to their original seat in the house, to one in the state senate, or to Congress. William Findley was elected to Congress in 1791 and, except for the fact that his personal influence was overwhelming, his success would seem to indicate that the section was democratically inclined.[33] Gallatin, who had received approximately two-thirds of the votes cast

[32] Pennsylvania, *House Journal*, 1790-91, p. 108-111, 145-147, 363; Pennsylvania, *Senate Journal*, 1790-91, p. 92.
[33] C. Schramm, "William Findley in Pennsylvania Politics," 81.

in his county in 1790, was reëlected to the state house in 1791 and 1792 practically without opposition. Smilie, Hoge, and Butler retained their seats in the senate without standing for reëlection. But in the lower house new faces, less democratic, appeared. Thomas Scott and Thomas Stokely, both of Washington County, and Thomas Morton of Allegheny County represented a gain for the Federalist ranks in the session beginning in December of 1791. The following year David Bradford was elected from Washington County, but he added little to the democratic strength because of his personal animosity for Gallatin. So great was his enmity that he, alone of the legislators from his region, opposed the election of Gallatin to the United States Senate in February of 1793.[34] The newly elected men were no less aggressive and coöperative upon measures for improving conditions in western Pennsylvania, but they displayed an increasing tendency to support Hamilton's program on the national stage.

The breach between Hamilton and Jefferson developed soon after the Virginian arrived in New York to assume the duties of the state department in 1790. They "rolled logs" to effect the passage of a measure for the assumption of the state debts by the federal government, but thereafter they were in disagreement upon nearly every policy, and Jefferson probably lived to regret his coöperation in the "log rolling." The establishment of the United States Bank in 1791 produced a definite gap between them; the passage of a federal excise on liquor in the same year increased the breach; the newspaper war conducted by John Fenno, Federalist, editor of the *United States Gazette,* and Philip Freneau, Democratic editor of the *National Gazette,* widened it still more; and the arrogant conduct of "Citizen" Genêt, which produced a climax in the heated controversies between the pro-English and pro-French sympathizers, extended the gap into a yawning chasm. Jefferson resigned from his post in the state department in December of 1793 and devoted himself to the formation

[34] Pennsylvania, *House Journal,* 1791-92, p. 3, 4; 1792-93, p. 3.

of a new political party with which to combat the Federalists.

Hamilton, probably a constitutional monarchist at heart, advocate of a strong central government based upon a substantial social class, and a devotee of commerce and industry, had already made great strides in forming a political organization. He organized the federal government and his party simultaneously. The payment of the public debt, both foreign and domestic, strengthened the government and drew the financial classes to him; the assumption of the state debts further increased the credit of the central government, tied the states to it, and increased the confidence of the financiers in him; and the creation of the United States Bank chained the bankers to the secretary of the treasury. Hamilton's advocacy of a tariff to protect industry was a gesture to manufacturers, and the strong central government, which was able to protect commerce, captured the commercialists. But this program would require money and some one would have to pay the fiddler. That problem Hamilton solved in two ways: he deferred payment of the national debt and proposed an excise on spirituous liquors, a tax that would fall more heavily upon farmers and distillers than on his wealthy commercial and financial friends. A letter to his prominent lieutenants in the states, a communication to the Society of Cincinnati, and an editorial from Fenno's pen were sufficient to put the secretary's ideas into motion. In Pennsylvania he relied upon James Wilson, Robert Morris, Thomas Willing, and William Bingham, men after his own heart and traditional rivals of back-country democracy.

Jefferson, an agricultural equalitarian, a states' right Republican, a leveler, politically and socially, was exasperated by the policies and practices of Hamilton. The Virginian's conception of a weak central government was unrealized; his scheme of a society in which agriculture would be dominant and an agrarian pay-as-you-go financial system would prevail was frustrated; his theory of equal rights to all seemed defeated; and his sympathy for the French was outweighed.

In fact, his most embarrassing situation in the state department was occasioned by the arrogant and ungracious conduct of the French emissary, Genêt, whom Jefferson actually wanted to aid. Genêt delivered Jefferson and the pro-French sympathizers, bound hand and foot, to the Federalists, who favored an understanding with England.

Jefferson's retirement from the cabinet gave him freedom to assemble his forces. He appealed to those classes that Hamilton forgot—the farmers, urban laborers, and an occasional planter or professional man. In Pennsylvania, David Rittenhouse and Benjamin Rush, professional men of Philadelphia, were responsive; but the most effective support appeared among the democratic politicians—Alexander J. Dallas of Philadelphia, Findley, Smilie, Gallatin, Baird, Todd—those men who had been fighting the conservatives of eastern Pennsylvania. The Virginian could hardly have known in 1794 that Gallatin, who had the temerity to offer a resolution in the Senate requesting a financial report from the secretary of the treasury, was soon to rise to the leadership not only of his region but of the national House of Representatives.

Thus the two earliest national political parties came into existence. Each consisted of a group of individuals with a permanent political organization with stated policies and principles, which the members hoped to put into practice by acquiring control of the governmental offices by means of elections. Each party reached out to the various states in the Union; national leaders relied upon lieutenants in the states, gave them political advice and aid, and in return expected the support of the state parties.

The crystallization of the two national parties was paralleled in the Quaker state and in the region of western Pennsylvania. Both Federalists and Democrats in the eastern counties realized the necessity of effecting an understanding with the leaders west of the mountains, and while Hamilton's friends controlled the state government and were increasing in numbers in Allegheny and Washington counties from 1790 to 1793, they were unable to crush the back-country democracy. The Federalists had few lucrative offices to extend to worthy party leaders even had they realized the possibilities of the spoils system. It is true that General Neville was made inspector of federal revenue for the district, but his office proved to be a political liability for him and for his party. Isaac Craig was appointed deputy quartermaster-general, the most influential of the posts because of the number of men with whom he dealt and the amount of government purchases to be made. James O'Hara and Abraham Kirkpatrick, industrialists and merchants, and John Wilkins, merchant, met other Federalists at the taverns in political parleys, which were probably as effective as any Federalist methods except the militia muster rolls. John McMillan preached religion and Federalism to his flocks. And all these leaders corresponded with their eastern friends on political questions. Certainly John and Presley Neville received the confidence, favors, and counsel of eastern friends. The growth of Federalism was slow, however, outside the towns of Pittsburgh and Washington.

The strength of the Democrats, or Republicans, in the eastern part of the state increased to such an extent by 1792, that they were in a position to challenge the supremacy of the Federalists. If the democratic farmers of the western counties would coöperate with the eastern Democrats, there was a possibility of wresting the control of the government from the Federalists. The western farmers were of the same political faith; only a closer and more effective understanding was necessary. Dallas, secretary of the commonwealth, assumed the task of cementing the alliance. From 1792 on, he wrote regularly to Gallatin; he displayed an interest in the problems of the western counties, suggested political alignments, and sent pamphlets and propaganda for distribution. On May 4 of 1792, an election year, he wrote a long letter to the Fayette County leader, expressing concern about the dangers of Indian raids and inquiring if General Arthur St. Clair would be acceptable to western men in the event that there should be a change in the secretary of the war department. Obviously catering to the western Democrats, he also asked Gallatin to convey felicitations to Findley and Smilie. On September 25, more than a month before the election, he again wrote Gallatin and sent political literature to be distributed. During the same year James Hutchinson, a political leader in Philadelphia, wrote three letters to Gallatin informing him upon political matters.[35]

At the same time Findley of the western leaders and General William Irvine of the eastern men were building up a coalition between the two sections. In a letter to Irvine, dated June 11, Findley discussed Indian affairs and reported a breach between the two Federalists, John Woods and Thomas Scott of Washington. Findley could not understand the reason for Woods's efforts to prevent Scott from winning a seat in Congress. A second letter, on August 17, reported that the people were rather indifferent to politics and predicted that the excise meetings that were being held would produce no results. The third letter from Findley to Irvine, written October 12, immediately after the election, recorded Westmoreland's vote for some of the congressional candidates. Findley had received 2,054 votes; Smilie, 2,009; Frederick Muhlenberg, 2,007; Irvine, 2,006; and William Montgomery, 2,005. The Federalist candidates were hopelessly beaten—Woods received 1,498 votes; Scott, 237; and John McDowell, 17.[36]

The Democratic leaders within the region also were exchanging ideas and advice. Findley and Gallatin were corresponding. Gallatin corresponded with James Marshel of Washington County. Even Judge Addison wrote to Gallatin to register a complaint and send him election statistics. This letter Gallatin turned over and on the back of the page computed the votes in various townships and counties. He was studying the detailed vote for reference in future elctions, ever the best of practical political methods. The exchange of information by letter was important and utterly necessary in

[35] Gallatin Papers, vol. 4.   [36] Irvine Papers, vol. 11, p. 17, 21, 33.

view of the fact that there was no paper to serve the interests of the Democrats in the region.[37]

The development of the Democratic societies, sometimes called "demoniacal societies" and frequently designated as "Jacobin Clubs" by the Federalists, was a boon to the organization of the Democrats. Western Pennsylvania Democrats were ripe for "Jacobin Clubs." John Scull had helped in preparing the people for this radical movement by publishing accounts of the French Revolution and the successes of the Revolutionists regardless of the fact that they were distasteful to him. He also had reprinted the constitution and principles of the parent society in his paper.[38] Brackenridge had done his part on July 4, 1793, when he had made an eloquent effort to extenuate the violence of the Revolutionists as a necessary by-product in a just cause.[39] At least two and probably three "Jacobin Clubs" were formed in the western counties. One was established at Mingo Creek and another at Washington. Each had a regular organization with officers and a constitution. They held meetings, considered political questions of local and national nature, and corresponded with the Philadelphia Society. "Democratus," a correspondent to the *Gazette,* on June 28, 1794, called attention to the society recently formed at the "mouth of the Yough," but the historian knows no more about that society today than the readers seemed to know then. Incidentally, none of the records of these societies seem to have been preserved, a fact that disturbs the student, because they were said at the time to have been chiefly responsible for the Whiskey Insurrection. Undoubtedly the societies were effective political instruments. They gave the Democrats an opportunity to congregate, to express their opinions, and to frame resolutions and remonstrances. In addition to formulating the policies of the Democrats locally, they aided in the in-

[37] Findley to Gallatin, August 20, 1792; Marshel to Gallatin, September 17, 1792; Addison to Gallatin, October 11, 1792, Gallatin Papers, vol. 4.
[38] *Pittsburgh Gazette,* December 26, 1789; July 27, 1793.
[39] Hazen, *Contemporary American Opinion of the French Revolution,* 246.

tegration of the party in the state and nation. They were invaluable in the development of Jefferson's party.

Back-country democracy in Pennsylvania was ready for its last desperate stand in 1794, and, as the American Revolutionists had rallied around the question of taxation a generation previously, so western Pennsylvania farmers rallied in resistance to federal excise on liquor. Opposition began as soon as the measure was suggested by Hamilton in his report to Congress in December of 1790. Democratic Congressmen were heated in their denunciations of the excise while it was still in the committee stage, and Gallatin, on January 22, 1791, introduced in the legislature of Pennsylvania a resolution against the general policy of an excise. Thereafter, west of the mountains there was an increasing resentment against the excise. The stoutest opposition existed among the farmers of Washington County in the vicinity of Mingo Creek and Washington where the Democratic societies were active. The farmers of Westmoreland, Fayette, and Allegheny were opposed to the measure but were more conservative, probably because they lacked the facilities for organization that the Democratic societies afforded. Too, the leaders of Westmoreland and Fayette were milder men than those of Washington County. Findley, Baird, Todd, Smilie, and Gallatin objected to the unpopular measure, but they were less virulent by nature than David Bradford, James Marshel, and other Washington County leaders. The people of Pittsburgh were inclined to favor the tax on liquor because they were Federalist generally and because few of them were distillers and liable to this particular tax.

From a passive political resistance in 1791 in which Democrats and Federalists could coöperate, the movement developed into an insurgency in 1794 in which the Democratic farmers opposed the Federalist townsmen and federal authority. Sentiment ran high against the tax, even against those who paid it, as William Cochran learned to his grief: "His still was cut to pieces; and this was humorously called, mending his still; and the menders, of course, must be tinkers." "Tom the Tinker" was the name assumed by those who uttered threats, advice, or commands "in measures with regard to the excise law."[40] The farmers attempted to prevent the enforcement of the measure by intimidating distillers who acquiesced in the tax and by persecuting the officers who served the summons.

On July 15, in the midst of the harvest season, the hottest and most irritating time of the year, David Lenox, United States marshal, arrived with a batch of summons to serve. Wisdom seemed the better part of valor, and he secured John Neville to accompany him in his duties. All went well until the marshal, leaving Neville on his horse in a lane, rode into a wheat field to read a writ to one Miller. Neville observed a group of men approaching on the run and urged Lenox to hurry. The two officials galloped off in safety, but the enraged farmers fired the shot that marked the beginning of the insurrection. The incident was the straw that broke the camel's back, the prick that loosed the pent-up wrath and indignation of these democratic farmers. They were conscious of eight years of defeats on every political measure that was dear to them; they were aware of an unfortunate situation for which there seemed to be no redress except open rebellion.[41]

For three months the atmosphere was tense in southwestern Pennsylvania, and one insurrectionary incident followed another in quick succession. On July 16, two days after the summons had been read to Miller by the federal marshal, a party of radicals attacked and burned "Bower Hill," the home of John Neville. In the melee one of the attackers was mortally wounded. About a week later, on July 24, a meeting was held at the Mingo Creek meetinghouse in which David Hamilton, a leader of the Mingo Creek society, David Bradford, and James Marshel, all radical Democrats, dominated the assembly and

---

[40] H. H. Brackenridge, *Incidents of the Insurrection*, 1:79.
[41] For extensive contemporary accounts of the Whiskey Insurrection, see H. H. Brackenridge, *Incidents of the Insurrection*, and Findley, *History of the Insurrection*. The best account is by Leland D. Baldwin, "Whiskey Rebels."

assumed a militant tone against the federal government and the Federalists of the Pittsburgh area. Insurrectionist leaders intercepted the Pittsburgh mail in order to learn who of the Pittsburghers were sending reports of events to Philadelphia.

On August 1 a meeting of volunteers from the militia was held on Braddock's Field with the purpose of punishing those people in Pittsburgh who favored the enforcement of the excise. Threatening to burn "Sodom," they marched upon the city, drank four barrels of Brackenridge's whiskey, burned a barn, and returned home. Two weeks later delegates from the four western counties met at Parkinson's Ferry (Monongahela City) to determine upon their course of action in dealing with the three federal commissioners, Senator James Ross, Jasper Yeates, a justice of the Supreme Court of the United States, and William Bradford, attorney-general of the United States. At Parkinson's Ferry Bradford and Marshel urged resistance to the federal government; Gallatin and Brackenridge advised acquiescence to the law. Again, at Brownsville on August 28, Gallatin and Brackenridge urged submission and in the midst of great danger won their point. By a vote of thirty-four to twenty-three the assemblage voted to accept the terms of amnesty extended by the commissioners. The signing of the required pledges began but was not carried out with sufficient speed to prevent the arrival of thirteen thousand federal troops, who found no revolutionary army to oppose them.

The events of the insurrection were not political, in the narrower sense of the word. In a broader sense the rebellion was political—its causes were political, and it had significant political results. On the national stage it represented the first definite challenge to the sovereignty and power of the federal government; and it also presented a definite challenge to the Federalist party. Jefferson had resigned from the cabinet less than six months before to create an opposition party; Gallatin, a western Pennsylvanian and the product of a European radicalism closely related to the philosophy of the French Revolution, had affronted Hamilton in requesting that the secretary of the treasury make a financial report of the treasury's condition; and frontier democracy, especially that of western Pennsylvania, had opposed the ratification of the federal Constitution only seven years prior to the insurrection. The prestige of the federal government and of the Federalist party was at stake. Under the circumstances, suppression of the insurrection was essential to Hamilton. In addition, the crushing of back-country democracy in western Pennsylvania would seem to discredit the Democratic party there, and open the opportunity for the development of Federalism in the region. Hamilton probably had expectations of ridding himself of the bothersome Gallatin and Brackenridge by putting them in the apparent position of traitors. A series of trials were held to consider the guilt of the "rebels," but the leaders escaped without impairing their political status.

In the political realm of the state, the downfall of back-country democracy would have enhanced the control of state politics, which the Federalist party already held. The Democrats, already a minority party in the state legislature, would have been reduced to a helpless position. But the suppression of the uprising did not crush the antipathy that the western farmers had for the excise, nor did it make Federalists of them; it merely increased their opposition to the party of Hamilton and taught them that they must utilize only political measures in seeking to improve their economic status.

The insurrection produced no great changes in the politics of western Pennsylvania. The democratic farmers who had actively opposed the excise on whiskey were still opposed to the principle of the tax. Their economic problems and their environment did not change, and their political philosophy did not change; but they recognized that violent resistance to the federal government was not a feasible means of obtaining redress. And apparently the number of Democrats did not decrease. The Federalists were exultant and hopeful in their triumph, but their immediate political gains were not appreciable. The merchants and townsmen were still outnumbered by a subdued and wiser agrarian population. Federalist leaders in the region anticipated, with justification, that the national leaders of their party would give them aid. John and Presley Neville, James Ross, Alexander Addison, and John McMillan had rendered valiant service to their party during the insurrection and deserved recognition. But Hamilton's recognition of his lieutenants in western Pennsylvania did not procure for them the favor of their own constituents.

The insurrection, however, did affect the careers of some individuals who had engaged in it. The more foolhardy men lost prestige. David Bradford fled down the Mississippi, thus permanently removing himself from the stage; and James Marshel was put in an unpleasant position that curtailed his political career. But except for the more radical leaders, the taint of insurrection proved to be no handicap. The saner and more conservative opponents of the excise, Findley, Smilie, and Redick, seemed not to suffer a loss of prestige from their activities; Brackenridge, a townsman of Democratic faith, sustained a loss of popular esteem, not because he consorted with the "whiskey rebels" but because he had seemed to vacillate between the opposing forces. The people questioned his sincerity. He was a Democrat and townsman with political ambitions who needed the votes of both the Democratic farmers and the Federalist townsmen. His apparent efforts to straddle the fence during the uprising did not please either group. Gallatin, on the other hand, consciously or unconsciously, conducted himself in such a manner that he increased his political strength. He had opposed the excise in principle; he had opposed it actively so long as constitutional measures were employed; and he had urged acquiescence to the government when submission seemed the better policy. He had behaved with less recklessness than David Bradford, whose rash statements necessitated his flight; and he had proceeded with less uncertainty than Brackenridge, whose wavering had made him unacceptable alike to Republicans and to Federalists.

Federalism under the direction of Federalist leaders in the state and nation had challenged the domination of back-country democracy in western Pennsylvania between 1789 and 1794 with indifferent success. It had made a conservative revision of the state constitution in 1790; it had sponsored an economic and financial system that was unsatisfactory to the democratic farmers of the West; it had passed a federal excise on whiskey that was odious to the farmers and distillers on the frontier, and when those farmers and distillers resisted its enforcement, the overpowering strength of the state and national governments had suppressed them. But the Democrats had not been won over to the Federalist party. They retained their political faith and awaited the rise of a national Democratic, or Republican, party strong enough to cope with Hamilton's organization.

THE STRUGGLE FOR SUPREMACY

CHAPTER SIX

Party lines were clearly drawn between the Federalist party of Hamilton and the Republican party of Jefferson by 1794. At that time the Federalists, dominant in the national government and in the state government of Pennsylvania, sought to consolidate their forces and perpetuate their powers. The Republicans were increasing rapidly and likewise sought to organize themselves and to oust their political adversaries. In no section of the United States was party rivalry more intense than in western Pennsylvania. Antipathies and animosities of the Whiskey Insurrection lingered on during the ensuing five years to intensify the conflict. Pittsburgh was the western citadel of Federalism, and Washington boasted many able men of that political faith. The townsmen, merchants, and a few Federalist farmers waged a merry battle to overcome the agrarian Democrats, or Republicans, as they were designated with increasing frequency, who were attracted to the party of Jefferson. As in previous years, local issues were prominent, but national issues, political tricks, and personalities played an increasingly important part in the outcome.

The issue was close in the election of October 14, 1794, which occurred before the excitement of the uprising had subsided. The Republicans emerged with a narrow victory. Westmoreland and Fayette counties chose Republicans for all the offices. The first-named county returned Benjamin Lodge, Michael Rugh, and George Smith to the lower house of the state legislature; and the latter elected Gallatin and John Cunningham as its representatives in that body. The senatorial district composed of those two counties chose John Moore and William Todd for the state senate. Allegheny County elected two Federalists, Presley Neville and Dunning McNair, to the state house of representatives. Washington County chose Craig Ritchie, Benjamin White, James Brice, and William Wallace, the first two Republicans and the latter two Federalists, to the lower house. The senatorial district of Allegheny and Washington counties returned Thomas Stokely and Absalom Baird, Federalists, to the upper house of the state legislature. Obviously the Federalists of the towns of Pittsburgh and Washington were dominant in the politics of their respective counties.[1]

The western counties were entitled to two national congressmen, one from the district of Westmoreland and Fayette counties and a second from the district of Washington and Allegheny counties. Findley, as usual, was elected with practically no opposition in his district. Four men, however, offered themselves for a seat in the lower house of Congress from the other district—Thomas Scott and John Woods, Federalists, and Daniel Hamilton and H. H. Brackenridge, Republicans. None of these candidates was wholly satisfactory to the voters. Scott had served in Congress before and had voted for the excise, a fact that rendered him unpopular with a great number of people in the region; Woods had opposed the insurrection and had sought to establish peace, but had suffered a loss of prestige from previous political defeats; Hamilton was unacceptable to conservatives because of his strong partisanship with the insurrectionists; and Brackenridge, who had appeared to straddle the fence in the insurrection, was described as a transformed preacher and a lawyer who used profanity.

Dr. John McMillan feared that Brackenridge would be

[1] *Pittsburgh Gazette*, November 1, 1794; Pennsylvania, *House Journal*, 1794-95, p. 4, 28; Pennsylvania, *Senate Journal*, 1794-95, p. 38, 125.

elected despite the fact that his popularity was waning and sought a strong man to defeat him. It is reported that McMillan was the instigator of a meeting, held at Canonsburg about ten days before the election, that suggested Albert Gallatin of Fayette County as a candidate for the districts of Allegheny and Washington counties. McMillan did not know Gallatin personally but was impressed with the sanity of his conduct in the insurrection. Supposedly, Gallatin's name was submitted without his knowledge or consent only three days before the election. It does not seem possible, however, that the information of Gallatin's candidacy could have been carried to the different election districts in so short a time. Regardless of this rare and unusual procedure in American elections, Gallatin, a Republican, living outside the congressional district, was elected to Congress. Conclusions upon this outcome are difficult; obviously many rabid insurrectionists who had resented Gallatin's tendency to temporize in the insurrection nevertheless voted for him; it is very likely that a number of Federalists, following Dr. McMillan's advice, voted for him; and it is more than probable that a majority of the democratic farmers voted for him because they sincerely preferred a Republican for the office. If, however, the Federalists' votes provided a margin for victory, they lived to regret their action.[2]

The success of the Republicans in the western counties was a disappointment to the Federalist party in the state. The Federalist leaders in the legislature had hoped that the Republican minority would be reduced further as a result of the election of 1794, and in their chagrin they resorted to a political trick to unseat the Republicans from the four western counties. A petition to the house of representatives from sixteen inhabitants of Huntingdon County and another from Washington County presented the opportunity to consider the legality of the elections in those counties.[3] From December 16,

[2] *Centenary Memorial of . . . Presbyterianism in Western Pennsylvania*, 397; Brackenridge, *Incidents of the Insurrection*, 2:44, 45.
[3] The petitions are in Pennsylvania, *House Journal*, 1794-95, p. 34, 79, 80.

1794, to January 9, 1795, the house of representatives and the senate deliberated upon this question. The legislators whose seats were contested were not permitted to vote, but Gallatin and Cunningham were given the opportunity to state their cases before the bar of the house. The former in a long speech, reviewed the causes and incidents of the insurrection, justified the right of the people to petition and to oppose by constitutional steps policies that they did not like, and asserted that the men of the western counties had submitted to the demands of the federal and state governments in sufficient time to make their votes legal. His effort was futile, however, because the Federalist leaders in control of both houses of the legislature voted to reject the western members on January 9, 1795.[4]

The ousted members, Republicans and Federalists alike, agreed to stand for reëlection in order to vindicate themselves. With one exception, John Moore, who did not choose to run, all of them were reëlected. Presley Carr Lane of Fayette County, Republican, was elected in Moore's place.[5] Gallatin, who during this interim was congressman-elect, returned to the state legislature and occupied his seat until the close of the session. Few measures of significance were considered during the remainder of the session, and aside from the aforementioned efforts of the eastern leaders to oust the western men, nothing of note occurred in the first part of the session.

The election of 1795 was quiet and produced very few changes. Apparently the Federalists and Republicans merely held their ground. Westmoreland and Fayette counties reelected all their assemblymen except Gallatin, who was replaced by John Smilie, a stanch Republican. Allegheny County chose Samuel Ewalt, a former Federalist, in the place of Dunning McNair, and Washington County elected John Minor and David Acheson to the seats held the previous year by James Brice and Benjamin White.[6]

[4] Pennsylvania, *House Journal*, 1794-95, p. 79, 80.
[5] *Ibid.*, 170, 174, 181; Pennsylvania, *Senate Journal*, 1794-95, p. 100.
[6] Pennsylvania, *House Journal*, 1795-96, p. 3-9.

The usual problems germane to the region, those pertaining to the ownership of land, to transportation, education, protection against the Indians, and to the navigation of the Mississippi River, were still present. But from 1794 to 1798 national affairs overshadowed the local questions in determining the politics of the region. Problems of diplomacy particularly interested western Pennsylvanians. The question of a commercial treaty with England and of a treaty with Spain that would settle the navigation of the Mississippi engrossed their attention.

The pro-English and pro-French sentiment that had been very strong in the United States in 1793 had subsided only a little by 1794. The fact that Hamilton and the Federalist party, English sympathizers, were in the saddle in 1794 had smoothed the way for an attempt to make a commercial treaty with England. Under ordinary circumstances western Pennsylvanians, far removed from the seaboard, would not have been deeply concerned with such a treaty. But the English forts along the boundary between Canada and the United States had not been evacuated, and the western pioneers believed that the English officers in command of those forts had stimulated Indians attacks upon the frontiers. Thus, a relationship between the local problem of defense against Indian attacks and the national problem of foreign affairs resulted. At the same time, however, western Pennsylvanians were deeply interested in the navigation of the Mississippi and became greatly agitated when the Federalist leaders sent John Jay to England. Jay was the same diplomat who had almost bartered away their rights to navigate the Mississippi a few years before.

The Jay Treaty with Great Britain was the first significant measure that confronted Congress in 1796. It had been confirmed by the Senate, but its provisions were such that the House would have to vote appropriations to make the treaty effective. Gallatin and Findley believed the treaty to be undesirable and thought that the president and the Senate were infringing upon the powers of the House, because the confirmation seemed to obligate the House to make an appropriation of money. Gallatin opposed the appropriations on constitutional grounds and led the fight in the House against the fulfillment of the provisions of the treaty. His constituents were divided upon the desirability of the treaty. The Federalists in and around Pittsburgh favored it upon commercial and political grounds, and many of the farmers, believing that Indian raids were instigated by the English agents along the Lakes, hoped that an acceptance of the treaty would diminish the number of attacks. But many of these same people did not want the executive branch of the government to overawe the House of Representatives.

On March 21 the members of the Allegheny County Grand Jury, then sitting at Pittsburgh, sent a petition to Gallatin in which they favored the treaty; David Redick on April 7 informed him of a meeting held at Washington that adopted a similar attitude; and on May 5 John McMillan, pastor of a church near Canonsburg, wrote to Gallatin commending him upon his resistance to executive aggression but imploring him to support the treaty and informing him that a meeting of McMillan's congregation would be held on the following Sunday to take the sense of the people upon the matter.[7] This meeting was held, and McMillan's congregation supported the treaty.[8] It is probable that McMillan's letter to Gallatin and the meeting of his congregation were due to the activities of Brackenridge and Addison, who favored the treaty. The former had written to Addison on April 30, 1796, suggesting that, "a small letter from McMillan to Gallatin would settle the matter, for it is on McMillan he counts, and is secure. It ought to be demanded of McMillan, that *as he sent him*, he should keep him right."[9]

Regardless of these communications and additional ex-

[7] Gallatin Papers, vol. 5.
[8] *Pittsburgh Gazette,* March 19, 1796.
[9] *Centenary Memorial of . . . Presbyterianism in Western Pennsylvania,* 399.

pressions from Westmoreland County,[10] Gallatin was not deterred from his purpose. Findley likewise opposed the treaty, but he and Gallatin were in the minority in the House of Representatives. Their efforts were not wasted, however, because it was upon the issue of the Jay Treaty that the Democratic-Republican party began to take shape, and the party centered about Gallatin in the House. Apparently, the Pinckney Treaty with Spain in 1795, which opened the Mississippi to western Pennsylvania with some restrictions, had mollified western men. They were more agreeable to the English treaty because they had secured the navigation of the Mississippi.

The Federalists were more than holding their own in the western counties at this time. Even Gallatin despaired of his reëlection to Congress in 1796. His campaign may be traced clearly through a number of letters that he wrote to his wife, who remained in New York while he made the journey to Fayette County during September and October of that year. He reported in a letter from Philadelphia that it appeared that William Findley would be reëlected from the congressional district of Westmoreland and Fayette but that he himself would probably be superseded by the Federalist, Thomas Stokely. He did not believe that his loss of popularity was due so much to the stand that he had taken on the treaty as to the fact that he did not reside in the district that he represented. The Republicans of his district were hesitating between James Edgar and Brackenridge. From New Geneva Gallatin reported that a number of scurrilous newspaper attacks had stimulated his friends to take up his cause again in order to vindicate him.[11]

The vigor of Gallatin's followers won the election for him but by a much smaller margin than in 1794. Federalism, although gaining in the district, was not dominant except in Pittsburgh and Washington and their vicinities; the party had not captured western Pennsylvania as has occasionally been asserted. Certainly the Federalists would not have drafted a

[10] *Pittsburgh Gazette,* July 9, 1796.   [11] H. Adams, *Life of Albert Gallatin,* 176.

Republican from another congressional district to represent them in Congress. Westmoreland and Fayette counties were undoubtedly Republican, with practically no Federalist strength in the first-named county and very little in the latter. Washington County had a more effective and more numerous Federalist constituency with such leaders as Alexander Addison, John Woods, Thomas Stokely, and John McMillan. Allegheny County, likewise, was well fortified in Federalism with such leaders as the members of the "Neville Connection," John Wilkins, General John Gibson, and James Ross, now a resident of Pittsburgh and a member of the United States Senate, to lead the party.

While the furor and excitement aroused by the Jay Treaty with England relegated local questions in the state legislature to the background, they did not completely submerge local issues. A number of problems, many of them continuations from previous years, were brought up for consideration. Western men were inconvenienced in making the journey to Philadelphia to sit in the state legislature or to visit the land office. They felt that the capital should be removed to a more centrally located site, and in March of 1795 they launched a movement to change the capital from Philadelphia to a location further west. Carlisle was unsuccessfully advanced as a site for the capital on March 28, 1795. Only McNair and Neville of the western men opposed the measure in the house of representatives, a fact that indicated that those two men were fairly well established in the Federalist party.[12] A year later, on January 7, 1796, a committee was established to consider a more central location. On January 28 a measure to move the seat of government to Reading failed by a vote of forty-two to thirty-four, with only Minor of the western men favoring the measure. Immediately afterward a measure to move the capital to Carlisle failed by a vote of fifty-five to twenty, with Neville and Ewalt the only western men favoring that site. On March 3 and 4 Lancaster was considered as a seat

[12] Pennsylvania, *House Journal*, 1794-95, p. 303-306.

of government in the lower house and accepted by a vote of thirty-nine to thirty-six, with Neville still opposed to it.[13]

Western Pennsylvania's representatives continued their fight to increase the fortifications in the West against the Indians. William Todd presented a petition in the senate on March 7, 1795, asking, "that the Legislature will take the unhappy situation of our frontiers into serious consideration, and devise some means that will grant the necessary protection," but this motion was tabled.[14] In December of the same year a committee in the house of representatives was proposed to consider a grant of land to the United States for a more eligible situation for a fort on French Creek, because the site of the old fort was deemed unsatisfactory.[15] As late as December 22, 1796, the governor's message to the legislature suggested that the defense of the frontier had seemed inadequate.[16] But the hitherto continual agitation concerning Indian attacks was practically at a close by that time, although the county militia was a necessary organization as events in the War of 1812 were to prove.

Another problem always of deep interest to western Pennsylvanians, the land problem, was considered frequently during the years from 1794 to 1799. William Todd brought in a petition from the people of Westmoreland County in February of 1795 praying that the land office "may be opened to all citizens on equal terms."[17] This petition was occasioned by the policy of the state to sell large grants of land to speculators and land companies. The Pennsylvania Population Company and the Holland Land Company had acquired great tracts of land in northwestern Pennsylvania in 1792 and 1793 respectively. Together they owned the greater part of the land now contained in the counties of Crawford and Erie. From that time on to 1836, there was constant trouble, involving land

[13] See Pennsylvania, *House Journal*, 1795-96, p. 88, 165-167, 293-300, 303, 304.
[14] Pennsylvania, *Senate Journal*, 1794-95, p. 133.
[15] Pennsylvania, *House Journal*, 1795-96, p. 27.
[16] *Ibid.*, 1796-97, p. 54.   [17] Pennsylvania, *Senate Journal*, 1794-95, p. 116.

titles, ejection, and litigation, between those companies and actual settlers.[18] A petition from Josiah Tannehill of Allegheny County was presented in December of 1795 asking for redress. He had built a home situated on a tract of land on the path leading from Fort Le Bœuf to Presque Isle. A survey had revealed that the tract fell within the state's reserved land. Consequently he had lost his land and his improvements, and he appealed for a special grant of four hundred acres adjoining to compensate for his loss. There were many cases similar to this, and many men received grants of land by special acts of the legislature.[19]

In February of 1796 a measure was passed in the house entitled, "An act for selling several reserved tracts adjoining the towns of Erie, Franklin, Warren, Waterford, Beaver; and also the reserve tract of two thousand acres at the mouth of Harbour Creek, below Presque Isle."[20] Throughout the time when these measures dealing with the sale of reserved lands and vacant lands were being proposed, western men stood solidly for the sale of such land to actual settlers.[21] Western representatives were assiduous in their efforts to procure land from the reserved tracts for settlers, to facilitate the settlers' opportunities to buy land, and to protect the actual settler, or even the squatter who had improved his land, against ejection or the loss of his tract through failure to complete his payment for it or to pay the taxes.

The westerners were equally diligent in their efforts to stimulate the building of roads and canals and to improve transportation by clearing the beds of the rivers for navigation. Scarcely a week passed between January, 1794, and March, 1797, while the legislature was in session, in which a measure dealing with some such project was not brought before the legislature for consideration. The Allegheny River was

---

[18] Reynolds, "Crawford County. A History of Its Growth and Development," in *Daily Tribune-Republican* (Meadville), centennial edition, May 12, 1888, p. 4.
[19] Pennsylvania, *House Journal*, 1795-96, p. 63.
[20] *Ibid.*, 262.   [21] *Ibid.*, 408, 409; 1796-97, p. 388.

declared a public highway in March, 1794; a few days later a committee recommended the granting of additional money for improving a road from Frankstown to Pittsburgh; among the unfinished business reported in December of the same year was a bill to authorize certain deviations in the road from Bedford to Pittsburgh; and the governor's message in December of the following year contained a survey of roads for the state.[22] With this encouragement roads were built, rivers were declared public highways, and internal improvements generally made progress although not as rapidly as western settlers had anticipated. Their representatives, however, were alert and were constantly pressing their measures in the Pennsylvania legislature.

Nor did they forget education. On a measure proposed in December, 1795, to establish schools throughout the state in order that the "poor may be taught gratis" every representative from the western counties voted affirmatively, and Lodge, Ritchie, Smilie, and Ewalt were named on the committee to draft such a bill. In this same session of the legislature, a petition was presented apparently without success from the trustees of the Canonsburg Academy asking for money to complete a spacious stone cabin. A year later, however, in December, 1796, a committee recommended a bill to grant relief to Washington Academy, and the following March the governor signed a bill affording such relief.[23]

The reorganization of election districts to establish more convenient voting places, the incorporation of towns, especially of Pittsburgh and Uniontown, and the division of Washington County to form the new county of Greene were also the subjects of many petitions and much consideration during these years. An act to erect the town of Pittsburgh was passed in 1794, and the good news was published in the *Pittsburgh Gazette* on May 17. It was two years later, however, on March 4, 1796, that the committee recommended that Union (now

[22] Pennsylvania, *House Journal*, 1794-95, p. 58, 281, 25; 1795-96, p. 10-20.
[23] *Ibid.*, 1795-96, p. 28, 235, 236, 368; 1796-97, p. 77, 399.

Uniontown) in Fayette County be incorporated.[24] In the same year, on February 9, the governor signed a bill erecting Greene County as a separate county from Washington, and the following year authorized the judges of the new county to hold court near Waynesburg.[25]

In their votes upon these measures that affected only their own region, the representatives of the western counties were generally in accord. Whether Federalist or Republican, they were deeply interested in anything that would improve the social or economic conditions of their region. Below the surface, however, there was a strong partisanship, which appeared in their reactions upon questions that were not purely local in their scope. On occasions a provincial attitude was displayed by the western representatives. An outstanding example of this provincialism occurred in February of 1797 when the state legislature considered the adoption of an address to Washington in reply to his farewell address, a copy of which had been received in the house of representatives on September 17, 1796. Every western representative, except Benjamin Lodge, opposed the drafting of an answer to the communication of the retiring president. It would appear on first thought that all of them except Lodge were Republicans.[26]

But the action of the representatives in opposing the address to Washington must not be taken as an indication that Federalism was dead in western Pennsylvania in 1797. In reality the Federalists were strong, and their strength increased during that year and the following year as a result of the diplomatic crisis between France and the United States. The Federalist party had assumed an anti-French attitude from the beginning of the French Revolution; the ratification of the Jay Treaty in 1796 had angered the French, and when the Federalist administration recalled James Monroe and sent a commission composed of John Marshall, C. C. Pinckney, and Elbridge Gerry to France in 1797, the French people were

---

[24] Pennsylvania, *House Journal*, 1795-96, p. 302.
[25] *Ibid.*, 244; 1796-97, p. 180.   [26] *Ibid.*, 127.

not appeased. Talleyrand, the French minister, anxious to feather his own nest, affronted the American commissioners and outraged the American people by insisting that Marshall, Pinckney, and Gerry "grease his palm" before he received them. Once again the French government had embarrassed Jefferson and Madison and the Republicans, who were friendly to it. On the demand of Republican leaders in Congress, Adams placed before the House the diplomatic correspondence revealing the insult that the French had inflicted upon the United States, concealing only the names of the three French intermediaries whom he designated as X, Y, and Z. The "X Y Z Affair" was a body blow to Jefferson and the Republicans; it raised the Federalist party to the peak of its strength in the country; for the first and only time, John Adams was popular, and the majority of the people of the United State would have gone to war with France to support him.

The "X Y Z Affair" cast its shadow over western Pennsylvania where so many of the farmers and Republicans had been sympathetic with the French Revolution. Federalists flared up in indignation, and even pro-French Republicans were swept off their feet by the outrage. Young Tarleton Bates, a Virginian and a brother of Frederick Bates, later a governor of the Michigan territory, and also of Edward Bates, who was to become attorney-general in Abraham Lincoln's cabinet, was then a young Republican living in Pittsburgh. He wrote to his brother Frederick observing that these were momentous times in politics. He reported that he was democratic but that he was a lover of his country.[27] Many other Republicans of the region reacted in a like manner, with the result that they were ready to join in a movement for war against France. The Federalists lost no opportunities to develop the fervor of a war and support for Adams. John Scull had dropped his pretense of nonpartisanship in his newspaper columns and aligned himself on the side of the Federalists.

[27] Mrs. E. M. Davis, "The Letters of Tarleton Bates, 1795-1805," in *Western Pennsylvania Historical Magazine*, 12:34(1929).

The *Pittsburgh Gazette* contained many columns on the "XYZ Affair"; in fact, on April 28, 1798, a special supplement of the *Gazette* was devoted to the instructions to Pinckney, Marshall, and Gerry. The people, carried away by the war hysteria, believed that the militia should be in readiness to respond to a call from the president. A general meeting of the militia of Allegheny County and a meeting of the officers of the Westmoreland County militia were reported in the *Gazette* on July 21. Letters of assurance were sent to President Adams, and letters of gratitude were received from him by the officers of the militia, all of which were printed in the *Gazette*. The militia of the four southwestern counties comprising the Third Pennsylvania Division were given orders to mobilize by Major General John Gibson of Allegheny County. The patriotic fervor of the people and the excuse for the meetings of the militia officers were factors that tended to promote the growth of Federalist numbers in the region. The officers were Federalists and capitalized upon the war furor, the patriotism of the people, and the militia musters to strengthen their political organization.

All this occurred in the months preceding the congressional election year of 1798. The anti-French sentiment afforded an excellent opportunity to strike at Gallatin, who was a Swiss-born, French-speaking, French sympathizer. A call for a borough meeting on August 2, 1798, to nominate "a suitable character free from foreign influence" for Congress was prefaced by the admonition:

At the moment when our infant Navy are contending with an imperious insulting *Foe,* when aggravated instances of unmerited oppressions have called forth the *Venerable Washington,* to meet the enemies of his country, when all hopes for accomodation have vanished—it is then a moment deeply interesting to Americans, and particularly enjoins them to be watchfull to prevent improper persons from managing their national interests during impending dangers.[28]

[28] *Pittsburgh Gazette,* July, 21, 1798.

John Woods, the Federalist lawyer and the unsuccessful candidate against Gallatin in 1794 and again in 1796, was pitted against him once more. Judge Addison and a number of Washington Federalists appeared to promote Woods's candidacy with great vigor. On July 21 Brackenridge in a letter to the *Gazette* sounded a blast against Woods. Gallatin was preferred by Brackenridge, who justified his opposition to Woods on the pretext that because of "the prejudice, however unreasonable, that exists against the profession of law" "it is not every day that we can get a lawyer elected"; and, on the other hand, Woods's limited education and political inexperience did not recommend him. This letter precipitated a bitter campaign with many recriminations.

Brackenridge further astounded the people by urging the candidacy of Presley Neville. The people immediately recalled that the wily lawyer had broken with the Neville family during the Whiskey Insurrection and had abused its members in his book on the *Incidents of the Insurrection*—an attitude that contrasted with his now apparent friendliness toward Neville's candidacy. Charges flew back and forth with sharpness and rapidity. The opponents of Gallatin harped upon the latter's friendliness to France. The Neville family was accused of having all the profitable offices in the county and of growing rich in the possession of them.[29] Brackenridge attempted in vain to explain away the hostile references to the Nevilles in the *Incidents*. One contributor, pungent and shrewd but less scholarly than Brackenridge, queried:

What is to be thought of all this? A man with half an eye may see what Brackenridge would be after. Woods and Neville he pitches to the devil . . . Gallatin is his man . . . a split division of the federal interests is his object, and we dread the success of his *management* . . . however, we must not despair, let us hope for the best . . . run but one man for Congress and let that one be John Woods, who was first proposed, and who appears to have by far the best chance. Brackenridge has his emissaries abroad, beware of them, dont put

[29] *Pittsburgh Gazette,* September 8, 1798.

it in his power, a second time to boast of having gulled the people.[30]

Bates wrote his brother on December 3 observing that electioneering ran high, adding:

It has put frowns upon the faces of friends and produced jarring and distrust where amity and concord subsisted. Illiberality is the watchword and the influence of party paramount to everything but an avidity after riches.[31]

But Neville took his candidacy seriously and refused to withdraw until nearly the eve of the election. On August 13 a group at Noblesburgh (now Noblestown), on Robinson Run, nominated Neville and endorsed his candidacy.[32] Almost two weeks later a communication from Federalists of Greene and Washington counties signed by John Hoge, David Hoge, James Allison, Alexander Addison, and David Redick, the former Republican, and addressed to a number of Pittsburgh Federalists, including John Gibson, Steele Semple, and John Wilkins, asserted that Greene County Federalists wanted Woods and condemned the aspirations of Neville. This communication was printed in the *Gazette* of August 26, which also contained similar communications indorsing Woods from the people of Presque Isle, Franklin, and Cussewago.

There is much about the whole affair that defies explanation. Brackenridge once more resorted to sophistry with the apparent purpose of splitting the Federalist party. A possible answer may be found in the fact that charges and countercharges of bad faith and chicanery were hurled between the Federalists of Pittsburgh and its vicinity on the one hand and those of Washington and Greene counties on the other. Such action suggests that the Federalists of Pittsburgh and Washington, now that success seeemed apparent, were fighting among themselves for advantage. If it was Brackenridge's purpose to accomplish Gallatin's election, he was successful, be-

---

[30] *Pittsburgh Gazette*, September 22, 1798.
[31] Mrs. E. M. Davis, "The Letters of Tarleton Bates, 1795-1805," in *Western Pennsylvania Historical Magazine*, 12:41 (1929).
[32] *Pittsburgh Gazette*, August 26, 1798.

cause Gallatin defeated Woods by a greater majority in 1798 than he had obtained in 1796. Washington County gave Gallatin 2,163 votes and Woods 714, while Allegheny gave Gallatin 1,304 and Woods 1,751; Gallatin thus had a total of 3,467 votes and Woods a total of 2,465. Smilie was elected without difficulty in the district of Fayette and Westmoreland to replace Findley, who retired ostensibly to enjoy the companionship of his family. In the returns for candidates for the state legislature, Westmoreland and Fayette counties chose Republican candidates; Washington County was divided with the Republicans in the ascendancy, and Allegheny County was carried easily by the Federalists.

The most promising opportunity for the Federalists had passed. Gallatin returned to Congress to ascend to greater heights and to solidify the Democratic-Republican party in the lower house. Brackenridge gleefully enjoyed the discomfiture of the defeated and surprised Federalists, and, rightly or not, Republicans in eastern Pennsylvania believed that Brackenridge was the leader of their party in western Pennsylvania; and he was soon to receive a reward for his services. James Ross wrote to Arthur St. Clair that there was not such a thing as a Federalist in Westmoreland County and only a small but firm little Federalist party in Fayette County.[33] John Scull and the Federalists continued to grumble and hurl charges in the files of his paper. The election had left an inheritance of ill feeling. Samuel Ewalt threatened to institute a libel suit against Scull because of a remark the editor had made about him in the *Gazette* of October 6. Ewalt himself was no less gentle in his remarks when he said about Scull that "whether a misinformed man or an intentional liar, clear it is from his language, *fool, knave, malice, harlot, apostate angel, bigot, midwifed, specious brat, &c* that this person is far from being a man of decent language."[34]

The blunder of the western Pennsylvania Federalists injured the party in the region, to be sure, but the inexcusable

[33] St. Clair, *Papers*, 2:423.   [34] *Pittsburgh Gazette*, October 20, 1798.

blunder that the national leaders made in that same year was much more disastrous to the future of Federalism. At the peak of their party's strength, they engaged in an internal quarrel concerning the ranks of the generals who were to command the proposed army to conduct the war against France. After President John Adams was forced to submit to the will of Hamilton and Washington in moving Hamilton from fourth position to second position in command, there was no war— there were only rankled feelings and resentment between Adams and Hamilton. Their greatest mistake, however, was that of passing the Alien and Sedition Acts to suppress the freedom of the press and the freedom of speech, not only of aliens, but of American-born citizens who attempted to criticize the government. These laws were obviously unconstitutional and met with sturdy opposition; the Republican leaders made great capital of the people's resentment and as a result were eventually able to displace their rivals in office.

Gallatin, Findley, Smilie, and other western Pennsylvanians had fought the suppression of the freedom of speech and the freedom of the press in the Pennsylvania Ratifying Convention of 1787, in the Harrisburg convention of November, 1788, and in the Pennsylvania Constitutional Convention of 1789 and 1790. They knew all the arguments and reiterated them without any hesitation. Scull, a Federalist, pathetically attempted to justify the laws even when he knew that they could be used as instruments to throttle his own paper; he referred to those people who would protest against this legislation as "deluded citizens." Furthermore he was impatient with the Virginia and Kentucky resolutions that condemned the Alien and Sedition Acts. He advised Virginia to "touch with cautious hands the cement of the union" lest she bring about her own dissolution.[35]

While the election of 1798 was a significant one for western Pennsylvania, the gubernatorial election of the following year was still more important to the region and vastly more signifi-

[35] *Pittsburgh Gazette,* September 29, 1798; February 2, 1799.

cant to the Republican party in the state. It foreshadowed and in some respects determined the outcome of the presidential election in 1800. Jefferson's margin of victory in his defeat of John Adams for the presidency at that time was a scant three votes. Without the eight electoral votes that Pennsylvania cast for him he would have failed; and because of a peculiar deadlock in the Pennsylvania legislature in 1800 no popular election was held to determine the electoral vote. The state election of 1799, therefore, was responsible for the Democratic-Republican majority in the lower house which fought for the electoral votes that Pennsylvania electors cast for Jefferson in 1800.

Federalist leaders in Pennsylvania seemed to sense the significance of the gubernatorial election in 1799 and sought to win it by capturing the votes of western Pennsylvania. To accomplish that end, they determined upon James Ross of Pittsburgh as their candidate. He was at the time a United States senator serving his second term; he was a prominent man with a majestic countenance and figure who had held himself with sufficient dignity to avoid the political brawls and "mud slinging" that were engaged in by so many of his colleagues; and as one of the United States commissioners in the Whiskey Insurrection he had taken a conciliatory and gracious attitude toward the rebels. There was no man better qualified to carry the votes of western Pennsylvania for the Federalist party in that year than he. The hopes of the party in the state rested in him and in his ability to win in the southwestern counties.

Ross's candidacy was announced in the *Pittsburgh Gazette* of March 23. His opponent was the eminent Thomas McKean, chief justice of the Pennsylvania Supreme Court from 1777 to 1789, a former president of the Continental Congress, and a signer of the Declaration of Independence. Scull began to canvass the grand juries of neighboring counties for their opinions of the candidates. The Bedford County Grand Jury reported unanimously for Ross, and the Allegheny County Grand Jury declared in favor of Ross with only one dissenting vote. These reports were published, and the editor proceeded with his program of building up the candidacy of his favorite.[36]

Despite Ross's popularity in the region, he encountered a blistering attack from the editor of a newly established Republican paper in Washington. John Israel, a capable Jewish editor, had established the *Herald of Liberty* the previous year and was not slow to hurl epithets at Ross or to close in a journalistic battle with the Pittsburgh editor. An address to "Fellow Citizens" in the files of the *Gazette* reveals the attacks upon Ross. It reads:

> Since Mr. Ross has been fixed upon as the next governor of this State, his opponents have laboured with incessant malignity to defeat his Election by circulating in the Newspapers, in Hand-bills and in Pamphlets, every Falsehood and Calumny which party-spirit, or personal enmity could suggest. They boldly assert that Mr. Ross is an open Reviler of Religion; a Deist; an Atheist; a Speculator, a Landjobber; an active Agent in exciting the Western Insurrection; and that in Public life he has been altogether under Foreign Influence. These charges will have no effect where Mr. Ross is known; but as a great portion of those who are interested in the choice of the Chief Magistrate are not personally acquainted with this Gentleman, it cannot be amiss for one who has known him intimately from early life to state his real Character and Conduct, in all the points where these anonymous Slanderers have attempted to attack him.

Scull attempted to refute the charges made against Ross, point by point, and a hundred eighteen leading men attached their names to the refutation. The names of Scull, John Wilkins, the two Nevilles, Isaac Craig, and Alexander Addison appeared among the list of signers.[37] The fact that among the names were those of approximately forty prominent merchants of Pittsburgh indicates that the merchants of the city were predominantly Federalist.[38]

[36] *Pittsburgh Gazette*, May 11, 1799. [37] *Ibid.*, October 5, 1799.
[38] Douds, "Merchants and Merchandising in Pittsburgh, 1759-1800," p. 72.

The *Gazette,* however, was not guiltless in its attacks upon McKean. He was described as "the man who had suffered his daughter to renounce her religion in order to form a connection with a Spanish nobleman"; he was referred to as "the father-in-law of the Spanish minister"; and the people were warned that if he were elected governor, his friend, Tenche Coxe, "the pilot of Lord Howe and his army to Philadelphia," would most likely become secretary of state.[39] The attacks upon McKean may have been effective in the region but they were insufficient to defeat him in the state.

The opponents of the Federalist party elected McKean governor by a margin of only 6,669 votes. Ross's strength, however, was evident in the vote of the western counties. Allegheny County gave him a majority of 1,130 votes; Fayette County cast 1,156 votes for Ross and 1,011 for McKean; Washington County gave McKean a majority of 751; and Westmoreland County returned a majority of 502 for McKean. Ross gained a majority of the votes cast in the four original counties of southwestern Pennsylvania, but his majority was a mere 122 votes.[40] The Federalist party was by no means dominant in western Pennsylvania. The candidacy of her favorite son, however, had frightened the Republicans, who had put forth a special effort to win the election in Westmoreland County. There William Findley, the county's most popular man, was virtually drafted as the senatorial candidate for the Republicans after he had announced his retirement from politics. The strategy was good, and his personal appeal probably produced the margin of victory for McKean in Westmoreland.[41]

This election marked the end of the struggle between the Federalists and the Republicans for the control of politics in the western counties. Never before or after did the Federalists register as many votes as they secured in this election in western Pennsylvania, but their national party had already passed its peak, and the Republicans under the masterful hand of

[39] *Pittsburgh Gazette,* Sept. 7, 1799.   [40] *Ibid.,* Nov. 2, 1799.   [41] *Ibid.,* Oct. 12, 1799.

Jefferson were steadily increasing in numbers and hopes. Furthermore, the Federalist party in the state of Pennsylvania no longer controlled the executive's post or the lower house of the legislature. It did control the senate, however, because senators were elected for three years, and not enough new ones took their seats in 1799 to wipe out the Federalist majority. But appointive offices would now go to the Republicans. The Federalists had good reasons to be gloomy, although Scull reported in the *Gazette* as late as October 12 that in New England a Democrat (Republican) was becoming as rare as a bear or a wolf and that Jacobinism, like the yellow fever, was on the wane in New England and would soon vanish.

The Republicans of western Pennsylvania were so happy over their victory in electing McKean that they held a "jollification dinner" at the tavern of Captain Smur in Pittsburgh on the evening of October 26. Hugh Henry Brackenridge served as the toastmaster for some forty or fifty who gathered there. In the midst of the drinking of toasts, the rumor spread that an armed party was gathering in front of the tavern to prevent a parade in honor of McKean. The banquet came to a close with unseemly haste, and the idea of a parade, if one had been planned, was dropped.[42]

A report was made, however, that five hundred soldiers had voted illegally for the Federalists in Pittsburgh. This rumor was printed in the *Philadelphia Aurora*. Scull answered the charge in a bitter reply:

In the Traitor's Repast, commonly called the Aurora, it is stated that five hundred soldiers voted at the last Elections, and that Mr. Ross was chased from the town. These are instances of Jacobin lies ... as no Jacobins can lie better than those of this town, it is probable that they have been fabricated here, and might have been one of the objects of Smur's hotel meeting.[43]

Brackenridge made little effort to answer Scull. The discomfiture of the Federalist party was great; his enemies had been defeated, and his sophistry apparently was the snag

[42] *Pittsburgh Gazette,* November 2, 1799.   [43] *Ibid.,* November 9, 1799.

upon which the Federalists had been wrecked; furthermore, party leaders in the state, and even Jefferson, seemed to consider him a political figure of significance. Brackenridge contented himself in his anticipation of political preferment and in a project for the establishment of another newspaper in Pittsburgh to rival that of Scull. Whether or not Brackenridge, Gallatin, Findley, and Smilie were aware of the fact in 1799, they had ended the struggle for the political supremacy of their region. The party of Jefferson now faced a future in the western counties that held promising prospects. The task ahead of the Republicans was that of solidifying and organizing their party and of combating effectively the Federalists who held offices in the boroughs of Pittsburgh and Washington.

JEFFERSONIAN DEMOCRACY ORGANIZES

CHAPTER SEVEN

THE achievement of the Democratic Republicans in electing Thomas McKean to the governorship in Pennsylvania in 1799 raised the hopes of the national party to hitherto unknown heights. The success of any national party during the early years of the Republic depended to a great extent upon the turn of political events in the four large states, Massachusetts, Virginia, New York, and Pennsylvania. The Bay State had been in the ranks of the Federalist party during the first decade and at the turn of the century remained solidly behind Adams. Virginia had swung to Jefferson and, since the death of Washington, had no son who could vie in popularity with the "sage of Monticello." New York had been under the thumb of Hamilton, but the Machiavellian hand of Aaron Burr was at work, suavely and ruthlessly undermining the structure of Federalism in the Empire State. The wresting of Pennsylvania from the Federalists in 1799, therefore, augured well for the Democratic Republicans. Apparently, New York and Pennsylvania were to be the pivotal states in the election of 1800. If the party of Jefferson were to succeed and endure, particular attention must be given to the organization and disciplining of his party within those states. McKean's margin of victory, 6669 votes, was too narrow to insure continued success in the Keystone State without additional and constant efforts to strengthen the party. The newly elected governor and the astute young secretary of the commonwealth, Alexander J. Dallas, set themselves to the task of consolidating their forces. Western Pennsylvania, with its hosts of democratic farmers, was a fertile field for cultivation.

The governor immediately launched into his program of strengthening the party. He was inaugurated on December 17, 1799. On the following day he appointed Brackenridge, whom he believed to be the leader of the party in the western counties, a justice of the Supreme Court of Pennsylvania.[1] The appointment was obviously a reward for political services that Brackenridge had rendered, but it was also a definite indication to western Pennsylvanians that their interests were to receive consideration. The following year, McKean designated John B. C. Lucas, a Republican and a French immigrant, as an associate judge of the Court of Common Pleas of Allegheny County.[2] This policy of elevating Republicans to the bench not only paid political debts but also served another purpose in tending to offset the preponderant weight of the Federalists in the judicial branch of the government. The appointment of these two particular men had disadvantages as well as advantages for the Republicans. Unfortunately, each of them had a vulnerable spot, which the Federalists were not slow to attack.

Brackenridge, long a legal and personal rival of Alexander Addison, president judge of the fifth judicial district of Pennsylvania, which included the four western counties, was reputed to be a profane and non-religious man, although he had served as a chaplain in the Revolutionary army. The Federalists quickly presented a mock petition for mercy to the new judge, addressing him as "President of the Jacobin Society, Protector of Chivalry, Privy Counsellor of the Governor of Bantam, Poet Laureate to the Herald of Sedition, Biographer of Insurgents, Auctioneer of Divinity, and Haberdasher of Pronouns."[3] Not only was the editor of the *Gazette,* Scull, shocked at Brackenridge's apparent lack of religion, but he

[1] Newlin, *Hugh Henry Brackenridge,* 213.   [2] Dahlinger, *Pittsburgh,* 47.
[3] *Pittsburgh Gazette,* December 21, 1799.

also gasped at the rumors of profanity and indecency on the part of the judge. It was reported that Brackenridge stamped into a tavern in Canonsburg, damned the tavern-keeper fifteen times, and, to the amazement of onlookers, disrobed himself. One correspondent to the *Gazette* lamented the fact that "a Supreme Judge and a sapient philosopher too, will so far lose sight of the reverence due to himself—to his station—and society, as to be seen almost 'stark naked and nearly stark mad' from too much tipple in the face of open day."[4] The new judge made little effort to deny the charge and was not much affected by it, because he removed to Carlisle soon afterward, and, except for the occasions when he rode his circuit in the western part of the state, did not come into personal contact with his enemies. It was not, however, the end of their complaints or blasts against him.

Lucas, reputedly an atheist who encouraged his wife to plow in the fields on Sunday, was vulnerable upon the score of his own religion and nationality. A Republican and a Frenchman, he encounterd the contempt and sneers of his judicial colleagues, who feared his political philosophy and deplored his religion.

Soon after Brackenridge's elevation to the supreme court of the state he is said to have prevailed upon the governor to dismiss James Brison, Federalist, from the position of prothonotary of Allegheny County, which he had held since September 26, 1788. Brison was a popular man in Pittsburgh, a captain of the Pittsburgh Troop of Light Dragoons, and secretary of the board of trustees of the Pittsburgh Academy. He was prominent socially and served as master of ceremonies on many important social occasions, among which was a ball given to "Light-Horse" Harry Lee, who commanded the expedition sent by Washington to suppress the Whiskey Insurrection. A few months before this ball Brackenridge had described Brison as a "puppy and coxcomb." Brackenridge and his wife received no invitation to the ball—a snub that

[4] *Pittsburgh Gazette,* August 16, 1800.

Brackenridge explained on the ground that it was a retaliation for the epithet that he had applied to Brison. In January of 1801 John C. Gilkison, who was a relative of Brackenridge, a scrivener, an owner of a bookstore and a library, and a Republican, was appointed prothonotary.[5] The idea, "to the victor belongs the spoils," was practical in 1800 even though the expression had not yet been enunciated. But the governor, despite the fact that county offices were appointive except for the commissioners, sheriff, and coroner, found an inadequate number of vacancies to fill. With Jefferson he might have said, "Few men die and none ever resign." These Democratic Republicans were politicians with fertile minds, however, and in 1800 conceived a project that opened up the possibility of many new appointments in that part of Pennsylvania west of the mountains—the part that was inhabited by a preponderance of democratic farmers.

The project consisted of the breaking up of the huge county of Allegheny, a Federalist county, into a number of smaller counties, thus increasing the number of county officials whom the governor could appoint. Furthermore, the organization of new counties would increase the number of voting places and thus enable the isolated farmers, who were Republicans, to vote with greater ease. In addition, the Federalist votes in Allegheny County could be submerged by yoking that county with the Republican counties of northwestern Pennsylvania in a new congressional district. Allegheny County would be whittled down in size, and its Federalists would be segregated and confined to county and borough offices; Greene and Fayette counties, comprising another congressional district, would assure a Republican victory. Obviously the plan suggested a shrewd bit of "gerrymandering" a dozen years before Elbridge Gerry reorganized the Massachusetts election districts, one of which Gilbert Stuart outlined on a map and said resembled a salamander, but that the bitter Federalist editor, Benjamin Russell, dubbed a "gerrymander."

[5] Dahlinger, *Pittsburgh*, 59.

Nine new counties were established by March 13 of 1800. Centre County was set up on February 13. Armstrong, Beaver, Butler, Crawford, Erie, Venango, and Warren counties were established on March 13. But the immediate gain to the Republican party was anticipatory rather than real, because the actual establishment of local county governments did not immediately follow. Even though the migration to northwestern Pennsylvania, that section north and west of the Allegheny River, had been stimulated by the activities of the Holland Land Company, which acquired land in Crawford and Erie counties in 1792, and of the Pennsylvania Population Company, which procured a grant in those same two counties in 1793, and by the opening of donation lands for ex-soldiers in other counties, the number of settlers was small. The fear of Indians was great until after the Treaty of Greenville in 1795, and it was not until then that the great influx of settlers began.[6]

Since it was not feasible to organize courts for each of the new counties at once, Meadville was designated as the site for a court to dispose of the cases in the northern counties, with the understanding that the citizens of Meadville would procure four thousand dollars for an academy. Consequently, that little town became a Mecca for judges and lawyers until 1805.[7] Previously a group of aggressive, prominent, and well-educated men had gone into Crawford County to represent the Holland Land Company and the Pennsylvania Population Company. Samuel and Alexander Forster managed the land sales there of the Holland Land Company from 1792 to 1796; Roger Alden, a Harvard graduate and a Revolutionary War veteran, succeeded them; Harm Jan Huidekoper replaced Alden when the latter's accounts became confused and continued to represent the company until its demise in 1836. Jabez Colt was the agent for the Pennsylvania Population

[6] Dick, "Recollections of an Early Settler," in *Daily Tribune-Republican* (Meadville), centennial edition, May 12, 1888, p. 11.
[7] See Reynolds, *Fifty Years of the Bench and Bar of Crawford County*, 3-34.

Company in Crawford County, and his brother, Judah Colt, was the company's representative in Erie County.[8] These men with many others, among them David Mead, founder of Meadville, and Samuel Lord, who donated the land for Allegheny College, had the benefit of a social training and cultural background that fitted them to be leaders in the Federalist party. As Pittsburgh was the Federalist stronghold in southwestern Pennsylvania, so did Meadville and Mead Township form the citadel of that party in northwestern Pennsylvania. There were a number of Federalists in Erie, but their strength was never sufficient to give them any appreciable voice in the political affairs of the region. There were Federalists, to be sure, in Franklin, Mercer, and Beaver, but those towns were so small that the Democratic votes of the farmers submerged the Federalist votes of the townsmen.

In 1800, then, the governor could appoint judges, justices of the peace, registrars of wills, and prothonotaries and he commissioned county militia officers. The farmers were in a position to elect county commissioners of their own political faith. Thus as the organization of the counties proceeded, a network of Democratic Republican local officeholders was constructed which served as the backbone for the party in western Pennsylvania.

Pittsburgh, Washington, Meadville, and, to a lesser extent, Erie were the centers of Federalism at the beginning of the century. The effectiveness of the Federalists in Pittsburgh and Washington, however, was decreased by the separation of Allegheny and Washington counties into different senatorial and congressional districts. The Federalists of Washington County were outvoted by the Democratic Republicans of Fayette and Greene counties; and the Federalists of Pittsburgh were outvoted by the Democratic Republicans of the northwestern counties. Nevertheless the attacks upon Pittsburgh and Washington Federalists were not ended.

[8] Reynolds, "Crawford County. A History of Its Growth and Development," in *Daily Tribune-Republican* (Meadville), centennial edition, May 12, 1888, p. 1-9.

JAMES ROSS

From an engraving of the portrait by T. Sully

Newspapers were established to combat the Federalist presses and to expound Democratic Republican ideas. The effectiveness of the Federalist presses, particularly the *Gazette,* annoyed the friends of Jefferson. Scull's paper undoubtedly had been the most widely circulated journal of western Pennsylvania during the first ten years of the republic. Furthermore, the second paper founded in the region, the *Western Telegraphe and Washington Advertiser,* published in Washington as early as August 17, 1795, was of the Federalist political faith. This journal was far less important than the *Gazette* in swaying public opinion, but its voice was heard in the town of Washington. Another early Federalist sheet of limited circulation was the *Fayette Gazette and Union Advertiser,* founded in 1797.[9]

Near the close of the century, however, as Jefferson's party became stronger in the western counties, Republican journals came into existence in the region to further the development of the party. Two such papers appeared in 1798. John M. Snowden founded the *Farmers' Register* in Greensburg during that year to give Findley, Baird, Todd, and other Westmoreland Democrats an opportunity to print their essays and articles on politics. Early that year, John Israel, a young Jewish editor, set up the *Herald of Liberty* in Washington and waged a long-range journalistic war with Scull. The *Westmoreland Democrat,* begun the following year, seems to have had a small circulation and little political influence.

After the gubernatorial campaign of 1799 and Scull's bitter attack upon Brackenridge and the Democratic Republicans, Israel decided to establish a Republican newspaper in Pittsburgh. Scull and the Federalists bitterly resented the founding of the new paper and accused Brackenridge of giving moral

[9] For a discussion of early newspapers in the region see Reuben G. Thwaites, "The Ohio Valley Press before the War of 1812-15," in American Antiquarian Society, *Proceedings,* 19:319-368 (1908-09), and Alston G. Field, "The Press in Western Pennsylvania to 1812" in *Western Pennsylvania Historical Magazine,* 20:231-262 (1937).

support and even material aid to the invading editor. Scull announced pathetically:

> For upwards of thirteen years, my best endeavors have been exerted to preserve the freedom and impartiality of the Pittsburgh Gazette and to render it useful. But my offense is of a nature not to be pardoned — my paper has not teemed with abuse of the government, its officers, and its supporters — on the contrary I discountenanced publications of that kind—in this I have offended —this is the unpardonable sin—and for this we are to be visited by what is modestly termed another Press.[10]

Brackenridge answered Scull in an open letter in which he indicated that he had told Scull some time before that he was dissatisfied with the general spirit of the *Gazette,* though not because it was favorably disposed toward the Federalists. The literary lawyer went ahead to explain that there was sufficient room for two presses and that the farmers who were not inclined to Federalism were entitled to have a press in which the political ideas of their own party could be expressed. Naturally they would look to another paper, since the *Gazette* did not have the political tone that they preferred.[11]

Israel established the *Tree of Liberty,* a four-column anti-Federalist sheet on August 16, 1800, in Pittsburgh. It is significant that this paper should have been founded at that particular time, only two months before a national election. This new journal probably played little part in the election of 1800 in western Pennsylvania, because the selection of the presidential electors that year was made by the state legislature, and a popular election was thus eliminated. But the paper became an effective tool for the Democratic Republicans in the next few years, and its editor became the storm center of a journalistic and political war.

Scull and his friends immediately opened an attack upon Israel and Brackenridge. One contributor to the *Gazette,* "A. W.," decried the formation of a new paper in Pittsburgh,

[10] *Pittsburgh Gazette,* November 30, 1799.   [11] *Ibid.,* December 7, 1799.

"especially in the present scarcity of cash when we can hardly get enough money to support our families." Israel was attacked from the standpoint of his religion; he was referred to as "the Jew"; and he and Brackenridge were accused of irreverence because they used the Bible to find a motto for their paper. Another contributor complained:

I am an old fashioned man. I reverence the Bible, and do not like, nay it shocks me, and I hope it does many others to see the word of God profaned. Messrs. Brackenridge and Israel have taken a motto to their paper from Revelations 22, 2 where the Holy Spirit, speaking of the Tree of Life says "and the leaves of the Tree were for the healing of the Nations." These sacred words they have profanely applied to their newspaper.[12]

Brackenridge, in reply to these accusations that he was sponsoring Israel and the *Tree of Liberty*, asserted that while he was friendly to Israel he had no connection with his newspaper. Little credit was given this statement, however, because Brackenridge's part in the founding of the *Gazette*, a few years previous, was known and remembered, and Scull took occasion to entitle a column, "Gross Lies in Judge Brackenridge's Tree of Liberty Detected."[13] Israel was unafraid, however, and he continued the publication of the *Tree of Liberty* in Pittsburgh and thus gave to western Pennsylvania a fourth Democratic-Republican newspaper. These four journals were invaluable in the development of the party, but others of similar political leaning were to be added within the next five years.

The election of 1800 indicated the strength of the Democratic Republicans in western Pennsylvania. In the contest for the state offices every Democratic Republican was elected. Each of the five southwestern counties gave sizable majorities to the party of Jefferson. Westmoreland gave a majority of 1,704 votes; Washington, 1,416; Greene, 257; Fayette, 305; and Allegheny, 1,059.[14] Thus a solid bloc of eleven members

[12] *Pittsburgh Gazette*, August 23, 1800. [13] *Ibid.*, September 26, 1800.
[14] *National Intelligencer* (Washington), November 15, 1800.

was sent to the state house of representatives from western Pennsylvania, a factor that greatly increased the strength of the party in the state. In addition, Albert Gallatin and John Smilie were returned to Congress, though Gallatin did not occupy his seat before he was elevated by Jefferson to the treasury department in 1801. Apparently the Democratic Republicans were well ensconced in the region and might have rested on their oars, but Jefferson and his cohorts were masterful politicians and realized the necessity of constantly rebuilding the fences. There was no lack of diligence on their part; actually, they extended themselves to even greater efforts in the next three or four years in order to solidify the party, not only in western Pennsylvania, but in the nation as well.

The Democratic Republicans pursued Federalism into its lair in Pittsburgh and sought to exterminate it there. From the formation of the borough, in 1794, to 1800 the borough offices, the federal post office, and the office of the deputy quartermaster-general had been in the hands of the Federalists. Their control was the result of the fact that approximately two-thirds of some sixty merchants in Pittsburgh belonged to the party of Hamilton. John Wilkins, James O'Hara, Isaac Craig, and John Scull were the more prominent of the business leaders in the town. They were ably supported by John and Presley Neville, the latter of whom had a town house, and by James Ross, Abraham Kirkpatrick, and others who were assiduous in the politics of the town. The economic and social positions of these men made their political positions almost invincible, but a new group of businessmen was arising on "Clapboard Row," or Market Street, who were to become worthy rivals.[15]

This group of men was referred to as the "Clapboard Junto." They were assiduous and partisan Republicans and divided their time between business and politics. Dr. Hugh Scott, popular and affable postmaster, was one of the leaders of this

[15] For a brief account of "Clapboardian Democracy" see Dahlinger, *Pittsburgh*, 127-134.

JEFFERSONIAN DEMOCRACY ORGANIZES 165

group. William Gazzam, an Irishman who had been in the United States only a few years, was one of the most effective of these local politicians—he was aggressive and ambitious and through his persistence had pushed forward in politics and had become brigade inspector of the Allegheny militia and a justice of the peace. General Fowler, another of this junto, whom Gazzam refused to support for Congress, described the Irishman as "a little man—in the most emphatic sense." Fowler insisted that Gazzam "under the cloak of Republicanism and religion was artfully aiming at offices."[16] Gazzam was a member of the Presbyterian church and apparently very narrow minded and orthodox; later in his career he left the church, it is said, because the minister gave out "two lines of a stanza to be sung instead of the time honored one."

Thomas Baird of the firm of Fulton and Baird was a member of the junto. Samuel Ewalt, Allegheny County's first sheriff, was associated with this group and aided in the war against the Federalists. Nathaniel Irish and Adamson Tannehill, former Revolutionary officers, inhabited "Clapboard Row" and swelled the ranks of the Republicans. Irish was a county commissioner in 1800 and was later appointed as inspector of flour for the western country.[17] Tannehill had at one time conducted a tavern on Water Street and had been president of the Pittsburgh Fire Company. In 1800 while holding office as a justice of the peace he was convicted of extortion and temporarily disqualified for that position, but in 1801 Governor McKean remitted the fine and again reappointed him.[18] Dr. Andrew Richardson also belonged to the "Clapboard Row" faction until he deserted the Republican party. But the ablest of this faction was young Tarleton Bates, who formed a friendship and a partnership with two brilliant young lawyers, Henry Baldwin and Walter Forward, to give

[16] *Pittsburgh Gazette,* September 4, 1801.
[17] *Tree of Liberty* (Pittsburgh), October 18, 1800; *Pittsburgh Gazette,* September 24, 1802.
[18] *Pittsburgh Gazette,* January 30, 1801; *Tree of Liberty* (Pittsburgh), February 7, 1801.

Republicanism in Pittsburgh the strongest leadership that it had held up to that time.

Bates was the eldest member of this trio both in point of years and of residence in Pittsburgh. Born in Virginia in 1775, he had come to Pittsburgh in 1793. He found employment in the quartermaster's department under Major Isaac Craig, at whose home he lived for a time. In 1801 he became a clerk in the prothonotary's office, serving under John C. Gilkison, whom he later succeeded. He was a dashing, handsome, popular young man who, in conjunction with Baldwin and Forward, helped to snatch the town from the grasp of the Federalists. The partnership of these three men lasted until Bates was killed in a duel in 1806.

Henry Baldwin was a Connecticut Yankee, born in New Haven, Connecticut, on January 14, 1780. He was graduated from Yale, studied law under the direction of Alexander Dallas, and was admitted to the bar in Philadelphia. He transferred his residence and activities to Pittsburgh, however, and was admitted to the bar of Allegheny County in 1801. Thereafter he became a leading lawyer and politician in western Pennsylvania. He served in Congress and later became a justice of the United States Supreme Court, a position that he held from 1831 to 1844.

Walter Forward, the third of the trio, was born in East Granby, Connecticut, in 1783. His family moved to the Connecticut Western Reserve and settled about 1800 in Aurora, Portage County, Ohio. He is said to have started his journey for Pittsburgh on foot with only the necessary wearing apparel and one dollar in his coat pocket. When he reached the Pittsburgh ferry he did not have enough money to pay his fare and induced the ferryman to carry him across the river in return for the gift of a horseshoe that he had picked up along the way for good luck. Once in Pittsburgh he sought the law office of Henry Baldwin, of whom he had heard but whom he did not know. The attorney was preparing to mount his horse when young Forward approached him and stated his desire to study

JEFFERSONIAN DEMOCRACY ORGANIZES 167

law. Baldwin gave him the key to his office and told him to take down Blackstone's volumes and go to work. Thus was formed a friendship between the two men that was to endure for forty years. Forward, like Baldwin, was a prominent lawyer and a member of Congress, and for a while served as secretary of the treasury of the United States in the cabinet of John Tyler.[19] During the early years of the century, before Bates's death, the triumvirate formed by the three young men gave astute and vigorous leadership to the Republicans in Pittsburgh.

In western Pennsylvania the Republicans were not slow to develop practical political methods for organizing and strengthening their party. One scheme that was effective in Pittsburgh originated among the "Clapboard Junto." It consisted of the formation of a committee composed of Thomas Baird, James Riddle, and Joseph McClurg to assist and encourage the naturalization of aliens.[20] A second scheme consisted in the establishing of committees of correspondence in each township and in each county to enable the leaders of the various counties to produce concerted action. Still a third plan provided for a "Committee of Order and Activity" in each district, whose duty it was to marshal the voters and protect the interests of the party on election days. So complete and effective were these practical devices that by 1805 the friends of Jefferson had virtually annihilated the despairing Federalists in western Pennsylvania, except for the isolated groups in Meadville, Pittsburgh, and Washington.

The Federalists in a negative way contributed to the success of their rivals because of their failure to propose a program and to organize themselves. Furthermore, the Federalist leaders, for the most part, were a group of older men, die-hards who complained about the success of the Republicans, pre-

[19] Ewing, "Hon. Walter Forward," in *Western Pennsylvania Historical Magazine*, 8:77 (1925); Sessa, "Walter Forward," 2, 15, 16. The latter source contains a detailed account of the life of Forward.
[20] Dahlinger, *Pittsburgh*, 128.

dicted dire results for the state and nation, and attempted to frustrate the action and program of the Republican legislature through adverse court decisions. Such action apparently was possible because the great majority of the judges were Federalists who had been given their appointments by Federalists and who held office for life or during the period of good behavior. Jefferson and his Republican followers recognized that the judicial branch was a stone about their necks and contemplated a general policy of impeaching and ousting Federalist judges. This idea found fertile ground in western Pennsylvania, and an effort was made to oust Judge Alexander Addison, who had served as the president judge of the fifth Pennsylvania district since 1791.

Addison had been accustomed to deliver political diatribes in his charges to the jury and to behave in an arrogant manner with the associate judges. In 1798, at the December session of the grand jury, he delivered a charge on the Alien Act justifying the constitutionality of that act and condemning the Virginia and Kentucky Resolutions.[21] Two years later, in the December session of the grand jury in the western counties, he delivered an address on the "Rise and Progress of Revolution," in which he pointed out that revolutions have three phases: first, the destruction of the Christian religion; second, the overthrow of government; and third, the disruption of society. He illustrated his points by using incidents from the French Revolution and emphasized the part that the Jacobins had played there, and he also referred to the Illuminati in Germany. He observed that the germs of revolution were in evidence in America and particularly in the western country. "The organization of the society of United Irishmen," said he, "somewhat resembles that of the Illuminati, and seems to be in operation here. That the Press is used, to promote the views of such societies, will not be doubted by any who see the unprincipled similarity of publications, at the same time, from New Hampshire to Georgia." Again he stated his fear of the

[21] See Addison, *On the Alien Act*.

proceedings of Virginia and Kentucky. This polemic, delivered under the guise of a charge to the jury, included also the observation that the recent election of McKean as governor of Pennsylvania was the result of the baneful influence of a revolutionary spirit.[22]

This charge was particularly offensive to John Lucas, who had just been named an associate judge in Allegheny County. Lucas had been trained in French law schools and, as has been noted, had been elevated to the bench that year by McKean, whose election, Addison averred, was the result of the insidious influences of the secret societies. Lucas was further humiliated by the fact that he was associated with John McDowell, another Federalist judge, who concurred with Addison. Together Addison and McDowell made an effort to embarrass Lucas and would not permit him to deliver a charge to the jury when he attempted to address the jurors.[23] On June 1, 1801, at a session of the court of common pleas, with only Addison and Lucas in attendance, the president of the court delivered a charge to a petit jury. Lucas again attempted to supplement the charges delivered by Addison and was brusquely stopped by the president. Later in the same day, when Lucas insisted upon his right to address the jury in his capacity as an associate judge, both McDowell, who appeared for this session, and Addison overruled him, and Addison threatened to take means to stop him if he did not desist.

Though Lucas did not continue his address to the jury, he did press his fight for the right to address the jury and insisted that an associate judge had an equal right with a president judge to deliver a charge. Already Lucas had made out an affidavit against Addison, who had first forbade him to address the jury in December of 1800, and the attorney-general had given his opinion that an associate judge or justice had equal rights with the president judge or justice to charge the grand jury. The supreme court of the state, however, had held that Lucas' affi-

[22] Addison, *Rise & Progress of Revolution*, 29-35; T. Lloyd, *Trial of Alexander Addison*, 50.   [23] T. Lloyd, *Trial of Alexander Addison*, 49.

davit had not indicated that the president judge had shown malice in stopping him and observed that no crime had occurred. Therefore the state supreme court had no question before it for decision.[24] Friends of Lucas came to his aid and on January 11, 1802, presented to the state house of representatives a petition signed by 384 inhabitants of Allegheny County, asking for the impeachment of Addison. On January 25 Samuel Ewalt presented additional petitions containing similar requests from 297 inhabitants of Allegheny, Beaver, and Butler counties.[25] In compliance with these requests the house of representatives made out articles of impeachment, and on March 29 presented those articles to the state senate.

The following December managers were chosen by the house to conduct the prosecution, and the trial of Addison began on January 17, 1803. Alexander J. Dallas served as chief of counsel for the prosecution. Addison acted as counsel for himself. John Lucas, Tarleton Bates, William Gazzam, William Thompson, John Redick, all Republicans, testified in behalf of Lucas. John McDowell alone testified for Addison. The essential facts brought out were that Lucas had been restrained from addressing the grand jury and that Addison had threatened to find means to stop him if he insisted. The testimony conflicted upon the point of whether or not Addison had been passionate in his restriction of Lucas; it seemed to be difficult to discern whether or not Addison was angry, because he ordinarily spoke in a loud tone. Some of the witnesses testified that the other gentlemen on the bench had laughed sneeringly and had shown contempt for Lucas after he had sat down. Addison, who was at a disadvantage in that he could not take a number of witnesses from Pittsburgh to Lancaster, attempted to introduce certificates containing the testimony of his friends upon his conduct, but he was denied the right to submit them as evidence. In his cross-questioning of Lucas he made an effort to establish the impression that Brackenridge was responsible for the filing of the affidavit by Lucas in his

[24] T. Lloyd, *Trial of Alexander Addison*, 69.   [25] *Ibid.*, 1-8.

appeal to the state supreme court. Again Dallas objected that the questioning was irrelevant to the guilt or innocence of Addison.

Addison summed up his case in a masterful address. His logic was clear, concise, and effective. He based his argument on the fact that the evidence did not show that he had malicious designs in stopping Lucas. Addison's premise may have been questionable, because ignorance of the law is not always accepted in a plea for acquittal. His case, regardless of its merits, was unlikely to receive any consideration, because this was a political trial of a political offense. Undoubtedly Addison was a narrow, harsh Federalist, who had used his office to expound the doctrines of his political faith and to embarrass Lucas, a Republican judge. He was brought to trial before Republicans and was convicted by a vote of twenty to four. This trial was merely one of many that Jefferson and the Democratic Republicans instigated for the purpose of getting rid of Federalist judges. Through Addison's fall Federalism suffered in western Pennsylvania, and Republicanism gained. It is probable, however, that the anticipations of the Republicans throughout the country were much greater than this political victory of Addison's impeachment warranted. If the Republicans had great expectations of prostrating the judicial branch of the government, those expectations were short-lived, because the following year, 1804, the state legislature of Pennsylvania failed to convict Edward Shippen, Jasper Yeates, and Thomas Smith, justices of the Supreme Court of Pennsylvania. Furthermore, in 1805 the Republicans were defeated in their efforts to oust the federal judge, Samuel Chase. These two defeats reacted unfavorably upon the party, and no further efforts were made to remove judges who were politically undesirable.

The star of the Republicans was in the ascendancy, however, and in 1803 one of the most fortunate diplomatic and political strokes of Jefferson's administration was accomplished. The territory of Louisiana was purchased from

France, almost against Jefferson's will; certainly he believed that the purchase was unconstitutional on the part of the government of the United States. The effect of the acquisition of that territory, which gave the jurisdiction and control of the mouth of the Mississippi to the United States, was an incredible boon to the party of Jefferson in the West. From the close of the American Revolution, western farmers had struggled for the right to send their products down the Ohio and Mississippi rivers without restrictions. The failure of the Federalist party to procure the right of the navigation of the Mississippi for them had disappointed the farmers, sown distrust among them, and caused them to contemplate arranging an understanding with the Spanish government that would have alienated them from the United States. The purchase of Louisiana therefore placated the western farmers, who were already inclined to democracy. They were now definitely tied to the Democratic-Republican party. The farmers of western Pennsylvania and even the merchants along the the western rivers who were sending cargoes to New Orleans were pleased because they could now engage in western commerce without the fear of foreign interference.

The efforts that Jefferson's lieutenants made to consolidate their forces in western Pennsylvania from 1799 to 1803 bore results in the elections. Their candidates to the state legislature were elected with increasing majorities and increasing ease until 1804, when the Federalists offered very little opposition. Scull, however, made ineffectual attempts to combat the rising tide of democracy during the year of 1801. On January 9, 1801, he observed in the *Gazette* that, "Jacobinism is a political pestilence—its effects upon towns are similar to those of yellow fever." Shortly afterward, however, he admitted that he was favorably impressed with Jefferson's conciliatory inaugural address.[26] Later in the year, on August 21, the columns of his paper contained protests against the rumored invitation to Thomas Paine, the Revolutionary radical, to

[26] *Pittsburgh Gazette,* March 27, 1801.

return to America upon a government ship. To Scull's alarm Israel inquired through the medium of the *Tree of Liberty*, "Why do they not blackguard James Ross for singing psalms over a card table? . . . O ye hypocrites: Ye Pharisees: Ye Federalists!"[27] Scull found room in his paper for voicing a complaint of Jefferson's general policy of appointing Republicans to office. Twenty-eight such appointments had been made, no one of which affected western Pennsylvania. With a dire shaking of the head, he published the names of the appointees, in an effort to stimulate alarm and fear among his readers.

The local elections for 1801 were generally favorable to the Republicans, although a few Federalists were elected to the state offices and the Federalist party carried the borough elections in Pittsburgh. In a special election William Hoge was sent to Congress by the counties of Washington, Greene, and Allegheny by a vote of 1514 to 755, and Thomas Morton was returned to the state senate by the narrower margin of 1306 to 1113. But Samuel Ewalt, Abner Lacock, and John McMaster, all Republicans, were sent to the state house of representatives from Allegheny County.[28] A complete delegation of Republicans was elected from the counties of Westmoreland and Fayette. Thus the election as a whole was a victory for the Republicans.

The following year the Federalists had even less hope of success in western Pennsylvania, although it was a gubernatorial year and James Ross was again put forward as the Federalist candidate for governor. Their despair was so great that many of them referred to themselves as Federal Republicans, to the disgust of the Democratic Republicans. In the district about Pittsburgh a combination ticket was put forward that contained the name of Thomas McKean, Republican, for governor; John Wilkins, Jr., Federalist, for Congress; and Andrew Richardson, a Republican who had

[27] *Tree of Liberty* (Pittsburgh), September 19, 1801.
[28] *Pittsburgh Gazette,* October 25, 1801.

been read out of the party, for the assembly. Apparently it was hoped that John Wilkins would be elected to Congress upon McKean's popularity.[29] The strategy was of no avail, however, because western Pennsylvania was swept in a smashing victory for the Democratic Republicans.

McKean's defeat of Ross in 1802 was decisive—the latter carried only three of the thirty-six counties in the state. William Hoge of Washington County was again elected to Congress and was apparently the lone Federalist candidate in the western counties to achieve success. John Smilie was elected from the congressional district of Fayette and Greene counties; William Findley, from the district of Armstrong, Westmoreland, and Somerset counties; and John Lucas, from the congressional district of Allegheny, Mercer, Beaver, Crawford, Erie, Warren, and Venango. Three of the four Congressmen were definitely Republicans, and Hoge, the Federalist, represented a Republican constituency, but the family name, which was connected with the founding of Washington, Pennsylvania, was sufficient to demolish party lines. To the state assembly, Allegheny County sent Ewalt, McMaster, and Lacock, all of whom had been elected the previous year; Washington County sent John Marshel, cousin of the James Marshel of Whiskey Insurrection fame, James Kerr, Samuel Agnew, and Joseph Vance; Fayette County sent Charles Porter, John Cunningham, and Samuel Trevor; Greene County elected Isaac B. Weaver; Westmoreland elected James Brady, James Montgomery, and Henry Alshouse; and the northwestern counties selected John Lytle, Jr., of Crawford County. Of the senators who stood for reëlection that year, Presley Carr Lane of Fayette and John Lyle of Washington were seated. Every successful candidate for the state legislature and for Congress, except Hoge, was a Republican.[30]

The despondency of the Federalist party was so great as a result of the election of 1802 that its leaders did not attempt to nominate candidates for all the offices in 1803. The party

[29] *Pittsburgh Gazette,* September 24, 1802. [30] *Ibid.,* October 22, 1802.

was not completely vanquished in Allegheny County, however, and a last stand was made in the election for county and borough offices. But the Republicans were successful even in Pittsburgh and for the first time won the borough offices. Federalism had been driven out of its lair. Only six Federalists were to be found in the newly elected general assembly of the state, one in the senate and five in the house of representatives.[31]

The following year the Democratic-Republican machine, now a well-oiled "steam roller," moved on relentlessly. John Scull, the Federalist editor, was elected to the council in Pittsburgh early in the year; but there was little solace in his success because the general Federalist ticket headed by James O'Hara, candidate for Congress, was hopelessly beaten in October.[32] Democratic Republicanism was at high tide in western Pennsylvania, and the Federalists were unable to elect one of their men to the more important offices, even on a combination ticket. Their outlook was hopeless, provided that the Republicans could maintain harmony in their ranks and perpetuate their strong organization.

[31] *Pittsburgh Gazette,* October 15, November 12, 26, 1803.
[32] *Ibid.,* March 23, October 19, 1804.

CONFLICTS AND CONFUSION

CHAPTER EIGHT

THE rise of the Democratic-Republican party in western Pennsylvania during the first administration of Jefferson was similar to its development throughout the entire country. The political gods smiled on Jefferson and his efforts from 1801 to 1805. Even in New England, his leaders were effective in winning the people and in organizing the party. In addition to those practical measures, however, policies, events, and issues conspired for the success of the Democratic Republicans. The repeal of the unpopular excise law, the purchase of Louisiana, the entrance of Ohio into the union of states, the administration's program of economy, and the democratic atmosphere in the Executive Mansion all appealed to the democratic voters and redounded to the credit of the president. Even the Hamilton-Burr duel proved to be a political boon to Jefferson. Burr and Hamilton were, at the time, two of his most powerful adversaries. Burr killed Hamilton and as a result of the duel was himself eliminated from the field of politics. There were, on the other hand, some discordant notes. John Randolph of Roanoke had been alienated, and his enmity eventually equaled his former loyalty; a few of Jefferson's appointments had created dissatisfaction; and Gallatin, who had been elevated to the treasury department, made many enemies in Pennsylvania by supporting the excise law which he had formerly opposed. But despite these rumblings and discords, Jefferson's reëlection in 1804 was a foregone conclusion.

CONFLICTS AND CONFUSION 177

The success of Jefferson's first administration, however, was matched by the grief of the second. The unfortunate impeachment and acquittal of Judge Samuel Chase; the unsuccessful effort to convict Aaron Burr of treason; the scandal attached to the Yazoo land affairs and John Randolph's increased bitterness as a result of it; the break in the state party in Pennsylvania between McKean and Dallas on the one hand and William Duane and Dr. Michael Leib on the other; and the organization of a group of malcontents known as Quids, including Duane, Leib, Randolph, Samuel and Robert Smith of New Jersey, and, later, James Monroe of Virginia, foreshadowed trouble for the party.

Foreign affairs, however, formed the rock upon which Jefferson's party foundered. The European conflagration in which England engaged in a life-and-death struggle with Napoleon led to a commercial struggle between England and France that eventually enveloped the United States. The officers of the English navy impressed American seamen into service; the British Orders in Council and the French Decrees disrupted American commerce; the United States government was unable to make an effective demand for a cessation of British and French depredations, because Jefferson's program of economy had materially weakened the army of the United States and limited the navy to a fleet of flat-bottomed gunboats. Consequently, the United States was forced to combat the British and French governments with economic reprisals. The Embargo Act was the supreme effort to bring those countries to their knees. This act, however, devastated American commerce and failed in its purpose. The economic and commercial disorder that resulted from it was the most significant disaster to Jefferson's party.

The discord that was evident in the national party was reflected in the state of Pennsylvania and in the region west of the mountains. Governor McKean and his henchman, Dallas, met stanch opposition from within the ranks in the state because of McKean's growing conservatism, which did not please the more radical Republicans, and because of his break with Duane and Leib on the question of appointments.[1] Once the Democratic Republicans had broken the power of the Federalists in Pennsylvania, they began quarreling among themselves. Not only did the Republicans in the eastern part of the state oppose each other but the Republicans of western Pennsylvania also developed local conflicts and engaged in controversies with the party leaders in eastern Pennsylvania. The people west of the mountains were greatly agitated about their courts and the judicial system, and the settlers west of the Allegheny River, in northwestern Pennsylvania, were anxious about the titles to their lands. These two problems received a great deal of attention and constituted the issues upon which the election of 1805 turned in western Pennsylvania.

From the days of the Whiskey Insurrection the men of the western counties had complained about their inability to procure prompt attention in the courts. In 1800 the fifth judicial district of Pennsylvania included the five counties of Westmoreland, Washington, Fayette, Allegheny, and Greene. In that year the new counties were formed in northwestern Pennsylvania and, as a part of the fifth judicial district, necessitated the presence of Judge Addison at Meadville.[2] The journey to Meadville was an inconvenient one for the president judge and could not be made frequently. Infrequent sessions of the court meant a delay in justice. Furthermore, courts were not established at once for the counties of Erie, Mercer, Venango, and Warren. Consequently, litigants in those counties were required to appear before the court at Meadville, often with great difficulty.

Governor McKean appeared to be unsympathetic with the desires of the people of the western counties to procure a more acceptable system of courts. The legislature in 1802 passed a bill transferring cases for recovery of debts not exceeding one hundred dollars from the courts to the justices of the peace.

[1] Walsh, "The Legal and Public Career of Alexander James Dallas," 55.
[2] Reynolds, *Fifty Years of the Bench and Bar of Crawford County*, 6.

CONFLICTS AND CONFUSION

The governor vetoed the bill saying that it "would devolve the jurisdiction, generally speaking, upon persons of incompetent skill in the law."[3] The following year petitions rolled into the legislature requesting a substitute system of referees for the regular courts.[4] The chief complaint of the petitioners was to the effect that much of the time was employed in the courts of quarter session in frivolous disputes of contentious people, to the prevention of a decision on civil actions. Governor McKean opposed this demand for a system of referees and warned the legislature that, "the spirit of litigation, the ruin of honest suitors, and the triumph of others equally culpable, can no longer be disingenuously ascribed to the machinations of a profession."[5] He continued to uphold the lawyers and the judges. Western Pennsylvanians were convinced that he was unsympathetic to the impeachment of Addison in 1803; but their resentment toward McKean was increased to a much greater extent when, in 1805, the members of the senate failed to convict the judges of the Pennsylvania Supreme Court, Edward Shippen, Jasper Yeates, and Thomas Smith. The radical Republicans believed that the acquittal of these judges was due to the efforts of McKean.

The impeachment of those three judges grew out of the general discontent of the people relative to the judicial system and out of the Democratic-Republican policy of striking at the judiciary. The specific incident which led to the impeachment was an action of the Pennsylvania Supreme Court in imposing a fine and penalty upon one Thomas Passmore, a Philadelphia merchant who had made a scurrilous attack upon an insurance company while awaiting a decision of the supreme court relative to a trial between Passmore and the company. Early in the year 1804 impeachment proceedings were begun in the house against the three judges, but the case did not come to trial until January of 1805. The senate was organized

---

[3] *Pennsylvania Archives,* fourth series, 4:496, 522 ff.; Pennsylvania *House Journal,* 1803-04, p. 28, 29.
[4] Pennsylvania, *House Journal,* 1803-04, p. 16.   [5] *Ibid.,* 1803-04, p. 28, 29.

as a court for the trial of the judges on January 7. Six western Pennsylvanians participated in one capacity or another in the proceedings. Abner Lacock of Beaver County was one of the managers of the prosecution for the house of representatives. In the senate, William McArthur from the district of Crawford, Erie, and Venango counties; Thomas Morton from the district of Allegheny, Beaver, and Butler counties; Presley Carr Lane from the district of Westmoreland, Armstrong, and Indiana counties; and John Piper representing Bedford, Huntingdon, and Somerset counties were the men from west of the mountains who sat in judgment of the supreme court judges and who, January 26, acquitted them by a vote of thirteen to eleven.[6] McArthur, Morton, and Piper cast votes for acquittal; Presley Carr Lane and James Brady found the judges guilty of the charges.[7] The failure to convict the judges and the belief on the part of the more radical Republicans that Governor McKean had used his influence in the behalf of Shippen, Yates, and Smith intensified the bitterness of the opponents of the judiciary toward McKean.

In that same session of the legislature, beginning in December of 1804, Lacock introduced petitions from inhabitants of Beaver, Butler, Mercer, and Crawford counties to the house of representatives asking that the number of judges of the supreme court be increased to facilitate the administration of justice in the northwestern counties. In February of the following year, Lacock presented a petition from Alexander Wright of Mercer County that complained of the conduct of Thomas Smith, one of the associate judges of the supreme court who had just been acquitted, and called the attention of the legislature to his behavior.[8] These petitions were fruitless in themselves but they probably contributed toward keeping alive the opposition to the Pennsylvania judicial system.

That opposition was increased a few weeks later when the governor vetoed a bill "Regulating the Administration of Jus-

[6] *Crawford Weekly Messenger* (Meadville), January 30, 1805.
[7] *Ibid.*, February 13, 1805. [8] *Ibid.*, January 23, March 20, 1805.

tice." The bill provided for the division of Pennsylvania into nine districts, four of which were to be located in the counties west of the mountains. It specified that the fifth district should include the counties of Franklin, Huntingdon, Bedford, Somerset, and Cambria; the seventh district was to be composed of the counties of Allegheny, Beaver, Washington, and Greene; the eighth district was to include the counties of Erie, Mercer, Crawford, Butler, and Venango; the ninth district was to contain the counties of Westmoreland, Fayette, Armstrong, and Indiana. Furthermore, the measure provided that there should be a president judge and two associate judges for each district and that there should be four terms of the session of the common pleas court.[9]

This bill would have facilitated and hastened the administration of justice immeasurably in the western counties. It would have guaranteed regular sessions of the court at stated intervals; it would have brought the courts closer to the people and eliminated difficult and long journeys on the part of the litigants; and it would have prevented a great number of cases piling up on the dockets. Together with the bill proposed in 1802 transferring cases for recovery of property of amounts less than one hundred dollars from the courts to the justices of the peace, this bill, had it been enacted, would have obviated the difficulties of the western men in procuring justice. But McKean had vetoed both measures; he had been suspected of using his influence in behalf of the judges in the impeachment trial; and he had indicated on all occasions that his sympathies rested with the lawyers and the judges whom the radical Republicans had attacked. As a result a strong opposition to McKean arose in western Pennsylvania. This opposition took form in the year 1805 in a movement among the radical Republicans to defeat McKean for the governorship and to revise the state constitution in order to change the judicial system.

The opposition that the people in the northwestern counties held toward the courts was tied up to no little extent with

[9] *Crawford Weekly Messenger* (Meadville), May 15, 1805.

their land problems. A particularly complex problem relating to the ownership of some tracts of land in Crawford and Erie counties arose as a result of the purchase of land along French Creek by the Holland Land Company. The completion of that purchase was effected on August 21, 1793, when agents of the company conveyed 34,860 pounds specie for 464,800 acres of land "situate on the north and west side of the Rivers Ohio and Allegheny and Conewango Creek in (then) Allegheny County granted to them by 1162 warrants of 400 acres each." In April of the previous year an act of assembly had provided,

That no warrant or survey to be issued or made in pursuance of this act for lands lying north and west of the Rivers Ohio and Allegheny and Conewango Creek shall vest any title in or to the land therein mentioned, unless the grantee has prior to the date of said warrant, made, or caused to be made or shall within two years next after the date of the same, make or cause to be made an actual settlement thereon ... Provided always, Nevertheless, That if any such actual settlers or any grantee in any such original or succeeding warrant, shall by force of arms of enemies of the United States, be prevented from making such actual settlement or be driven therefrom, and shall persist in his endeavor to make such actual settlement as aforesaid, then in either case, he and his heirs shall be entitled, to have and to hold the said lands, in the same manner as if the actual settlement had been made and continued.[10]

The provision of the law that required an evidence of actual settlement upon a tract within two years time of the acquisition of the warrant was the basis for many misunderstandings and legal suits relating to possession of land for the next fifteen years. The Holland Land Company was unable to comply with that provision because, as a result of Indian uprisings, Crawford County was practically abandoned in 1792, and again in 1793. Little progress could be made or attempted

---

[10] Huidekoper, "Holland Land Company," 5, 6. Mr. Huidekoper is a descendant of Harm Jan Huidekoper, an early agent for the Holland Land Company, and he was in possession of the Huidekoper Papers when he prepared this article. It is in the form of a legal brief of the case of the Holland Land Company in its efforts to retain possession of the land.

until after the ratification of the Treaty of Greenville on December 22, 1796. Thereafter the company made surveys, built mills and a storehouse, and provided for improvements upon the tracts. Many settlers, however, came into the region, squatted upon the land, and built crude homes. These settlers, desiring to hold the land and their improvements, contested the validity of the patents of the Holland Land Company. A trial case to determine the ownership of the land was held before the Supreme Court of Pennsylvania, sitting at Sunbury, on November 25, 1802. Chief Justice Shippen was of the opinion that the state of hostility and danger shown to have existed after the taking out of the warrants was a sufficient legal excuse for non-performance of settlement and that the company was entitled to its patents. Justices Yeates and Smith, however, held that the hostilities shown only deferred, but did not excuse, a subsequent performance of the conditions. As a result of the ruling of this court, therefore, actual settlers could take out warrants for their improved land, and the company was powerless to eject them.

The Holland Land Company was not to be outdone, however. Since the question of whether or not the state had violated a contract arose, the company was entitled to carry its case to the federal courts. It made an appeal to the Supreme Court of the United States in the case of Harm Jan Huidekoper's "Lessee *v.* Douglas," which was tried at the April term of the United States Circuit Court of Pennsylvania in 1805 before Chief Justice John Marshall and two associates. The chief justice delivered the instructions to the court. He explained that the law provided that if hostilities prevented the actual settlement upon the land that the grantee or his heirs "shall be entitled to have and to hold the said lands, *in the same manner as if the actual settlement had been made and continued.*" In other words, Marshall held that hostilities excused the non-performance of actual settlement, and the jury, agreeing with him, rendered a verdict favorable to the company. Thereafter the company could legally eject the actual settlers who had improved their land and had felt secure in their ownership. Again the courts had disappointed the farmers of western Pennsylvania. The actual settlers could see nothing but gross injustice in the loss of their lands and in the attitude of the courts.[11]

This decision, while rendered in behalf of the Holland Land Company, laid down a principle that was valid for the Pennsylvania Population Company as well. Both companies were in a position to evict the settlers and sell the land, thereby reaping for themselves the benefit from the improvements made upon the land. The settlers who had built homes for themselves had no legal recourse. Steps were soon taken, however, to alleviate their distress. Even before the decision had been rendered by the federal court, McArthur introduced a petition in the Senate of Pennsylvania asking that aid be given to the settlers to enable them to hold the land upon which they had settled but for which they had not yet paid.[12] On July 1 James Gibson, agent for the Pennsylvania Population Company, gave notice to the persons seated on the company's lands in Beaver and Mercer counties that the company would not take advantage of the improvements if the settlers would apply for and purchase the lands by September 14 of that year. If, however, the settlers did not avail themselves of that opportunity, the company would proceed to eject them. These measures for relief were not wholly satisfactory and did not prevent injustices or solve the difficulties, because hundreds of land sales for taxes and for warrants were made within the next two years.[13] The attitude that the Democratic Republicans, many of whom were actual settlers in northwestern Pennsylvania, assumed upon the land problems and their opposition to the legal system in western Pennsylvania can easily be understood. They approached the election of 1805 with bitterness toward the courts and toward McKean. Like the radical

[11] Huidekoper, "Holland Land Company," 10.
[12] *Crawford Weekly Messenger* (Meadville), February 13, 1805.
[13] *Ibid.*, May 14, July 1, 1805.

Republicans in the southwestern counties who were opposed to the conservative governor, they felt that a constitutional convention to revise the state constitution was necessary.

The election of 1805 was one of the most bitter and most confused of any election in all the history of the Keystone State. The Republican party was divided into two factions: the radical Republicans, who favored a constitutional convention, a reorganization of the courts, and the election of Simon Snyder, on the one hand, and on the other the conservative or constitutional Republicans, who opposed the revision of the constitution and who favored the reëlection of the conservative McKean to the governorship. The Federalists, no longer able to cope with a united Democratic-Republican party in the region, were in a position to give effective aid to one of the warring factions. Naturally they preferred the more conservative wing of the party that was led by McKean. Thomas Atkinson, editor of the *Crawford Weekly Messenger*, on April 17 predicted great warmth for the next election and expressed disgust with the governor's behavior. The governor, on his part, was reported to have called those people who wanted the constitution revised, "Clodhoppers, stupid Geese, rascals and Villians."[14] Tarleton Bates, on May 10, wrote to his brother Frederick observing that, "*We* are just beginning our political violence. God knows when it will end."[15] The prediction of Atkinson and the observation of Bates were well borne out in the ensuing election.

Not only was the feeling of the people intense in this election, but the interest in the election extended to a greater number of people than in previous elections. This widespread interest was the result of the development of political machinery and political propaganda. The beginnings of committees of correspondence reached back into the closing years of the previous century. The origin of the caucus, likewise, existed prior

[14] *Crawford Weekly Messenger* (Meadville), May 1, 1805.
[15] Mrs. E. M. Davis, "The Letters of Tarleton Bates, 1795-1805," in *Western Pennsylvania Historical Magazine*, 12:51 (1929).

to 1800. Both institutions developed rapidly and by 1805 were very effective. Simon Snyder was nominated on April 3, by a caucus comprised of fifty members of both houses of the state legislature; Snyder received forty-two votes, McKean seven, and Samuel Maclay one.[16]

But the organizations within the townships, the counties, the districts comprised of counties for the election of an assemblyman, the senatorial districts, and the congressional districts formed the backbone of the party's strength. Each township had a committee of correspondence which met, published an address to the citizens of that particular township, and selected delegates to a county meeting. The delegates from the various townships convened in a county meeting, chose a county committee of correspondence, which published an address to the people of the county, selected candidates for the county offices, and chose delegates to attend a district meeting to nominate a candidate for the Pennsylvania House of Representatives, and in years when state senators or congressmen were to be chosen, delegates were sent from each of the counties in the district to select those officers. The committees of correspondence in the various counties west of the mountains corresponded with each other, exchanging their reasons for supporting their candidates and giving moral support and advice to each other. The addresses that they wrote to the people of their counties were published in the newspapers that were favorably inclined to that particular party or in any other paper that would publish the address. Thus the party organizations were carried to every township in every county in western Pennsylvania. Furthermore, this type of organization became prevalent throughout the United States, especially for rural communities, and remained the dominant form of party organization for over a century—until the direct primary modified it to some extent.

The increasing effectiveness of this party organization and the increasing interest in the election of 1805 in western Penn-

[16] *Crawford Weekly Messenger* (Meadville), July 24, 1805.

CONFLICTS AND CONFUSION 187

sylvania are explained in part by the founding of newspapers at that time. In addition to the papers already mentioned, the *Pittsburgh Gazette*, the *Herald of Liberty*, the *Tree of Liberty*, and the *Farmers' Register*, two additional papers appeared in 1805. Both of them were Democratic-Republican papers; both of them wielded great influence in the election of that year; and both of them were excellent papers for their time.

The paper established first in point of time was the *Crawford Weekly Messenger*, which was published in Meadville. Thomas Atkinson and W. Brendel brought out the first number of this journal on January 2, 1805. Shortly afterward, Atkinson assumed full ownership and control, and he continued to edit the paper, with short interruptions, for over a quarter of a century. Atkinson was a Democratic Republican whose personal inclination was toward McKean, but the files of his paper indicate that he made an effort to be nonpartisan; he accepted the articles and essays from radical and constitutional Republicans alike. The *Messenger* was unusually significant during the first decade of its existence because it was the first newspaper in northwestern Pennsylvania and because it included political information for all the counties north and west of the Ohio and Allegheny rivers. The editor kept his readers informed of the activities of the party organizations in each county of the congressional district; and he reprinted the notices of the activities of the Democratic Republicans in Allegheny and Westmoreland counties as the accounts appeared in the *Tree of Liberty*, in the *Commonwealth*, and in the *Farmers' Register*.[17]

[17] Reynolds, "Crawford County. A History of Its Growth and Development," in *Daily Tribune-Republican* (Meadville), centennial edition, May 12, 1888, p. 2. The *Crawford Weekly Messenger* was significant to the people in the region from 1805 to 1831; it is significant to students of history in the present day because the complete file of this little journal is available. No issues appeared for a short period during the War of 1812, when the editor deserted his printing office for a few weeks to rush to the defense of Erie. Atkinson was a man of literary ability and was just as meticulous in preserving and filing his papers as he was in printing them. The files from 1805 to 1831 were bound in eleven volumes, and when Joseph Kennedy took over the paper in 1831, he preserved them with the same care. Eventually

The second of the newspapers, the *Commonwealth,* was established in Pittsburgh on June 24, 1805, by Ephraim Pentland, a Democratic Republican and a future son-in-law of Abner Lacock, who was later elected to the United States Senate. The young editor used his paper to further the cause of constitutional revision. Atkinson reported in the *Messenger* on August 7 that he had received the first and second numbers of the *Commonwealth,* and he made the comment: "From the zeal and ability displayed by its editor, we have reason to believe, it will be the means of adding strength in the western country, to the cause of Snyder and the convention." Undoubtedly young Pentland was prevailed upon by Lacock and other radical Republicans to provide a journal that would aid the cause of Snyder in the convention because in 1805 the *Tree of Liberty,* as well as the *Pittsburgh Gazette,* was supporting McKean and the constitution.

Pentland lost no time in opening a journalistic war with the *Tree of Liberty.* John Israel was still the owner and nominal editor of the latter journal, but it was suspected of being under the control of Bates, Forward, and Baldwin. Pentland urged that the *Tree of Liberty* change its name to the "Weekly Recorder of Apostacy." Obviously, these three young men who had wrested the borough of Pittsburgh from the Federalists and who were now conservative Republicans were using the *Tree of Liberty* very effectively. Pentland believed that Bates and Baldwin had purchased the paper from Israel and that Forward was doing the editorial work.[18] The two journals traded blast for blast so vigorously that early in the following year the controversy led to the duel in which Bates was killed.

The committees of correspondence and the newspapers in the region opened the political campaign early in the year of 1805. The selection of candidates, while somewhat cumbersome, was more democratic than in previous years. On May

---

they fell into the hands of Kennedy's half-brother, William Reynolds, who in turn presented them to the public library in Meadville.

[18] *Commonwealth* (Pittsburgh), December 25, 1805.

18 a circular call from Pittsburgh, published by a committee composed of William McCandless, Tarleton Bates, John Johnston, Adamson Tannehill, and William Wirsthoff, specified that the Democratic Republicans of Allegheny County should meet at the township election places on Saturday, June 22. The purpose of the meeting was to elect two delegates for a county meeting to be held at the "sign of President Jefferson" on Tuesday of the June court for the purpose of nominating one assemblyman, two commissioners, and three delegates who would meet at James Dixon's house on Franklin Road on Wednesday, July 31, to confer with the delegates from Beaver and Butler counties to nominate a state senator. The call also recommended that the counties of Butler, Mercer, Erie, Crawford, and Venango send delegates to a conference on August 1 at Colonel Robert Reed's on Franklin Road to nominate a candidate for Congress to succeed John Lucas.[19]

A few days later, on May 22, a meeting of citizens at Beaver voted upon the question of changing the state constitution and by a vote of sixty-five to seven opposed the change. By a similar vote, the members recommended McKean for governor, after which a committee of correspondence was chosen. Another meeting at Meadville, on May 28, opposed the calling of a convention by a vote of 127 to 24. This meeting also resolved to support McKean. In addition, it chose delegates for Crawford, Warren, and Venango counties to meet those from Mercer and Erie counties at Meadville on the third Monday in June to select nominees for that district. It further resolved to transmit its resolutions to the *Tree of Liberty*, the *Pittsburgh Gazette*, and the *Crawford Weekly Messenger*.[20]

A similar meeting was held about the same time at Mercer. The people voted to support the constitution by a vote of 121 to 1 and to support McKean. They established a committee of correspondence to communicate with the constitutional Republicans of Crawford, Erie, and Venango counties and to

[19] *Crawford Weekly Messenger* (Meadville), June 5, 1805.
[20] *Ibid.*, May 22, June 8, 1805.

agree on candidates, with the provision that no revisionist was to be supported. The resolutions of this meeting were to be published in the *Tree of Liberty* and the *Crawford Weekly Messenger*. The constitutional Republicans of Erie also held a meeting, on June 5, opposed the convention by a unanimous vote of 47, agreed to support McKean by a vote of 46 to 1, chose delegates to meet in Meadville for the purpose of nominating candidates, and transmitted their resolutions to the *Tree of Liberty,* the *Gazette,* and the *Messenger.* A similar meeting of the constitutional Republicans in Berlin, Somerset County, was reported in the issue of the *Messenger* for June 12; another such meeting at Greensburg, comprised of three hundred people of Westmoreland, Armstrong, and Indiana counties, met at the courthouse on June 19 and agreed to support the constitution and McKean. A group of five hundred or more constitutional Republicans met at the courthouse in Pittsburgh on June 28 and reported that there were only ten dissenting votes on the question of supporting the constitution and six dissenting votes on the question of supporting McKean.[21]

The friends of McKean and the constitution took opportunity to meet on a more convivial and congenial occasion. On July 4 some forty-five people assembled at a cool clear spring near Mercer and ate heartily. In liquor more potent than spring water they drank twenty toasts, which seemed to be the traditional number for Fourth-of-July celebrations. Among others, they drank toasts to the fair sex, the army, the navy, President Jefferson, and McKean—particularly McKean, for his firmness in upholding the state constitution. Such celebrations as these increased the anticipations of the conservatives for shortly afterward predictions were made that McKean would be elected. A little later, reports were spread that his followers wanted to bet that he would be reëlected. A thousand dollars was available in Lancaster County for a wager upon McKean, and five hundred dollars in Crawford

[21] *Crawford Weekly Messenger* (Meadville), May 29, June 12, July 3, 1805.

County.[22] The constitutional Republicans pressed their campaign vigorously and had good cause for anticipating success. William Findley and John Smilie, the old war horses of Westmoreland and Fayette counties, were friends and associates of McKean and were growing conservative. Age was mellowing the virulence of these two men who had gone through the Revolution and had seen the formation of the Constitution. In Allegheny County, Bates, Forward, and Baldwin, pro-McKean men, were appealing to the Federalists in an effort to elect the constitutional Republican candidate for governor, and the conservative Republicans in northwestern Pennsylvania were also well organized and active. But the democratic or radical Republicans matched them in the intensity of their partisanship and were almost, if not quite, as well organized.

The first call for a township meeting of the radical Republicans appears to have been made on June 19, through the columns of the *Messenger*. The Republicans of Mead Township, Crawford County, were requested to meet at the home of Henry Hurst on June 22. At that meeting the members selected delegates to the county meeting and resolved to recommend Simon Snyder as their candidate for governor, William McArthur for reëlection to the senate, and Wilson Smith of Waterford, Erie County, for the state house of representatives. The township delegates of Erie County met in Erie on June 29 and chose delegates for the district meeting of Crawford, Mercer, and Venango counties to be held in Meadville on July 6. They likewise resolved to support Snyder for the governorship and to oppose the constitution. The district meeting was held at the home of Henry Hurst on July 6, at which time the delegates of the counties of Crawford, Mercer, and Erie completed the nomination of William McArthur for the state senate and Wilson Smith for the state house of representatives and chose delegates to meet at Reed's house on August 1, to designate a candidate for Congress.[23]

[22] *Crawford Weekly Messenger* (Meadville), July 17, 24, August 7, 1805.
[23] *Ibid.*, June 26, July 10, 17, 1805.

The delegates who met at the home of Robert Reed on Franklin Road to nominate a congressional candidate were divided between the radical and constitutional Republicans. Nine of those present favored Snyder for governor and five favored McKean. This division indicates that while the local differences in the individual counties were sharp, the Democratic Republicans, whether radicals or constitutionalists, considered themselves the regular party. Nathaniel Irish was nominated as the candidate for Congress from the district composed of Allegheny, Beaver, Butler, Crawford, and Erie counties. A few weeks later Irish, in answer to a query concerning his preference for governor, published an open letter indicating that he intended to vote for McKean. Thereafter, the radical Republicans in the district supported Samuel Smith of Waterford, a brother of Wilson Smith, for Congress.[24]

Thus three Republican tickets were presented to the people in western Pennsylvania in the election of 1805. The constitutional Republicans favored McKean and the retention of the constitution; some of the Democratic Republicans supported McKean but the majority favored Snyder and a revision of the constitution; and in Pittsburgh a Federal Republican ticket was arranged, which was headed by McKean for governor; James O'Hara, Federalist, for Congress; and Samuel Ewalt, a former Democratic Republican, for the state senate. In the southwestern counties the issue was between McKean and Snyder. Findley of Westmoreland and Smilie of Fayette stood by McKean, their old friend and associate.

Throughout the campaign the chief bone of contention was the question of revising the constitution. As early as March 20 a remonstrance was circulated through the state condemning the constitution and pointing out the weaknesses of government under it. The term of the senators was too long, the patronage of the governor was too large, the delay in procuring justice for citizens was too long, and the disparity be-

[24] *Crawford Weekly Messenger* (Meadville), August 7, September 5, October 3, 1805.

HENRY BALDWIN
From an engraving in the possession of Mr. and Mrs. John E. Reynolds of Meadville

CONFLICTS AND CONFUSION 193

tween the rich man and the poor man before the bar of justice was too great. These circular remonstrances were deposited in public places where those who wished to sign the protest could do so.[25] Articles and essays from both points of view, both original and copied, appeared in each issue of the newspapers. The Philadelphia *Aurora* published much pro-convention and anti-judiciary material. An article from that paper written by "Regulus" was reprinted in the *Messenger* on April 10, 1805. The grand jury of Crawford County passed a resolution by a vote of fifteen to three against the calling of a convention. Abner Lacock defiantly announced that the report that he favored the calling of a constitutional convention was correct.[26] An "Address of the Society of the Constitutional Republicans" of Philadelphia, six columns long, was reprinted in the *Messenger* of July 31 and continued in the issue of August 14. The editor of that paper in a public notice to the "Mercer County Democratic Farmer" explained that it was impossible to publish the Farmer's essay because of the preponderance of articles submitted opposing the constitution and that he wanted to give space to both sides and was forced to reject much good material.[27] Articles and essays appeared in the *Farmers' Register*, the *Tree of Liberty*, the *Commonwealth*, and probably in the *Gazette*, although the files of that newspaper are scare for the year 1805. It is reasonable to suppose, however, that Scull was carrying on the fight for McKean and the constitution.

In addititon to the issue of a constitutional convention and a revision of the constitution, attacks were made upon individual candidates. Samuel Smith of Erie County, the radical Republican candidate for Congress, was attacked with great vigor by conservative Republicans in Pittsburgh. A communication to the *Crawford Weekly Messenger* entitled "Samuel Smith of Erie County" averred that he was a man of

[25] *Crawford Weekly Messenger* (Meadville), March 20, 1805.
[26] *Tree of Liberty* (Pittsburgh), July 5, 1805.
[27] *Crawford Weekly Messenger* (Meadville), July 31, 1805.

extensive education; that the charge that he was a coward was untrue; and that the charge had been made by six Irishmen of Pittsburgh and a convicted justice of the peace, which indicated that William Gazzam and Adamson Tannehill probably were known in the extreme northern part of the state. William McArthur, the senatorial candidate from the northwestern counties, was accused of being an ingrate. It was said that David Mead had picked him up and made him a deputy surveyor, giving him a start in life, and that thereafter he had been unfair to the actual settlers.[28] Throughout the region there were many such bitter recriminations; the controversy between the *Commonwealth* and the *Tree of Liberty* has been cited. The influence of Findley in Westmoreland and Smilie and Lane in Fayette was sufficient to prevent a spirited contest on the part of the radical Republicans in those counties. In Washington County the preponderance of radical Republicans obviated a close contest, although there were heated arguments between the members of the two wings of the party.

McKean won the state by the slender margin of 5115 votes. Samuel Smith of Erie County and General John Hamilton of Washington County, radical Republicans, were elected to Congress by their respective districts.[29] Apparently, the two factions of the Republican party in the western counties divided the spoils fairly evenly, especially in the county and legislative offices. An analysis of the votes in the twelve counties west of the mountains including Somerset, which has not been included generally in this study, reveals that McKean received 8115 votes and Snyder 7077, a difference of 1038. In the six counties north and west of the Ohio and Allegheny, McKean had a majority in only one. Beaver gave him a scant margin of 34 in a total of 996 votes. Northwestern Pennsylvania, then, was virtually solid for the radical Republicans. Of the six counties of southwestern Pennsylvania, McKean received a majority of the votes in four—Somerset, Westmore-

[28] *Crawford Weekly Messenger* (Meadville), August 21, October 3, 1805.
[29] *Ibid.*, October 30, 1805; *Pittsburgh Gazette,* October 19, 1805.

land, Fayette, and Allegheny. The margins of those majorities in Allegheny and Somerset counties were not impressive; Westmoreland and Fayette, however, did give him substantial majorities of 1952 and 530 respectively. Washington and Greene counties were decisively in the ranks of the radical Republicans.[30]

In other words, the northwestern counties, more recently settled, more generally agricultural, and more closely familiar with frontier conditions, were more democratic and radical than the southwestern counties, particularly the older counties of Westmoreland and Fayette, in which the people had grown conservative. In addition to the old Jeffersonian Republicans in the southwestern counties, the Federalists who had no general slate in this election cast their votes for McKean. It must be concluded that the Federalists throughout the state and, to a considerable extent, in western Pennsylvania were responsible for McKean's success. Tarleton Bates with a sigh of relief reported to his brother Frederick that, "We have carried McKean by about 5000, nearly the same as in 1799, though not the same persons. The Feds have done nobly."[31]

The people of the northwestern counties had lost in a good fight, but they were not satisfied with the fact that they had made a good showing. The unsatisfactory legal system and the uncertainty of the ownership of land about which there was a question of title, still remained. The Federalists were not contented and they could assume no credit unto themselves as a party; they did enjoy the discomfiture of the Republicans, who were fighting among themselves, but there was less satisfaction to be obtained from aiding and abetting the fight among their opponents than there would have been in controlling the offices themselves. Consequently, the Federalists were unlikely to support the conservative Republicans in the

[30] *Crawford Weekly Messenger* (Meadville), November 13, 1805.
[31] Mrs. E. M. Davis, "The Letters of Tarleton Bates, 1795-1805," in *Western Pennsylvania Historical Magazine*, 12:52 (1929).

future if the Federalists themselves could procure the offices. While the constitutional or conservative Republicans were successful in this election, they had little assurance that they would be able to gain victories in the future unless they obliterated the troublesome problems of the courts and of land ownership.

Governor McKean, recently reëlected and knowing that he was serving the last term permitted him by the constitution, was adamant in his opposition toward a reorganization of the courts. In his message to the legislature on December 3, 1805, he condemned the judiciary bill of the previous session. But his Republican friends, still conscious of the close margin in the recent election and anxious to eliminate the vexing question of the courts before another election occurred, produced a bill in the session that began in December of 1805 that was eventually signed by the governor and was reported in the *Crawford Weekly Messenger* of April 17, 1806. This judiciary act divided the state into two districts for the purpose of the administration of justice by the Pennsylvania Supreme Court. Twenty of the western counties were included in the western district for which a court sat annually at Pittsburgh. The reorganization obviated only a part of the complaints that the men of the western counties registered against the judicial system, but it nevertheless served as a safety valve and quieted their demands for a constitutional convention. It was not until 1810 that an act known as the "Justice of Peace Act" was passed granting to the justices of the peace jurisdiction in all cases of contracts not exceeding one hundred dollars, except in cases where land titles or tenement cases were involved.[32] The latter act apparently satisfied the most extreme demands of the western men and terminated their contentions relative to the courts. Snyder, however, had succeeded McKean as governor by that time.

The controversy between the actual settlers and the warrantee land owners was fully as virulent for three or four years

[32] *Crawford Weekly Messenger* (Meadville), April 25, 1810.

CONFLICTS AND CONFUSION 197

after the election of 1805 as it had been before, and it continued to be bothersome for at least a decade after 1805. The Erie County commissioners served notice on May 12, 1806, that all unseated lands on which the taxes had been due for two years or more would be seized and sold within two months unless the taxes were paid. A petition from "Actual Settlers" requesting a federal amendment to the Constitution to prevent federal courts from settling the land question was forwarded to Samuel Smith to be presented in Congress. The petitioners, uninformed of any congressional action, suspected that Smith had not presented the petition and requested an explanation from him. He presented evidence, however, to indicate that he had read the petition in Congress.[33]

Public officials and officers were not the only ones who were accused of a lack of fairness and sympathy in these controversies over land. A nasty rumor had it that Samuel Lord, a Federalist and prominent citizen of Meadville, had evicted one John Rogers and his wife from their land, putting them out in the snow while the woman was in labor. Lord openly denied the rumor and procured a certificate from David McKee asserting that Rogers and his wife denied that they were evicted but maintained that they had left of their own accord while the sheriff was absent. Unsavory reports were bandied about concerning Harm Jan Huidekoper, agent for the Holland Land Company, who had his office in Meadville. It was rumored that he had said that if any efforts were made to procure relief for the actual settlers through legislative means he "would damn this country." Another charge was made against him that he had unfeelingly forced Michael Seeley, a farmer with an invalid wife and children, to sell his horses to pay for his land. It was alleged that Huidekoper, representative of a company with a capital of five million dollars, had taken advantage of a poor man.[34]

The resentment of the people toward Huidekoper was

[33] *Crawford Weekly Messenger* (Meadville), July 3, 10, September 25, 1806.
[34] *Ibid.*, September 25, 1806, April 19, 1807.

doubtless occasioned by the fact that there were hundreds of forced land sales during these years. The county commissioners were selling tracts of land for the purpose of collecting taxes, but they represented local government, and the animosity toward them was less, though evident, than it was toward the representatives of a foreign country who hoped to profit through the misfortune of the farmers. A spirit of resentment existed, likewise, against the Pennsylvania Population Company, which held land extending over into Beaver County. In a trial in that county in 1806, twelve jurors, local citizens, found a verdict in favor of the actual settlers. This verdict was set aside, however, by Justice Yeates of the state supreme court sitting at Beaver. The Supreme Court of Pennsylvania in 1807 upheld Yeates's decision, and the actual settlers were helpless.[35]

The farmers were very bitter as a result of this decision, and the feeling in Beaver County was unusually tense. An effort to eject one William Foulkes, a resident of seventeen years, led to the fatal shooting of James Hamilton by a young man named Aitken, a friend of Foulkes. Aitken was brought to trial and acquitted by a jury of local men.[36] Apparently, this was the only instance in all the controversy relative to the ownership of lands in western Pennsylvania in which a loss of life occurred. But Ennion Williams, agent for the Pennsylvania Population Company in Beaver County, departed from the county shortly after the slaying of James Hamilton, because of the intense feeling of the settlers. Some of them burned his home soon after his departure.[37]

While this excessive bitterness subsided to some extent in the ensuing years, it did not disappear immediately. In 1810 Patrick Farrelly and others petitioned the state legislature asking for a settlement of the still troublesome land ques-

---

[35] *Crawford Weekly Messenger* (Meadville), October 8, 1807.

[36] *Commonwealth* (Pittsburgh), November 19, 1807.

[37] *Crawford Weekly Messenger* (Meadville), April 14, 1808.

CONFLICTS AND CONFUSION 199

tion.[38] But it was not until the following year, 1811, that the legislature formulated a bill for the purpose of alleviating the difficulties of the actual settlers. This bill, brought out on March 7, 1811, provided that when actual settlers had made previous arrangements with the warrantees and had been unable to meet those arrangements in due time, the settlers might now have an opportunity to do so; that if the settlers had not made such arrangements but had made improvements on their land, they should receive 150 acres from the state— apparently as payment for the improvement; that settlers who had improved their land and then left it might return before June, 1813, to fulfill the requirements; that those who had been evicted might also return and resume the fulfillment of the qualifications; and that where no acutal occupation had occurred settlers were permitted to establish rights any time before June of 1814.[39] Thereafter, the controversies over land ownership decreased but did not disappear. As late as 1817 controversies still existed,[40] but they did not precipitate political issues after 1811.

The court system and the land question, significant as they were, could not hold the complete attention of the people of western Pennsylvania throughout the years from 1805 to 1807. Aaron Burr, the dashing, fascinating former vice president, who was then under a cloud, seemed to cast a spell over the young men, many of whom were sons of prominent people in the region, and to draw them to himself through some scheme of conquest that was probably as vague to them then as it is to the historian now. Burr was reported to have tarried only a day in Pittsburgh, early in 1805, before sailing down the Ohio and Mississippi rivers for the rumored purpose of relieving William Claiborne as governor of the Louisiana Territory.[41] Whatever Burr's fantastic scheme may have been, the fact that so many prominent men of the region attached themselves to him, and the fact that there was a mysterious atmos-

[38] *Crawford Weekly Messenger* (Meadville), February 7, October 1, 1810.
[39] *Ibid.*, March 27, 1811.   [40] *Ibid.*, February 5, 1817.   [41] *Ibid.*, May 8, 1805.

phere about his adventure, created a furore in the western country. The columns of the newspapers were heavily loaded with opinions, both favorable and adverse to Burr's project. Frederick Bates writing from Pittsburgh on December 3, 1806, reported that Burr's plans seemed complete and that most of the young men in the community, respectable by birth, education, and property, were descending the river.[42] Even in northwestern Pennsylvania, Jabez Colt, agent for the Pennsylvania Population Company, was intimately friendly with one Davis, who was openly known to be Burr's emissary in that region.[43] So great was the excitement in the northern counties that the Republicans gathered before the courthouse in Meadville, listened to an address by Patrick Farrelly condemning Burr, and burned Burr's effigy.[44]

Regardless of the amount of space given by the newspapers to Burr, to his enterprise, and to the young men who joined him and regardless of the excitement that existed in the region, the Republicans apparently were unable to make a great amount of political capital from the incident. They assumed that the majority of the young men who had attached themselves to Burr were Federalists or sons of Federalists and had implicated themselves in a treasonable venture. Fortunately, those who had dabbled in the project escaped without any serious blights to their careers or reputations.

The more virulent and radical Republicans found no advantage in implicating their rivals in treasonable ventures, however, because the tardiness of the constitutional Republicans in settling the legal system and the land problems was sufficient to wipe out the small majority that the latter had received in the election of 1805. The schism in the party became less noticeable; the Democratic Republicans utilized the political organizations in the townships and the counties; and the tide of success rolled in for them for the ensuing three years,

[42] F. Bates, "Letter," in *Michigan Pioneer and Historical Collections,* 8:557 (1886).
[43] *Crawford Weekly Messenger* (Meadville), March 19, 1807.
[44] *Ibid.,* March 5, 1807.

with the exception that William Hoge, a Federalist in Washington County, was elected to Congress in 1806. He had resigned his seat in 1804, and his brother, John Hoge, a Republican, had been elected to complete the unexpired term and had served from November 2, 1804, to March 3, 1805. John Hamilton, a Democratic Republican, had then represented Washington County from March 4, 1805, to March 3, 1807. The fact that the Hoge brothers, one a Federalist and the other a Republican, alternated in representing their district in Congress suggests that neither of them was extreme in his partisanship and that both of them were popular leaders in their county. Evidently the personalities and the prestige of these two men were bigger than party lines. Allegheny County in the same year gave 1059 votes to John Wilkins, Jr., candidate for Congress, and only 837 to Samuel Smith, the Erie County Republican, who was seeking reëlection. But Allegheny County was yoked to Beaver, Butler, Mercer, Crawford, and Erie counties in a congressional district, and every county, except Allegheny, gave a majority to Smith, with the result that he was reëlected by a vote of 3339 to 2621.[45]

Findley and Smilie were reëlected from their districts without serious opposition. Those two men had become fixtures in the House of Representatives and in the scheme of Jefferson's national party. Both of them enjoyed the confidence and respect of the leaders in Congress, and Findley had taken a part in the technical organization of Congress just as he had aided in setting up the organization of the state house of representatives in his own state in 1790. It was he who was instrumental in introducing the institution of a committee on ways and means in the House of Representatives in 1803.[46] The fact that Findley and Smilie were administration men helps to explain their support of governor McKean in the election of 1805. The conservative Pennsylvania governor was

[45] *Crawford Weekly Messenger* (Meadville), October 23, 1806.
[46] Findley, "An Autobiographical Letter," in *Pennsylvania Magazine of History and Biography*, 5:447 (1881).

attacked in that election by Duane and Leib, who were likewise attacking the administration. Because the two veteran Congressmen from western Pennsylvania were growing conservative through age and experience, because McKean had been associated with them for a long time, and because they stood with the administration in its fight against Duane and Leib, they were conservative Republicans in the memorable election of 1805. But when the unfortunate results of the Embargo Act of 1807 gave the Federalist party a new lease on life and that party became active again in the election of 1808, both in the nation and in western Pennsylvania, these two Democratic-Republican stalwarts, finding party blood thicker than water, preferred to stand with the more radical Republicans than risk the possibility of a Federalist victory in the state and nation.

The Embargo Act of December, 1807, a futile gesture on the part of the United States in its attempt to retaliate against England and France for the British Orders in Council and the Decrees of Napoleon, was devastating to the commerce of the American seaboard. At first glance it would seem that the embargo should not have had a ruinous effect on the economic conditions of the hinterland, but the prices of farm products fell, and there was a tendency toward stagnation in the commerce of even the western counties of Pennsylvania. The friends of Jefferson, however, out of loyalty to the party and believing themselves to be patriotic, supported the president to an extent that was unknown in New England or even in the middle colonies along the seaboard. The Federalist papers in western Pennsylvania, particularly the *Gazette,* voiced a protest against the embargo. Scull was gleaning many of the ideas of eastern newspapers, upon which he was relying. As a result, the members of the "Federal and Constitutional Republican Group" in Pittsburgh met at the home of Samuel Peebles to take stock of the economic situation that had been produced by the act restricting American commerce. In this meeting the conclusions were reached that farmers were confronted by a dreadful economic future and that trade and commerce were stifled, since "All exportation is prohibited under severe penalties."[47] "Fabius," speaking to the "people of the Western Country" through the columns of the *Gazette,* predicted certain ruin and poverty and explained that the embargo was passed in obedience to the commands of the French emperor.[48] Unquestionably there was opposition to the embargo from some quarters of western Pennsylvania, but in the end, patriotism led even the Federalists to support Jefferson's administration and that of his successor in the foreign policy that led to the War of 1812. The Democratic Republicans, with but few exceptions, bore the aftermath of the embargo with patient fortitude.

The election of 1808 in Pennsylvania loomed as one of significance at the beginning of the year. Except for a few seats in the senate nearly all the offices would be vacated in that year, and the election of candidates for the governorship, the lower house of the legislature, the various county offices, and even presidential electors would be required. Furthermore, in the national scene Jefferson's second administration was drawing to a close, and the series of disappointments that he had encountered had made him weary; like Washington he concluded that two terms in the presidency should be the extent of a man's eligibility for that office. Madison, upon whose shoulders the mantle of responsibility fell, was left a heritage of economic stagnation and political dissatisfaction. In fact, Madison had apprehensions about the possibility of his election. The split between the constitutional and radical Republicans in Pennsylvania was one of those irksome problems that confronted him.

The apparent rejuvenation of the Federalist party led to the fear that the Federalists in Pennsylvania might carry the state provided they could appeal to a sufficient number of conservative Republicans. Duane, Leib, and Snyder had waged such a relentless warfare on the unyielding McKean for three

[47] *Pittsburgh Gazette,* April 26, 1808.   [48] *Ibid.,* May 24, 1808.

or four years that there seemed to be little probability that the two wings of the party could coöperate. In bestowing the federal patronage the administration leaders wavered and hesitated in making a choice between the two factions of the party in Pennsylvania. But fortunately for the welfare of the party, the leaders of the two groups of Republicans in the state, anxious to procure that federal patronage, attempted to align themselves with Madison. The outcome was a truce, in so far as a truce was possible, between the radical and the conservative Republicans, with the result that they coöperated in the election to defeat the Federalists in the state. Apparently a deal was made that terminated the party rift even though it did not eradicate all the individual personal animosities.[49]

The nomination of gubernatorial candidates began early in the year. A few friends of Snyder met in Meadville on January 1, nominated Snyder, passed resolutions against a state convention for nominating gubernatorial candidates, and established a committee of correspondence. A group of constitutional Republicans in Greensburg recommended John Spayd of Reading for governor on February 19. On March 5 a Federalist meeting was held in Pittsburgh which nominated James Ross for governor. A number of constitutional Republicans in Pittsburgh also nominated James Ross on March 15.[50] Thus it appeared that there were to be three candidates for the governorship. The Federalists and the Quids, the name some times used to designate the constitutional Republicans, had separated; James Ross received the support of the Federalists; John Spayd attracted the votes of the majority of constitutional Republicans and received the nomination from a number of people in Greensburg described as the "Westmoreland Whigs"; and Snyder was assured the undivided vote of the radical Republicans. Early in May there was an indication that the Federalist party could expect little support from the

[49] Stanwood, *History of the Presidency*, 2:92.
[50] *Crawford Weekly Messenger* (Meadville), January 7, March 3, 17, 1808; *Pittsburgh Gazette*, March 29, 1808.

Quids, or constitutional Republicans, whom they supported in 1805.[51]

The Federalists, nevertheless, conducted their campaign with more vigor in western Pennsylvania than they had displayed at any time since 1800. May 28 the Meadville Federalists met at the "Sign of the Buck," nominated James Ross for governor, Alexander Forster, a Meadville attorney, for Congress, John W. Hunter for the lower house of the state legislature, and Samuel Torbett for county commissioner. And since the *Crawford Weekly Messenger* had been placed at the disposal of the Republicans, a Federalist newspaper, the *Mirror*, was established in Erie to give the party an instrument for propaganda in the northern counties. Its specific task appeared to be that of attacking Samuel Smith, the Republican Congressman. The *Mirror* wanted to know what Smith had done with the petition of the citizens of Erie that asked the federal government for six thousand dollars for opening a harbor at Presque Isle. Smith explained that he had presented the petition but that the committee on manufactures had opposed it. Also he justified his vote for the embargo.[52] Scull regained a little of his former vigor in this campaign and once more used the *Gazette* to further the candidacy of James Ross. The *Crawford Weekly Messenger* for August 18 contained a four-column address from the Pittsburgh committee of correspondence, of which Scull was a member, attempting to refute an attack upon Ross by the Republican committee of correspondence of Beaver County.[53] Public meetings were held in Pittsburgh to swell the boom for the Federalists' favorite son. James O'Hara presided at one of these meetings of naturalized Irishmen and made an address to the Irish voters in behalf of Ross.[54]

But the efforts of the Federalists appeared indifferent and feeble in comparison to the activities of the Republicans in

[51] *Crawford Weekly Messenger* (Meadville), May 12, 1808.
[52] *Ibid.*, June 8, 16, 1808.   [53] *Ibid.*, August 4, 18, 1808.
[54] *Pittsburgh Gazette,* March 1, September 21, 1808.

western Pennsylvania in this campaign. In every county there was a vigorous Republican committee of correspondence; even the townships in the counties were well organized. The *Crawford Weekly Messenger* was definitely at the service of the Republicans, and its editor was a member of the Crawford County Republican committee of correspondence.[55] A recently established paper, the *Minerva* (Beaver, 1807), added its weight to that of the *Commonwealth* and of the *Farmers' Register* to present the cause of the Democratic Republicans. The Republicans held a county meeting in Westmoreland on February 25; in Erie on April 6; in Venango on May 2; in Mercer on May 27; and at Beaver late in July, at which time a vicious attack was made upon James Ross.[56] In each of these county meetings the leaders worked effectively and smoothly, tightening the party reins and preparing addresses to their constituents.

The attacks upon the Federalist candidates, especially Ross, contained in the addresses of the committees to their people, and those thrusts appearing in the Republican newspapers were telling. In the northwestern counties, Alexander Forster, candidate for Congress, was a favorite target. Atkinson jubilantly enumerated the many Republican meetings and sarcastically made the report of a Federalist meeting:

MARK THE CONTRAST!!

The Federalists held a meeting in Franklin during the same week —and not withstanding every exertion to marshall their forces— with the aid of that dreadful monster, *embargo*, sounding in every direction—Behold! no less than ELEVEN gathered together—organized themselves—and unanimously (we suppose) resolved to support James Ross for governor—Alexander Forster for Congress —and Judge McKee for general assembly! Flattering prospects indeed![57]

At another time Atkinson called attention to the fact that all

[55] *Crawford Weekly Messenger* (Meadville), May 19, 1808.

[56] *Ibid.*, March 28, May 5, 12, June 16, August 5, 1808.   [57] *Ibid.*, June 30, 1808.

the Federalist candidates for state offices in Erie, Crawford, and Warren counties were lawyers—he was playing upon the farmers' antipathy toward the members of the bar. Pentland in the *Commonwealth* in a comparison entitled, "Take your choice," listed in two columns the respective positions of Ross and Snyder upon a number of questions. He described Ross as a Federalist, a member of the party to which belonged all the "old tories, traitors and apostate whigs," an "enemy of liberty," an "advocate of standing armies," the "Enemy of Irish, German and other emigrants," the "Enemy of peace," an "Enemy to Christianity," and a man desirous of pomp and parade. Snyder, on the other hand, according to Pentland, was a Democrat, a friend of his country and "equally the enemy of France and Britain and their respective adherents," an "Enemy of every law restricting freedom to express opinions," an "advocate of republican economy," a friend of those who fled to the United States from the oppression of European tyrants, "Friend of Peace," "Believer in God," and a mild unostentatious man.[58]

In the southwestern counties the campaign was less caustic but no less effective. The people there had outgrown the radicalism of the Whiskey Insurrection days, and, too, their leaders, Findley, Smilie, and Lane, had the political situation well in hand and as usual opposed their old Federalist rival, Ross. Everywhere in western Pennsylvania the Republicans were strong.

The election was a complete success for the Snyderite Republicans. Every county west of the mountains was carried by Snyder and his ticket, and even Allegheny County, which had been the stronghold of Federalism in the West, cast 2118 votes for Snyder and only 1249 for Ross, her own eminent son. Spayd, the constitutional Republican, received 65 votes, scattered through four western counties.

The outcome of this election may be explained by many factors. Probably first in importance was the high-powered or-

[58] *Crawford Weekly Messenger* (Meadville), July 21, September 22, 1808.

ganization of the Democratic Republicans in the counties and townships; secondly, the failure of McKean and the conservative Republicans to make a satisfactory reorganization of the courts and to accomplish a settlement of the land question; thirdly, the understanding that was effected between the constitutional and radical Republicans in the state as a whole in which it was agreed that the McKean slate of presidential electors would be supported by the Snyderites and that the followers of McKean would support Snyder for governor; and finally, the Democratic atmosphere of the more recent frontier of northwestern Pennsylvania. All these factors aided in this sweeping Democratic victory. Madison assumed the presidency in 1809 with a feeling of complacency about the status of the party in Pennsylvania.

PASSING THE BATON

CHAPTER NINE

THE period from 1808 to 1815 or 1816 was really a twilight zone in the political development of the country, a transitional period in which the old order was passing and a new one arising. The party of Jefferson, with Madison at the helm, still retained nominal control of the offices in the nation, in Pennsylvania, and in western Pennsylvania. But the policies of Jefferson, which Madison attempted to continue, were badly warped by younger and more vigorous political leaders who were just arriving on the scene. The old Revolutionary political leaders, men who had been young and able in 1776, were rapidly fading out of the picture; after the election of 1816 few of them remained active in politics. Likewise, the economic order that had obtained in 1776 was undergoing changes, which, in turn, brought about social and political changes. Yet at no specific year in this period could it be said that the old order was dead and that the new order had arrived. Rather, the changing may be compared to the passing of the baton in a relay race. The fresh runner, vigorous and anxious, stands waiting in his lane a few yards from the tape; as the weary team mate approaches, the fresh runner gathers his stride, eagerly grasps the baton, and dashes out on a new lap, while his worn comrade staggers along a few steps across the finishing line and drops out, exhausted. So smoothly has the baton been passed from the old runner to the new that the onlooker can scarcely determine the exact spot in which the change occurred. The task of designating the spot becomes much more difficult when three or four relay teams are involved. The time of the passing of the political, economic, and social batons to the new generation is no less difficult to determine.

The simple explanation of the fact that the political leaders who had precipitated and accomplished the American Revolution were withdrawing from politics in this period lies in their age. If one accepts the ordinary calculation of three generations to the century, the conclusion is that approximately thirty-three or thirty-four years may be assigned to a single generation. By the simple arithmetical process of adding thirty-three or thirty-four years to the date of 1776 one arrives at 1809 or 1810. The ranks of the prominent political leaders of the American Revolution were growing thin at that time. Washington, Franklin, John Hancock, Samuel Adams, Patrick Henry, and Hamilton were long since dead. Jefferson, John Adams, Harrison Gray Otis, the Pinckneys of South Carolina, William Branch Giles, Aaron Burr, and many others who were political leaders in 1790 had yielded the leadership to younger men and from their places of retirement merely cast their shadows across the paths of their successors.

Some of the old Revolutionary leaders continued in the race beyond 1810, and a few like Monroe were in the running even beyond 1816. James Madison held the office of president until March, 1817; Monroe, who had been a mere youth during the Revolutionary days, followed in the footsteps of Madison and carried on until 1825; but the glorious group of political leaders was a mere shadow of its former self. Those who still remained in office lacked the fire and determination that had driven Washington, Patrick Henry, Samuel Adams, and Charles Thompson to risk their lives and fortunes in order to give birth to a new nation. In fact, in the period from 1808 to 1812, Jefferson and Madison hesitated to enter a war to complete the task of the formation of the nation. As they stood hesitating, a group of young "war hawks," elected to Congress in 1810, rashly snatched the baton from their trembling hands and plunged the United States into a war which, however ignominious, it may have been, furnished the unifying thread necessary to the development of the nation.

The new leaders just arriving on the national political stage were destined to dominate the government until 1850. Henry Clay and Richard M. Johnson of Kentucky, Peter B. Porter of New York, Felix Grundy of Tennessee, William Lowndes, Langdon Cheeves, and John C. Calhoun, South Carolinians, were elected to the House of Representatives in 1810. Daniel Webster arrived to take his place with them in 1813. William Harris Crawford of Georgia, already a United States Senator, later minister to France, was to become secretary of the treasury in 1816. And Andrew Jackson of Tennessee, who had been in the United States Senate in 1798 and had later dropped into political oblivion, became a national figure again in 1813 and, as a result of his victory at New Orleans in January, 1815, a national hero. These young men were seizing the political baton from the older generation between 1810 and 1815, but for a time they were unable to run with it, because the War of 1812 temporarily obstructed the efforts of any particular party.

In Pennsylvania, too, the old Revolutionary leaders were dropping out. In addition to Franklin, the Morrises, reduced in financial circumstances, had declined in influence near the turn of the century; James Wilson had died after leaving the state to escape his creditors; Arthur St. Clair, broken in wealth but not in spirit, retired to a mountain cabin near Ligonier; Thomas Mifflin had drowned himself in drink; and George Bryan, Thomas Willing, William Bingham, and many others of their vintage had either died or retired from active life. In western Pennsylvania the political leadership had experienced a similar change. John Neville was dead, and his son Presley had removed to Ohio to fight against poverty in his old age. Gone from active politics were Thomas Scott, John Morton, John Gibson, James Marshel, Edward Cook, Nathaniel Breading, William Todd, and John Lucas.

Many others ended their political careers during these years. Ross made his last gesture in the race for the governorship in 1808; neither William nor John Hoge's name appeared in Congress after 1809; Samuel Smith of Erie closed his career in Congress in 1811; Scull relinquished the editorship of his paper to his son in 1816, and, although he held the offices of county commissioner and justice of the peace after that, his political influence was practically negligible. Adamson Tannehill, whose success came late in life, was first elected to Congress in 1812 but was an unsuccessful candidate for reëlection in 1814, and he returned to his farm where he died in 1820; John Woods, a willing candidate for office from 1790 to his death, was elected to Congress in 1814, but never qualified or attended, and died in Pittsburgh in 1817. Hugh Henry Brackenridge, whose name was a household word in western Pennsylvania politics from 1786 to 1799 and in the Pennsylvania judiciary after 1799, died in 1816. William Findley retired from Congress in 1817 but from his home in Youngstown continued to cast his shadow over the Republican party in Westmoreland County until his death in 1821. Smilie died in harness in 1812. Albert Gallatin, although he maintained a nominal home at Friendship Hill near New Geneva, had long since withdrawn from western Pennsylvania politics to serve as secretary of the treasury for Jefferson. He had transferred his activities from partisan politics to diplomacy before the end of this period. The old generation was rapidly approaching the end of its lap of the race and was passing the baton of leadership to younger men.

Among the new generation in western Pennsylvania were many men who had begun their political activities in a humble way near the beginning of the century and by 1808 had already attained some prestige. In Pittsburgh the two young lawyers, Baldwin and Forward, had wrought havoc with the Federalists in the borough even as early as 1804. They were effective political and civic leaders from that time forward but neither of them rose to the eminence of a congressman until

Baldwin was elected to the House of Representatives in 1816. William Wilkins, of a prominent commercial family in Pittsburgh, was ready to take up the banners of the Federalist party by 1810. Aaron Lyle of West Middleton inherited the mantle of the Hoges in Washington County in the election of 1809. Isaac Griffin of New Geneva was elected to fill the vacancy of Representative-elect John Smilie and took his seat on May 24, 1813. Abner Lacock, who had been very active in western Pennsylvania from 1805 on, was elected to the House of Representatives in 1810 and was reëlected in 1812, but he resigned his seat in the House when he was elected to the United States Senate. Thomas Wilson of Erie, a brilliant young Democrat, was then elected to Lacock's vacant seat in the House of Representatives.

In Meadville, Patrick Farrelly, another brilliant lawyer, was prominent in local politics as early as 1810 and was serving in the state house of representatives in 1811 and 1812. He was unable, however, to secure an election to Congress until 1820, after which time he served in the lower House continuously until his death in 1826. Robert Moore, treasurer of Beaver County from 1805 to 1811, was elected to Congress in 1816 and served two terms in that body from 1817 to 1821. In Westmoreland County, David Marchand was groomed to fill the position of Findley, which he took over in the election of 1816 and occupied until 1821. All these young men proved to be worthy leaders, but Henry Baldwin of Pittsburgh became the most prominent because of his advocacy of a protective tariff, which was becoming more desirable to the manufacturing interests of western Pennsylvania.

The protective tariff as a political issue became increasingly important during these years because the old economic order was changing along with the old political leaders. Those people who had been economic leaders in the days of the American Revolution were yielding their economic and financial control to a new generation. The Revolution in itself produced no new social classes; the planters in the South, the merchant princes in the North, and the merchant princes and landed gentry of the middle states still comprised the American aristocracy in 1783. In the South, however, the planters of the older generation fell upon evil days, and various factors cooperated to impair their financial leadership by 1810. Some of the planters were left in dire straits by the English and the colonial armies. The price of tobacco fell between 1783 and 1793, and the fertility of the soil decreased noticeably during that decade. The southerners were in straitened circumstances when the invention of the cotton gin, in 1793, led to the development of cotton raising instead of tobacco growing. But the older men were hesitant to take up the production of a new and different crop, and that task fell to the younger men who migrated toward the West. By 1810 a group of rich cotton planters sprang up, and it was these men who sent the young "war hawks" to Congress.

In New England the merchants found that the treaty with England in 1783 did not guarantee commercial intercourse with England, and commerce proved to be far less lucrative in an independent United States than it had been in the colonial days even with the commercial restrictions that the mother country had imposed upon commerce. The Napoleonic wars, however, opened up a great carrying trade to New England merchants and shippers, which by 1806 had brought them affluence. The older merchants and shippers were wealthy and politically powerful and dominant, but the Embargo Act of 1807 paralyzed their commercial activities. They were too firmly set in their commercial pursuits to enter into another field of activity. They loaned their money to younger men, who built factories and developed industry in the New England states. Consequently there developed a group of new-rich families in New England who were interested in industry and in Congressmen who favored the protective tariff, as Daniel Webster was later to learn.

Likewise, the economic leaders of the middle colonies grew older in years, experienced the depression of the 1780's, and achieved some affluence from the rising prices and commerce of the Napoleonic wars. In western Pennsylvania the same period of depression affected the merchants and even the settlers, because prices were lower and money was scarce. Likewise, the rising prices of farm products at the turn of the century and the increased exportation of those products to Europe improved the economic conditions in the region. Yet the decline and rise of prosperity were less marked in western Pennsylvania than along the seaboard, because the people lived in a frontier region that was to a considerable extent self-sufficient. There was the same evidence of developing industry in western Pennsylvania, however, particularly in Pittsburgh, where it began in the closing years of the eighteenth century, pressed forward in the early years of the nineteenth century, and increased noticeably from 1808 to 1816.

The surge of industry in the Pittsburgh area during the period under consideration was undoubtedly aided by the fact that the embargo disrupted commerce and required the manufacture of many articles that had formerly been imported. But others factors were also at work to stimulate manufacturing at the forks of the Ohio. The inadequacy of the roads and the inconvenience of transporting heavy articles over the mountains or upstream against the current of the Mississippi, made for the growth of local manufacturing.[1] Then too, during the first and second decades of the nineteenth century, a great migration toward the West occurred. Since the Ohio River was one of the finest channels for this migration and since Pittsburgh was located at the junction of the two rivers that formed the Ohio, thousands of people passed through Pittsburgh yearly on their way toward the West. These migrants required tools and implements to establish their homes in the wilderness and found it advisable to buy them in Pittsburgh. If they purchased their supplies there, they were relieved of the necessity of transporting them across the mountains. At the same time, Pittsburgh merchants were relieved of the diffi-

[1] W. J. Bining, "The Glass Industry of Western Pennsylvania, 1797-1860," p. 1-6.

culties of importation when they could procure those manufactured products in or around Pittsburgh.

Furthermore, the increase of river trade placed greater demands upon manufacturing in western Pennsylvania. The development of steam power and its application to river boats facilitated the progress of the upstream traffic. While the actual miles in distance between Pittsburgh and New Orleans remained the same, the length of time consumed in passage either up- or down-stream was much less, and the possibility of bringing cargoes from New York to Pittsburgh produced a greater two-way trade than that which had existed before. But the New Orleans traffic or trade was only a part of the Ohio and Mississippi commerce after 1810. Great quantities of manufactured products were taken to the settlers who had gone up the tributaries of the Ohio and even of the Mississippi. To meet these demands for supplies for settlers going West and for those who had already settled in the West and for outfitting soldiers and furnishing supplies for the army in the War of 1812, an industrial expansion was obviously necessary.

The War of 1812 stimulated industry in western Pennsylvania. Supplies were needed for the western armies, and Pittsburgh was in a position to furnish some for the soldiers just as it was in a position to sell to the settlers who went through the region. Many of the supplies that were used by Commodore Perry in the building of his fleet on Lake Erie were made in Pittsburgh, and practically all of them were shipped through Pittsburgh.[2]

Manufacturing had begun, of course, when the first settlers began making their own furniture, tools, and utensils for domestic use. The manufacturing of products for commercial purposes, however, had begun at the turn of the century. Iron and glass were being made as early as 1800. Isaac Craig and James O'Hara had established the first glassworks in the Pittsburgh district in 1798. Joseph McClurg founded the

[2] Dick, "Recollections of an Early Settler," in *Daily Tribune-Republican* (Meadville), centennial edition, May 12, 1888, p. 12.

earliest successful iron foundry in 1805, although iron furnaces had been in use before that date.[3] By 1807 the *Pittsburgh Gazette* carried advertisements for Anthony Beelen's Pittsburgh Eagle Foundry, George Miltenberger's Copper and Tin Ware Manufactory, and many other such enterprises.[4] Albert Gallatin established a glassworks at New Geneva near Uniontown as a part of a model industrial and agricultural community that he was planning to develop.[5] He and his partner, Badollet, had also manufactured iron there early in the century, for Gallatin made an effort to get contracts to supply equipment for the United States army.

The woolen industry received attention in 1808. A subscriber wrote to Scull indicating his "infinite pleasure" at the manufacturing spirit in Pittsburgh and boasting that no inland town in the United States contained more "industrious patriotic and persevering mechanicks" than Pittsburgh. He continued by expressing the desire to see the manufacture of woolen cloth introduced there and suggested that sheep raising, with the best breeds of sheep chosen, should be encouraged.[6] Apparently the suggestion took root, for the following year Scull stated in an editorial:

The spirit of manufacturing these articles [*woolen goods*] we find is increasing rapidly throughout our country: as evidence of which, fulling mills are erecting in much greater ratio than has hitherto been the case, and some little pains are beginning to be bestowed on the breed and management of sheep by our farmers.[7]

By 1813 advertisements for woolen manufacturers took a prominent place in the *Gazette*.[8]

While the Pittsburgh locality appeared to be the foremost of the industrial centers, it did not have a monopoly of industries. A glance at the little town of Meadville, which had a

[3] E. C. Schramm, "General James O'Hara," 69.
[4] *Pittsburgh Gazette,* April 21, 1807.
[5] *Tree of Liberty* (Pittsburgh), May 7, 1803; W. J. Bining, "Glass Industry in Western Pennsylvania, 1797-1860," p. 16.
[6] *Pittsburgh Gazette,* June 28, 1808.   [7] *Ibid.,* Nov. 8, 1809.   [8] *Ibid.,* May 1, 1812.

population of 300 in 1810 and was located in Crawford County, the population of which was only 6,150 at that time, shows the progress of industry there. In the county there were 2,142 horses, 5,389 cows, 4,120 sheep, 934 spinning wheels (one for every 6.5 of the inhabitants), 313 looms (one to every 20 inhabitants), and 166 male weavers and 181 female weavers—a total of 347, or one weaver to every 18 people. A list of manufactures for the year included linen cloth, 53,330 yards; woolen cloth, 16,818 yards; cotton cloth, 3,212 yards—a total of 73,360 yards of textiles produced or twelve yards *per capita*. Seventy thousand pounds of maple sugar were refined during the year. The list of exports for the same year included whiskey, black salts, and lumber and staves, most of which were exported to New Orleans.[9]

The application of steam to the river boats not only increased the speed and volume of commerce but stimulated shipbuilding. The first of the steamboats was built in Pittsburgh in 1811.[10] Within the next five years many steamboats were launched in the city, including the "Comet" and the "Vesuvius" in 1813, the "Buffalo" in 1814, the "Etna," and the "Franklin."[11] Shipbuilding, iron manufacturing, woolen industries, rope making, saddle making, manufacturing of hats, shoes, and nails, and the printing of books gave a new tone to the economic atmosphere of the region.

It cannot be said that during the period from 1808 to 1816 the old economic leaders in the Pittsburgh region were either dead or retiring as were most of the political leaders, because James O'Hara, one of the first business men in Pittsburgh, was active from 1796 to well beyond this period. It is true that John Scull retired in 1816 and that William Wilkins assumed the place of his brother, John Wilkins, in the affairs of his family; and it is true that a host of young men came into the communi-

---

[9] Reynolds, "Crawford County. A History of Its Growth and Development," in *Daily Tribune-Republican* (Meadville), centennial edition, May 12, 1888, p. 4.
[10] *Pittsburgh Gazette,* October 25, 1811.
[11] *Ibid.,* July 16, December 3, 1813; January 3, 1814; March 4, 1815; April 20, 1816.

ty to vie with the older men. Nor can it be said that agriculture or commerce had run their race and were pasing the baton to industry. In fact, agriculture and commerce increased with an incredible acceleration for several decades. But it is true that an industrial development was taking place in which young men threatened to seize the baton of economic leadership from the older leaders and to emphasize industry to such an extent that agriculture could no longer completely monopolize the region.

The growth of industry, commerce, and agriculture was materially benefited by a change in monetary and financial conditions in the region. From the time that Pittsburgh had been established as a British post in the wilderness to 1800, there had been a scarcity of actual money in western Pennsylvania. Spanish gold, Continental currency, currency of the state of Pennsylvania, and even sight drafts had been used. None of these forms of money had proved entirely satisfactory, however. There had been an insufficient amount of Spanish money; the Pennsylvania certificates or currency and the Continental currency had depreciated in value, and the sight drafts were acceptable only among those merchants and millers who had agreed to use them. In reality, barter was more common than the use of money in commerce at the close of the century. Before 1804 Philadelphia had been the nearest banking point, and exchange was accomplished by Pittsburgh merchants aided by two or three brokers, or by the transfer to and from Philadelphia of various notes, bonds, and certificates.[12]

The first bank west of the Alleghenies, a branch of the Bank of Pennsylvania, under the presidency of John Wilkins, Jr., was opened for business in Pittsburgh on January 9, 1804. It also served as the Pittsburgh office of discount and deposit of the Bank of the United States.[13] The Bank of Pittsburgh was

[12] Holdsworth, *Financing an Empire*, 1:137; Wagner, "The Economic Conditions in Western Pennsylvania during the Whiskey Insurrection," 38.
[13] Holdsworth, *Financing an Empire*, 1:138.

founded in 1810 under the banking laws of 1808, but when those laws were amended, the bank was forced to cease operations. It was reorganized again, however, under the name of the Pittsburgh Manufacturing Company, and William Wilkins was again elected president of the organization. After new legislation, Wilkins was able to reëstablish the Bank of Pittsburgh in 1814.[14] A third banking venture was launched in Pittsburgh in 1815 when John Scull founded the Farmers' and Mechanics' Bank of Pittsburgh. Three years later, however, the bank was robbed of a sum so great that its credit was undermined and it was found advisable to discontinue operations.[15] In 1814 the Northwestern Bank of Pennsylvania was established in Meadville, the first bank north of Pittsburgh west of the mountains. Subscription books were opened at the home of Samuel Torbett on May 4, and on October 28 the stockholders elected a board of directors. The Northwestern Bank served the people of Erie, Venango, Warren, Crawford, and Mercer counties until its liquidation in 1822.[16] By 1816 there were two banks in Fayette County and one in Washington County.[17]

The founding of banks in western Pennsylvania created changes in finance and in financial transactions that were as evident as the changes that occurred in political leadership and in the economic and industrial life of the region. As the older leaders, whether in politics, commerce, industry, agriculture, or finance, gave up the baton, they yielded it to fresh new men who carried on the burden of leadership with the traditions of the past generations hovering over them but with new factors and new ideas facing them. These factors and ideas produced political theories and social changes that were anathema to Thomas Jefferson but that would have pleased Alexander Hamilton.

[14] Slick, "The Life of William Wilkins," 14-16.
[15] Thurston, *Allegheny County's Hundred Years*, 252.
[16] Reynolds, "Crawford County. A History of Its Growth and Development," in *Daily Tribune-Republican* (Meadville), centennial edition, May 12, 1888, p. 4.
[17] *Crawford Weekly Messenger* (Meadville), February 28, 1817.

Henry Adams' assertion that "the details of State politics are not a subject of great interest to the general public, even in their freshest condition, and the local politics of Pennsylvania in 1790 are no exception to this law,"[18] may very well be applied to the period from 1808 to 1815 in western Pennsylvania. Simon Snyder had been elected governor in 1808 with an avalanche of votes from the counties west of the mountains—western Pennsylvania was solidly Democratic. Snyder was reëlected in 1811 and again in 1814, not without opposition, but with a safe margin in each case. Western Pennsylvania remained Democratic throughout those years, but there were occasional breaks in the ranks of the Democratic Republicans; there were issues that created controversies and contests, and, as has been indicated, there was a depletion in the ranks of the old leaders. The Federalist party continued its activities to 1816, but, like an old man whose heart beats with less vigor, except for unusual occasions of excitement, the spirit of the party waned and its hopes for a return to power grew small. In other words, both the Republicans and the Federalists carried on during these years on the momentum that they had accumulated in previous years. Naturally, the momentum of the Democrats was greater than that of the Federalists. Furthermore, the organization of the party of Jefferson and Madison was more effective and more vital in the counties and the townships west of the mountains. There were decided differences of opinion between the members of the two parties on the question of foreign affairs and on the War of 1812, but for the most part the story of politics in the region during these seven or eight years centers around the inter-county and local bickerings that arose in the struggle for the control of local offices.

The selection of representatives for the lower house of the state legislature and the election of county officers were the chief considerations for the electorate in 1809. Under the circumstances issues played a small part. The personalities of the

[18] H. Adams, *Life of Albert Gallatin*, 84.

candidates were more significant. Snyder, to be sure, drew some condemnation on himself because he had attempted to tighten his political organization through the appointment of a great number of prothonotaries and recorders in the counties.[19] Then a few of the old "Conventionalists" of 1805, now that Snyder was in office, entertained a futile hope that the constitution could be revised. The *Recorder,* a Democratic newspaper of Washington, Pennsylvania, contained an editorial, "On the Call of a Convention," which was reprinted in the *Crawford Weekly Messenger* of July 7, 1809. The editorial asserted that conditions had improved but that the constitution was not perfect and could be revised with benefit to the people. The land office and the judiciary needed improvement, the article asserted. But there was little response to this effort to revive the issue that had plagued McKean in 1805. The judiciary had been reorganized in 1806; the land question was well on the way to a solution; and, too, Snyder and his followers who had demanded the constitutional amendment in previous years were now in office. It is possible that the latter fact had much to do with quieting the demands for changing the constitution.

Despite minor splits in the Democratic-Republican ranks in the counties, rifts that were purely local in nature and that resulted from the desires of the followers of different candidates to put their men in office, western Pennsylvania was preponderantly Democratic in 1809. Roger Alden, a Federalist, was elected to the state house of representatives from Crawford, Erie, and Warren counties, and three representatives listed as Federalists were elected from Westmoreland County, where the people were now growing conservative.[20] These four men were the only Federalists elected to state offices by the counties west of the mountains. The complexion of the state legislature as a result of the election in this year stood as follows: senate—twenty-two Democrats, six Federalists, three doubtful; assembly—seventy-one Democrats, nineteen Fed-

---

[19] *Crawford Weekly Messenger* (Meadville), February 2, 1809.
[20] *Ibid.,* October 19, November 2, 1809.

eralists, five doubtful. At the close of the year the editor of the *Crawford Weekly Messenger* observed that there seemed to be a laudable harmony among the recently split Democrats.[21]

The following year, however, political agitation increased as a result of the depression that followed the Embargo Act and the administration's conduct of foreign affairs. Scull had allowed his party allegiance to influence him in opposing the policy of Jefferson, and later that of Madison, in regard to foreign affairs, a policy that seemed inimical to England. Regardless of Scull's attitude, however, sentiment in Pittsburgh ran high when the English man-of-war, the "Leopard," fired on the American ship, the "Chesapeake," in 1807. Even Scull was stirred by the incident.[22] But in 1809 and thereafter the Pittsburgh editor found fault with the policy of Madison because of the latter's apparent tendency to vacillate; and his opposition to Madison increased down to the approach of the War of 1812.[23] Only a minority of the people in the region reacted as did Scull, however, and Madison could have heard resolutions supporting his policies had he so wished. Early in 1810 meetings of Democratic Republicans were held that passed resolutions commending Madison for his firm stand in rebuking the arrogant James Jackson, British ambassador to the United States.[24]

The election of 1810 was more significant than that of the previous year because it was a congressional election year and because a number of senators stood for reëlection at that time. The outcome of the election indicated that there was very little change in the relative strength of the parties. William Findley of Westmoreland for Congress; William Friedt, Thomas Pollock, and John Lobenger, that county's delegation to the state house of representatives; and Roger Alden of Crawford County, representative in the lower house of the state legislature, were the only successful candidates listed as

[21] *Crawford Weekly Messenger* (Meadville), December 27, 1809.
[22] *Pittsburgh Gazette*, August 25, 1807. [23] *Ibid.*, March 27, 1812.
[24] *Crawford Weekly Messenger* (Meadville), February 1, 1810.

Federalists from the western counties. The results of this election were significant, however, from the standpoint of the advent of new leaders. In addition to the Federalists already named, the following individuals were elected: to Congress, John Smilie for the district of Fayette and Green counties, Aaron Lyle for Washington, Abner Lacock for the district composed of Allgeheny and the counties to the north; to the state senate, Presley Carr Lane for Fayette County, Abel McFarland for the district of Washington and Greene; to the state house of representatives, James Patterson, William Marks, Samuel Scott, and John Negley for the district of Allegheny and Butler; John Lawrence for Beaver; John Phillips for the district of Crawford, Erie, and Warren; Christian Tarr, Isaac Griffin, and Samuel Trevor for Fayette County; Riese Hill for Greene; John Colmery, Andrew Sutton, Thomas Hopkins, and Joshua Dickerson for Washington County.

Findley, Smilie, Lane, Lobenger, and Scott are the only names on the list that can be associated with western Pennsylvania politics in the 1790's, or even in the early 1800's. The name of Lobenger is misleading in this connection because it only revives the names of the family—John Lobenger was a son of Christopher Lobenger; and the name of Samuel Scott merely suggests Thomas Scott, who was western Pennsylvania's first congressman in 1789. Only Findley and Smilie of the older generation of politicians remained. Some of the men elected were successful candidates for the first time in 1810; others had been elected the year before; but only a few antedated the year 1808.[25] Among them one looks in vain for a single name that became nationally prominent, yet they represent a new generation of politicians in western Pennsylvania.

The gubernatorial election of 1811, at first thought, would seem to be sufficiently important to arouse the sentiment of the people, but it proved to be a drab and commonplace affair. Governor Snyder had built up his party so effectively that

[25] *Crawford Weekly Messenger* (Meadville), November 12, 1810.

WALTER FORWARD

From a portrait by J. R. Lambdin in the possession of the Historical Society of Western Pennsylvania

there was practically no opposition to him in this campaign. The momentum of the party was so great that it swept on to success with a minimum of local bickering in the counties. The vote for the gubernatorial candidates as reported in the *Crawford Weekly Messenger* of January 8, 1812, stood as follows: Snyder, 52,319; Tilghman, 3,609; scattered votes, 1,675. In such a landslide the candidates of the Democratic party for local, county, and state offices rode into office on Snyder's popularity and by means of the strength of the party organization.

Before the election of 1812 occurred, the War of 1812 had been declared, and the war fever seized western Pennsylvanians. Political activities did not cease during the duration of the war but they were subordinated to the more important task of upholding the nation's honor and bringing the war to a successful culmination. The majority of the people in the region, particularly those who were Democratic Republicans, were patriotic and held a traditional antipathy toward England—an antipathy engendered by their memory of the English forts along the boundary between the United States and Canada and by their political faith, which caused them to sympathize with the French Revolution. There were old Federalists in the region, however, in whose hearts the pro-English sympathy lingered. They were not disloyal, but they believed that Madison had been weak and ineffective in his conduct of foreign affairs prior to the summer of 1812; they further believed that the president did not press the war with sufficient vigor after it had begun; and they still entertained hopes of rejuvenating the Federalist party in the region.

Among these Federalists was John Scull, whose attitude toward the embargo and the administration's policy has already been noted. He bestirred himself to greater vigor in behalf of the Federalists in the campaign of 1812 than he had demonstrated in the campaigns of the years immediately preceding. The *Gazette* of June 25, 1812, announced that war had been declared on June 18. In the following issue, that of July 3, the editor reflected the feverish anxiety of the western people relative to their lack of preparation and reported that hasty preparations were being made to improve the defense of Erie. On August 28 he bemoaned the fact that John Hull had surrendered his army at Detroit. This unfortunate capitulation of Hull was a shock to the western people, and it offered an opportunity to stimulate anti-Republican sentiment, especially in Pittsburgh. About the middle of September a group of people there "who disapproved of the ruinous War into which the United States have been plunged by the President and Congress attended a meeting at the house of William Morrow." Out of this meeting emanated a "Peace Ticket," which was headed by John Woods for Congress; John Gilmore for the state senate; John Darragh, James Semple, William McClure, and Ephraim Harris for the lower house of the state legislature.[26] This ticket was backed by the *Gazette* and by the people of Allegheny County, who gave a majority of nearly 200 votes to it, but the people in Butler County, yoked to Allegheny in a congressional district, turned to Adamson Tannehill, who had waited long for his opporunity, and elected him to Congress by a majority of 257 votes.[27]

The Federalist majority that Allegheny gave Woods represented the Federalist party's nearest approach to success in the western counties in 1812, because the Republicans, despite the fact that they lacked the unity of the previous year, swept western Pennsylvania again, although the Federalists made slight gains in the state as a whole. For a time before the election, the Federalists had held some hopes of succeeding, because of the lack of unanimity of their opponents on a candidate for the presidency. It cannot be said that Madison enjoyed the same party allegiance that had been accorded to his illustrious predecessor, nor can it be said that he was decisive in his handling of foreign affairs. Consequently, when the astute and ambitious De Witt Clinton sought to gather up the loose ends of the disgruntled Republicans and the remnants

[26] *Pittsburgh Gazette,* September 18, 25, 1812.
[27] *Ibid.,* October 23, 1812; *Crawford Weekly Messenger* (Meadville), October 21, 1812.

of the Federalist party to oppose Madison for the presidency in 1812, the ambitious New Yorker's success was alarming to the Democratic Republicans.

The coöperation of the anti-war Republicans and the Federalists throughout the nation to support the ticket headed by Clinton was reflected in western Pennsylvania. Madison had been nominated by a caucus, and Clinton by the state legislature of New York. The followers of Clinton immediately attacked the caucus method of nominating a candidate, although they had readily acquiesced to the nomination of Jefferson and later that of Madison by the same method. Clintonian Republicans and Federalists reiterated the objections to the caucus. At a meeting of so-called Democratic Republicans of the borough of Pittsburgh at the house of John McMasters on September 18, 1812, resolutions were adopted, and an address was prepared for publication. It was resolved that the declaration of war against England was justifiable; that the war should be prosecuted with vigor; that there should be no peace except on terms compatible with the interests, rights, and honor of the United States as a neutral nation; that there should be a change in the administration of the general government; and that De Witt Clinton would be the candidate "of the freemen of the United States" for the presidency and Elbridge Gerry for the vice presidency. In an address these citizens deplored the fact that they lacked confidence in the leadership of the president to carry on the war in an effective manner; they insisted upon a speedy conclusion with an honorable peace; they avowed that the caucus method of nominating a candidate for the presidency opened the field for corruption; and they requested western Pennsylvania Republicans to vote for Clinton.[28] Their activities accomplished nothing except to excite those who supported Madison, because the entire Madisonian electoral ticket was carried in Pennsylvania by a majority of 10,863.[29]

[28] *Address of the Democratic Republican Committee of the Borough of Pittsburgh.*
[29] *Crawford Weekly Messenger* (Meadville), November 18, 1812.

The Federalists were not without hope, however, as the setbacks of the American forces piled up and as the dissatisfaction and lack of coöperation on the part of Federalist New England increased. Undoubtedly the Federalists in western Pennsylvania sincerely regretted the discouraging military failures of 1812. But there is the suggestion that the early defeats brought them a little satisfaction in that their condemnations of Madison's partisanship and inefficiency seemed justifiable. Certainly Scull's pleasure in Perry's victory on Lake Erie was not limited to mere relief at the safety assured by the British defeat. Scull congratulated the people on the victory, and when he learned that Perry was a Federalist his joy was unlimited. "We state this with greater pleasure," he asserted, "as all the disgrace and defeats which our armies have met with were solely owing to the treachery, cowardice, or incapacity of their Democratic commanders."[30]

Something of the virulence of the partisanship existing between members of the two parties was carried into the ranks of the militias engaged in the defense of Pennsylvania. The various county militias were mobilized at Meadville, where Samuel Lord, an old Federalist, graciously granted the use of his land for a camp. Republicans greatly outnumbered Federalists in the militias, and there seem to have been but one or two companies that could be designated as Federalist. Some unthoughtful and uncontrolled Republicans abused the hospitality of their Federalist host. They barbecued his hogs and used his fence rails for the fire. When he complained to the company commander, the soldiers became truculent and threatened to retaliate for his complaints. The Federalist companies, feeling that the injustice to Lord was great enough to deserve redress, became embroiled in the quarrel, and an open fight between a Federalist and a Republican company was averted by the narrowest possible margin. It might be observed that the animosity between the Federalists and the Republicans in the militias seemed greater than the animosity between the militia

[30] *Pittsburgh Gazette,* October 28, 1812.

and the British, because the militias of western Pennsylvania were no more inclined to leave the state and carry the war to the British in Canada than were the militias of the state of New York.

In the election of 1813 the Democrats again carried western Pennsylvania, although the Federalists' hopes had been higher than they had been for some years. And again in the following year, when Snyder ran successfully for reëlection to the governorship, the Democrats carried the elections generally, although the Federalists managed to break through in Allegheny and Butler counties. There John Woods, who had run for Congress on three occasions in the 1790's, finally won the coveted seat by twenty-three votes.[31] It was the last time that the Federalists dared to hope for success in western Pennsylvania. Before another election could be held the Treaty of Ghent was signed, and the New England Federalists, in the Hartford Convention, threatened to leave the Union and by the threat put themselves and their whole party in an embarrassing and unexplainable position. Furthermore, Jackson's victory over the British at New Orleans on January 8, 1815, raised the self-respect of the American people and gave at least a modicum of justification for the contention of the Democrats that they had rescued the United States from a disgraceful war and had preserved the honor of the country.

In fact, there seemed to be little reason for the continuation of a Federalist party, because by 1815 the Democratic Republicans were making use of the policies of the old Federalist party and welding them into a program that resembled the Hamiltonian program of the 1790's so closely that the two programs cannot be distinguished one from the other, unless they are accompanied by dates. One historian has very aptly said that the Republicans out-federaled the Federalists. In 1816 the new program was to go into effect, and while it contained nearly everything that the old Federalists of the region had clamored for, a few of them, whose hearts still beat a little

[31] *Crawford Weekly Messenger* (Meadville), October 26, 1814.

faster at the mere name of the Federalist party, refused to accept these principles for which they had once fought, because they were sponsored under the name of Democratic Republicanism.

The passing of the old leaders, the rise of manufacturing and commerce, the decline of Federalism, and the confusion within the ranks of the Democratic Republicans in western Pennsylvania gave the younger men an opportunity to seize the baton of leadership and to carry it forward in their own way. For virtually a decade they chose to align themselves with their young contemporaries Henry Clay, John Calhoun, and John Q. Adams even though the shadows of Hamilton and Jefferson still hovered over them.

THE AMERICAN SYSTEM

CHAPTER TEN

THE political behavior of the people in the United States during the decade that immediately followed the War of 1812 presents one of the most interesting studies in American history. The younger men who had risen to prominence and leadership in the period from 1805 to 1815, utilizing the political organization that had been so highly developed by Jefferson and Madison since the beginning of the century, reached back to the 1790's for the political theories of Hamilton and integrated them into a program that has been called the American System. A protective tariff, a second United States Bank, and a program of internal improvements that included the building of roads and canals, the improvement of harbors, and the clearing of river channels were the chief features of the American System that was advocated by Henry Clay, John Quincy Adams, John C. Calhoun, Henry Baldwin, and other Republican leaders. This program, they explained, would constitute the government's contribution toward the economic and social integration of three rather distinct sections within the United States: industrial New England, the cotton-growing South, and the newly developed agricultural West. The integration of those sections was a significant task at the close of the War of 1812.

The war that had been urged, and even imposed upon the United States by a group of young men from the agricultural South and West to protect the commerce of the people of the North and East, who did not want a war to protect their commerce, had many strange features. The military events of the war were not especially gratifying to the American participants. There were too many disasters and too few victories; in fact, the only significant victory accomplished by the land forces occurred after the treaty of peace had been signed. The Treaty of Ghent did not mention any of the grievances for which the Americans asserted they had gone to war. And, furthermore, near the close of the war, the New England Federalists, who had failed to support the prosecution of the war with sufficient vigor, met in the Hartford Convention and considered the policy of withdrawing from the Union unless military activities ceased and some nine amendments to the Constitution were adopted. They even sent commissioners to Washington to convey their demands to the government. Yet by December of 1815 the American people and their leaders were buoyant with hopes and enthusiasm.

This strange psychological reversal by the Americans, who had been so despondent and disorganized only the year before, can be explained in part by Jackson's victory at New Orleans on January 8, 1815, after the treaty of peace had been signed. The success of Old Hickory's backwoods warriors over the "pick of the British troops" saved the self-respect of the Americans. There was an element of humor in the victory too; the Americans had struck the last blow, and, like an individual who shouts the last word in an argument, they felt that all previous humiliations had been wiped out. Within the next few years an "Era of Good Feeling" developed in the United States during which even the disgruntled New England Federalists, who had approached perilously close to treason in their Hartford Convention of 1814, were anxious to further the American System and integrate the American nation.

The result was a spirit of nationalism that permeated every community in each of the three sections of the still young republic. Cotton raisers in the South, farmers in the West, and mill workers in New England were conscious of the fact that their destinies were linked together. They believed, furthermore, that a glorious future faced them; all that was necessary was coöperation in the development of their economic possibilities. The national government, they believed, should encourage home manufacturing by the protection of industry against foreign competition by means of a tariff; it should facilitate the exchange of goods by developing roads, canals, harbors, and river transportation; and it should stabilize finance. The Republican party attempted to accomplish this program, but federal aid was necessary, and nationalism, rather than democracy, was the keynote in determining their activities. Hence the Democratic-Republican party of Jefferson became the National-Republican party of the period from 1816 to 1829. It was the only party of any significance from 1815 to 1823 and encountered little opposition during those eight years, because the Federalists had virtually committed suicide by engaging in the Hartford Convention at an inopportune time, and because the National-Republican party in its program offered everything that the most rigid Federalist could want.

Western Pennsylvania accepted the American System in nearly all its phases. The people in the region were enthusiastic about the protection of manufacturing because of the developing industries of iron, glass, and textiles; even the farmers believed that the protection of industry, and especially the protection of hemp and woolen enterprises, would benefit them. The people in the western counties not only wanted but clamored for the development of roads, canals, harbors, and river transportation. They acquiesced readily in the establishment of the second United States Bank but soon became antagonistic to that institution when they realized that it would destroy their local "wild-cat" banks, which, however unsound they may have been in a system of national finance, provided a circulating medium for the particular community in which they existed. Furthermore, within the region, as within the nation, there was only one strong party, the National Republican, although remnants of the Federalist party, at times calling themselves Federalists and at other times using the term of Federal Republicans, continued to exist. There were contests and differences of opinion among the political leaders, but it was not until a fervor for Jackson arose in 1824 that there was any noticeable opposition to the National Republicans in Pennsylvania.

The principle of protectionism was not new in western Pennsylvania when the tariff measure of 1816 was enacted. Even in the early colonial period the people in the Quaker colony had sponsored the household manufacture of textiles, and, as the eighteenth century unfolded, they made an effort to enhance the production of iron, paper, and leather. Many iron furnaces sprang up east of the mountains, and as early as 1789 a furnace was erected west of the Alleghenies in what is now Fayette County.[1] The enthusiasm for the encouragement of manufacturing continued throughout the colonial, Revolutionary, and post-Revolutionary periods; and when the Constitution, which permitted Congress to levy duties on imported goods for the purpose of raising revenues, was put into effect in 1789, Pennsylvania congressmen were not slow to grasp the fact that the power of Congress to place duties on incoming goods presented the opportunity to place the rates of these duties at such a level that they would protect American industry. Thomas Scott was awake to the situation when the first bill was under consideration in 1789. He sought a duty on hemp and suggested to Congress that "agriculture is entitled to its proportion of encouragement." When Thomas Fitzsimons, an eastern Pennsylvania congressman, opposed such a duty on the ground that it would be a burden upon American shipping, Scott reiterated his demand for the protection of hemp and expressed his opposition to a duty on salt, which he considered an article of universal necessity.[2] It is obvious that the Pennsylvania representatives were not unified upon the objectives of a tariff in their debates upon

[1] Eiselen, *Rise of Pennsylvania Protectionism*, 16.
[2] *Annals of Congress*, 1 Congress, 1 session, 1:154, 159, 165.

THE AMERICAN SYSTEM   235

the first tariff act. The industrialists, however, supported the tariff principle; the farmers acquiesced in it; but the merchants were skeptical about it.[3] Consequently there was no sustained unanimity among the Pennsylvania leaders upon the tariff question prior to the War of 1812.

Perhaps the most effective agency in the encouragement of manufacturing before the War of 1812 was that of the societies for the "Encouragement of Manufactures and the Useful Arts." Such organizations sprang up throughout the state, and as early as 1807 the "Society for the Encouragement of Manufactures and Arts" was established in Meadville and offered a liberal advance in money for the founding of a fulling mill within ten miles of the town. There is little evidence to indicate that similar societies were organized in western Pennsylvania in this decade, but the Meadville society was active and rendered great service to both manufacturing and agriculture in that community for at least a score of years.[4] These societies as well as the people who were interested in particular industries such as iron, textiles, or glass, sent in petitions to Congress requesting protection for their enterprises, but Congress, apparently, was not swayed to any appreciable extent by their pleas.

Pennsylvania congressmen before 1815 were generally, though not unanimously, protectionists. Twenty-seven revisions of the tariff were made between 1789 and 1816, many of which increased the duties levied but all of which were for the purpose of raising revenue. Gallatin in 1797 opposed the increase of the tax on salt and, like Scott before him, offered as his reason that it was an article of common necessity. The western part of the state, which he represented, was still importing its supply of salt and paying a price that was already high.[5] A revision of the tariff in 1804, which resulted in a real

[3] Eiselen, *Rise of Pennsylvania Protectionism*, 25.
[4] Reynolds, "Crawford County, A History of Its Growth and Development," in *Daily Tribune-Republican* (Meadville), centennial edition, May 12, 1888, p. 3.
[5] Eiselen, *Rise of Pennsylvania Protectionism*, 30.

protective duty on window glass, received the support of western Pennsylvania because the glass industry was rapidly developing in the region at that time. The Pennsylvania delegation in the House of Representatives registered a fourteen to one vote for the measure.[6] Likewise, in 1809 the representatives of the Keystone State gave votes that were just one or two short of unanimity on a protective measure and did so again in 1812 on a measure to double all existing duties in order to procure sufficient revenue to conduct the war with England. This substantial vote of congressmen favoring protectionism was the result of the demands of their industrial constituents for the encouragement of infant industries, the hope of the farmers that rising prices would improve their own economic condition, and the popular preference for an indirect tax to raise the revenue rather than a direct tax or an excise. The merchants, originally opposed to the principle of the protective tariff, grew indifferent when the Napoleonic wars brought them a deluge of trade; moreover, the War of 1812 drew their attention to other grievances.

The period following the close of the war, however, saw the rise of an aggressive and militant protective movement in western Pennsylvania. The prosperity of the industrialists, the merchants, and the farmers ceased with the advent of peace and the arrival of European goods that were dumped on the American markets. The effect of the unloading of cheap foreign commodities was undoubtedly a great factor in stifling American industry and commerce, yet it was not the only agency that injured the economic status of western Pennsylvania. Financial conditions as a result of the wild-cat banks, inflation, and the establishment of the second United States Bank, which brought about the failure of the unsound state banks, likewise played a prominent part in producing the depression that hovered over western Pennsylvania and the nation from 1817 to 1821. Western men were inclined to attribute their economic distress to the failure of the govern-

[6] *Annals of Congress,* 8 Congress, 1 session, p. 1205.

ment to provide protection for them and gave less emphasis to the financial conditions.

The intensity of the distress of the westerners was sufficient to stimulate strenuous efforts on their part to obtain redress. The industrialist interests in the region were hard pressed from 1816 to at least 1821. A committee reported in 1816 that "the manufacture of cottons, woolens, flint glass, and the finer articles of iron, has lately suffered the most alarming depression. Some branches which had been several years in operation have been destroyed or partially suspended, and others of more recent growth, annihilated before they were completely in operation."[7] This depression increased during the succeeding years. Morris Birkbeck, an English observer who visited Pittsburgh in 1818, observed that "the manufacturers are under great difficulties, and many are on the eve of suspending their operations owing to the influx of depreciated fabrics from Europe."[8] A comparison of industrial conditions in 1815 with those in 1819 in the *Pittsburgh Gazette* of January 11, 1820, indicated that employment in Pittsburgh and its vicinity had decreased from 1,960 employees in 1815 to 672 in 1819, and the value of the output had fallen from $2,617,833 to $832,000—in other words, this committee's report indicated that the output was virtually a third in 1819 of what it had totaled at the close of the war.

The production of the glassworks in Pittsburgh had declined in this period to a little over one-sixth of the former production—the value of the output had fallen from $235,000 to $35,000. Furthermore, the decline in the production of glass came at a time when the glassmakers had been expanding and tying up their available capital; they had practically no financial reserves and a growing accumulation of glass on their hands. James O'Hara, the pioneer glassmaker in western Pennsylvania, was forced to reduce the prices upon boxes of window glass from twelve to seven dollars and to resort to bar-

---

[7] *Niles' Weekly Register*, 12:130 (April 26, 1817).
[8] Birkbeck, *Notes on a Journey in America*, 41.

ter and auction sales to complete transactions. He attempted to sell his landholdings in Illinois to procure working capital, but it is probable that he would have been financially ruined had it not been for the aid of his friend, James Ross.[9] The glass firm of Bakewell, Page, and Bakewell, another Pittsburgh enterprise, was also in dire financial straits. The managers found it difficult to pay their workmen and impossible to carry insurance on their property. They faced a debt of $50,552 on September 1, 1818, and could accumulate a cash balance of only $1,155. Thomas Bakewell, who was to have become a partner of the firm at that time, declined the partnership because of the dismal outlook and continued with a salary until 1823.[10]

The ironmasters, likewise, suffered severe losses in the aftermath of the War of 1812. Since many furnaces were located in Fayette and Westmoreland counties and a few in Allegheny, western Pennsylvanians favored the tariff to prevent the importation of iron products from England. James O'Hara, the glass manufacturer, suffered a loss in a venture that he made in the iron industry. He had bought the property of Arthur St. Clair, which had been sold to satisfy the debts against it. About 1815 he reopened the Hermitage Furnace, which St. Clair had built in the period from 1803 to 1806 on Mill Creek, about two miles northeast of Ligonier. O'Hara's venture was a failure, however, because of increasing losses and falling prices, and in 1817 the deficit amounted to twenty thousand dollars.[11]

The woolen industries, the woolgrowers, and the farmers experienced the same distress. The influx of English textiles soon glutted the American market after the cessation of war and stifled the industry, a condition that worked a particular hardship on western Pennsylvania. Washington County was easily the leading county in the production of wool, although

[9] W. J. Bining, "The Glass Industry of Western Pennsylvania, 1797-1860," 46; Brownson, *James Ross*, 46.
[10] Benjamin Page to John Hammond, January 3, 1825, Denny-O'Hara Papers.
[11] Agnew, "Address to the Allegheny County Bar," in *Pennsylvania Magazine of History and Biography,* 13:55 (1889).

sheep were raised in many of the western counties. Not only the woolgrowers, who were farmers, but also the farmers who produced the grain products suffered from the depression. The decline in prices caused a decrease in the wages of laborers. The prices of farm products fell and the landlord could not procure as much rent for his property as formerly. The woolen manufacturers, the sheep raisers, and the farmers joined hands with the ironmasters and glassmakers to further protectionism, in the hope that it would lead them to prosperity.

In October of 1815, before Congress had time to convene and consider the general question of protecting American goods against the low-priced goods of Europe, a movement for protective measures was launched through the *Pittsburgh Mercury*. One writer declared,

Should it not, therefore, be the hope and the wish of every true friend to the genuine interests of our country, that the confidence manifested by our manufacturers in the government during the war, by increasing their different establishments to the utmost of their ability . . . should not in time of peace be found to be misplaced founded as it was, on the hopes they entertained, that on the restoration of peace, the fostering hand of the constituted authorities would be immediately extended to their relief, support and patronage . . . Congress will do their duty; they will realize all the reasonable expectations of their manufacturers . . . by continuing the double duty on articles imported.[12]

The sentiment expressed in this editorial seems to have been widespread, because the principal objective of protectionism at the opening of Congress in December, 1815, appeared to be that of aiding the textile industries in their competition with English goods. But the iron industry and the glass industry received practically as much attention as did the manufacturers of textiles.

Despite the above plea and many similar ones for the retention of the double duties as levied in 1812, the number of protective tariff men in Congress was insufficient to secure an

[12] *Pittsburgh Mercury,* October 21, 1815.

act incorporating the rates established by the act of 1812. It was resolved that the double duties were to be in force only until June 30, 1816, although one member of the House proposed that they be continued to January 1, 1817, on the ground that an abrupt termination would "alarm the whole manufacturing interest, which was now looking up to the Government for additional support, instead of expecting an early reduction of the existing duties."[13] The protectionists, however, were sufficiently strong in number to effect the passage of a tariff measure in this session that gave them rates that were more advantageous than those that had existed prior to 1812.

Secretary of the Treasury Alexander J. Dallas, the Pennsylvania Republican of the days of Thomas McKean, prepared the report that served as the basis for the revision of the tariff in that year. He suggested that the rates of revenue applied to the goods should fall within three classes. High rates should prevail to protect thoroughly the goods already produced in sufficient quantities in America to satisfy the home demands; duties "as will enable the manufacturers to meet the importer in the American market upon equal terms of profit and loss" should obtain upon manufactures not yet adequate to meet domestic requirements; and rates for revenue only should be placed upon articles produced in small quantities or articles that were not produced at all in the United States. The revision, as recommended by Dallas, lowered the rates on hammered bar iron from seventy-five cents to forty-five cents per hundred weight, and were a disappointment to the iron interests of the state. Despite this unsatisfactory rate, the Pennsylvania delegation gave a vote of seventeen to three in favor of the tariff with all of western Pennsylvania's congressmen voting in the affirmative.

While the revenue on the rolled bar iron, which was not produced in the United States, was one dollar and fifty cents per hundred weight, a really protective rate, the forty-five cent

[13] *Annals of Congress*, 14 Congress, 1 session, 675, 676.

duty per hundred weight upon the hammered bar iron represented approximately eighteen per cent of the average price of that commodity in England and was a comparatively low rate.[14] The rate on window glass, however, was thirty per cent *ad valorem* because it was considered an article already produced in sufficient quantity to satisfy domestic consumption and therefore one that should be thoroughly protected. On all other kinds of glass the rates were low or non-existent.[15] The tariff of 1816 proved to be a disappointment to western Pennsylvanians, and in the following year glassmakers, textile industrialists, and iron manufacturers joined in petitions to Congress for higher duties. One such petition, over the signature of Ebenezer Denny of Pittsburgh, was sent to the Speaker of the House of Representatives.[16] Walter Lowrie of Beaver County introduced a resolution in the state senate on February 14, 1817, in which he described the results of imports upon iron, glass, and textile industries in the state. He asserted: "The citizens of this state have already embarked extensive capitals in manufacturers, particularly in iron and glass, woolen and cotton goods. But the large and unprecedented importation of foreign articles, has given a shock to our infant manufactures, unprotected as they now are, by discriminating duties."[17]

The dissatisfaction in western Pennsylvania relative to the tariff of 1816, the continued decline of manufactured articles and the generally adverse economic conditions, created in part by the failure of local banks and the depreciation of their currency, increased the sentiment for protection in western Pennsylvania in 1818, and the efforts to stimulate support for domestic industries were intensified. The Bakewell, Page, and Bakewell Company made a set of cut-glass tableware for President Monroe and urged the people to follow the presi-

[14] Scrivenor, *History of the Iron Trade, throughout the World*, 377, 407, 409.
[15] W. J. Bining, "The Glass Industry of Western Pennsylvania, 1797-1860," p. 43.
[16] *Niles' Weekly Register*, 12:130 (April 26, 1817).
[17] Pennsylvania, *Senate Journal*, 1816, p. 234, 235.

dent's example in refusing to purchase foreign articles if similar articles were manufactured at home.[18] The *Mercury*, with a sly insinuation that Messrs. Bakewell and Page had found a rare opportunity to advertise their products, hoped that "the glass that sparkles on the President's 'board' [may] operate as a talisman on our representatives, to stimulate them to unremitting exertions in favor of manufactures."[19] The insinuation contained in the *Mercury* did not deter Bakewell, Page, and Bakewell from making further gifts, however, because the following year they sent to the editor of *Niles' Weekly Register* a pair of glass decanters as a token of esteem for that paper's many publications upon protectionism.[20] The program of creating a sentiment favorable to the tariff in western Pennsylvania was not without results in 1818, because in the congressional election of that year, a battery of western Pennsylvania congressmen favorable to the tariff was elected. Among them was Henry Baldwin, erstwhile Democratic Republican, who ran on the Federalist ticket in this election and was reëlected on an almost exclusively protection issue. A few weeks later Walter Lowrie of Beaver was elected to the United States Senate by the state legislature.[21] Thus two western Pennsylvania congressmen, one in the House and one in the Senate, took their places in December of 1819 to labor for a higher tariff.

The Congress that convened in December of 1819 was favorably disposed toward the tariff; the protectionists were strong enough to establish for the first time a standing committee on manufactures, and Henry Baldwin of Pittsburgh was named chairman of that committee.[22] Baldwin's committee promptly brought out three bills that comprised a complete program for the amelioration of the conditions of production of the manufacturing interests. A tax on sales by

[18] *Pittsburgh Gazette,* October 6, 1818.
[19] *Pittsburgh Mercury,* November 10, 1818.
[20] *Niles' Weekly Register,* 17:34 (September 18, 1819).
[21] *Pittsburgh Mercury,* October 9, 1818; *Crawford Weekly Messenger* (Meadville), December 13, 1818. [22] *Annals of Congress,* 16 Congress, 1 session, 1:710.

auction, the payment of import duties in cash, and the complete upward revision of the tariff from twenty to one hundred per cent on nearly all articles manufactured in Pennsylvania were suggested by the committee. Baldwin, in a long and effective speech, defended the tariff bill. He boldly asserted that the measure was protective in principle and expressed the hope that he would see the time when the interests of the United States would be free from foreign competition. He believed that adequate protection for every article that could be produced at home should be provided and that if there was a deficit in the revenue it should be made up by an excise tax on the protected manufactures in the United States. In response to the attitude of his fellow congressmen that he was overzealous in behalf of the interests of his own city, he declared,

This has been called a Pittsburgh, a cut-glass bill, local, partial in its operations; and I have been charged with framing it from interested motives.... I tell the house frankly, that I have not lost sight of the interest of Pittsburgh, and would never perjure myself if I had; but the charges shall be met plainly, and if you are not convinced that the interests of that place are identified with the nation; that cut glass can be defended on national grounds, then I agree that Pittsburgh, its Representative, its favorite manufacture and the tariff, may go together.[23]

He asserted that he approved the increased duties on iron, regardless of the fact that the people of his congressional district were dependent upon external sources for their supply of that commodity. He neglected to say that he was actively interested in the production of iron and was part owner of an iron furnace on Bear Creek in Butler County, just outside his district. He maintained, however, that he supported the proposed bill on national principles rather than on local selfish grounds.

The bill passed the House of Representatives with the

[23] *Annals of Congress*, 16 Congress 1 session, 2:1916 ff.; Eiselen, *Rise of Pennsylvania Protectionism*, 55.

unanimous vote of the western Pennsylvanians favoring it, but the Senate voted by a majority of one to postpone the consideration of the measure until the following session. Walter Lowrie and Jonathan Roberts, Pennsylvania senators opposed deferring the measure, which in effect meant that they favored the tariff.[24] In the following session Baldwin again presented a tariff bill from the committee on manufactures, but the measure seemed to arouse little interest, and the session closed without changing the rates.[25]

The tariff issue declined in public interest in 1821 not so much because of an anti-protectionist sentiment as because the depression was lifting and a general industrial recovery was producing a rise in prices. There was, however, a reaction toward high duties. William H. Crawford, secretary of the treasury, reported in the president's cabinet that even in Pittsburgh an opposition to the high duties was developing.[26] Western Pennsylvania was beginning to ship linen, glass, and iron products to Philadelphia and Baltimore.[27] Nevertheless the protectionists continued their efforts to procure a higher tariff in the session of Congress beginning in December of 1822. Baldwin was not present in this Congress, having resigned because of ill health. Walter Forward of Pittsburgh, long a close friend and associate of Baldwin, was elected to fill his seat in Congress;[28] and John Todd, a Democratic Republican of Bedford County, filled Baldwin's place on the committee of manufactures. James Buchanan, recently elected to Congress from Lancaster County, made his maiden speech on the tariff bill and seemed to take the leadership of Pennsylvanian protectionists. He suggested moderate protection, however. But the House as a whole was opposed to protection, and the bill was overwhelmingly defeated.[29]

---

[24] *Annals of Congress,* 16 Congress, 1 session, 1:672; 2:2155.
[25] Eiselen, *Rise of Pennsylvania Protectionism,* 56, 57.
[26] J. Q. Adams, *Memoirs,* 5:411.
[27] *Democratic Press* (Philadelphia), April 14, 1821.
[28] United States Congress, *Biographical Directory,* 981.
[29] Eiselen, *Rise of Pennsylvania Protectionism,* 58, 59; *Annals of Congress,* 17 Con-

Although the glass manufacturers were on the road to prosperity by 1823, the ironmasters in western Pennsylvania were distressed because the price of English bar iron had fallen more than ten dollars a ton while American prices remained stationary.[30] Consequently, the iron manufacturers sought legislative assistance, and the committee on manufactures, in the session of Congress beginning in December of 1823, recommended that the rate on hammered iron bars should be raised from seventy-five cents to a dollar and twelve cents per hundred weight. A stanch opposition to this proposal arose. The contention was made that the ironmasters of Pennsylvania were already prosperous and that they alone sought higher duties.[31] Buchanan apparently led the protectionists' forces of Pennsylvania in this fight, but Andrew Stewart of Uniontown, who had been elected to Congress in 1821, was an able lieutenant for him. Stewart asserted that if Congress would not raise the duty on iron for the sake of the manufacturer, then he "asked it for the sake of the farmer; for the sake of the revenue; for the merchant; for the nation; it was demanded by every thing *American*—by every proud and patriotic feeling." The rate of ninety cents per hundred weight was finally adopted, although every western Pennsylvanian opposed the rate since it was lower than the one they sought.[32] An effort to have the rate on pig iron increased from fifty to seventy-five cents per hundred weight met with no success.[33] In the final vote upon the tariff of 1824, every representative from western Pennsylvania voted in the affirmative.[34]

The tariff rates under the act of 1824 were lower than the rates recommended by the committee on manufactures but they represented a gain that was acceptable to western Pennsylvanians. The following year the iron industry in Allegheny and Fayette counties regained something of its former activi-

---
gress, 2 session, p. 1015.
[30] Scrivenor, *History of the Iron Trade, throughout the World*, 377, 406-410.
[31] *Annals of Congress*, 18 Congress, 1 session, 2:1706, 1707.
[32] *Ibid.*, 2:2275, 2287.   [33] *Ibid.*, 2:1751.   [34] *Ibid.*, 2:2429.

ty,[35] probably because of an appreciable increase in prices both in the United States and in Europe. Not only was the iron industry booming but the glass industry in western Pennsylvania was also enjoying great success—one Pittsburgher observed that glass from the region was sold from Maine to New Orleans.[36]

Thus closed the first cycle of protectionism in western Pennsylvania. Textile manufacturers, glassmakers, ironmasters, and even the farmers had been convinced that their economic interests could be improved by governmental assistance in the protection of infant industries against low-priced foreign competition. And western Pennsylvania's congressmen reflected the opinions of their constituents throughout the era from 1815 to 1824. Henry Baldwin, in particular, had been the champion of the western manufacturers, but he was supported by his colleagues from west of the mountains in practically every protectionist move that he made. On other phases of the American System, however, the people of western Pennsylvania were not so completely in accord.

The question of finances and banking proved to be just as troublesome to the people of the western part of the state during the years from 1815 to 1823 as it had been in the last two decades of the 1700's. They had always believed themselves to be at the mercy of eastern bankers. Findley and Smilie epitomized western animosity against the Bank of Pennsylvania when they voted for the discontinuance of the charter in 1786; Gallatin, Findley, and Smilie again represented the western attitude when they objected to the chartering of the first United States Bank in 1791; and the merchants in the vicinity of Pittsburgh constantly believed that the rate of exchange was unfair to them even after the branch bank of the Bank of Pennsylvania and the office of discount and deposit of the United States Bank were established in the western city during the first decade of the nineteenth century. Their re-

[35] *Democratic Press* (Philadelphia), January 7, 1825.
[36] Jones, *Pittsburgh in the Year Eighteen Hundred and Twenty-six,* 69.

sentiment was not unjustified, but it was created probably as much by the inconvenience that western men encountered in banking and by the unfavorable balance of trade between western and eastern Pennsylvania as it was by the actual evils of the banking system.

The opposition to eastern banks and eastern financiers produced a general sentiment in the western counties against the rechartering of the first United States Bank in 1811. The state legislature early in the year adopted a resolution requesting the Pennsylvania congressmen to oppose the rechartering of the bank. The resolution was passed in the house of representatives by a vote of sixty-eight to twenty, with only two men from the western counties, Alden and Lobenger, voting in the negative. In the senate every western man opposed the rechartering of the bank.[37] The members of the state legislature, however, addressed their opinions to unreceptive ears, because Findley and Smilie, long since the deans of western Pennsylvania politicians, had grown conservative and, like Gallatin, now believed that the institution that they had once opposed was constitutional and expedient. Findley justified his reversal of opinion in a speech on the floor of the House in which he said:

The question of the Constitutionality of the bank solely depends upon the question, whether it is necessary and proper for conducting the moneyed operations of Government. So great a change has taken place on that subject within twenty years past, that it is supposed that question is now settled. Not only the moneyed transactions of the United States, but, it is believed, of all the State governments, are carried on through the respective branches, as well as commercial transactions ... Pennsylvania, formerly so much opposed to banks, has since that period incorporated many, and for seventeen years has connected banks with the Government, and conducts her moneyed transactions by their assistance.[38]

But the three Pennsylvanians who had been in the minority

[37] *Crawford Weekly Messenger* (Meadville), February 4, 1811.
[38] *Annals of Congress*, 11 Congress, 2 session, 2:1811.

in their opposition to the bank in 1791 now found themselves in the minority in supporting the bank in 1811, because younger men, less removed from the frontier in point of time and distance, killed the bank measure.

The death of the first United States Bank was the signal for a rush to establish state banks throughout the Union. Pennsylvania joined in this movement. As early as February 13, 1811, the applications for five such banks were considered in the state legislature, and in every case the charter was granted by a small margin.[39] Between 1811 and 1818 the number of banks in Pennsylvania increased from three to fifty-nine. The majority of these banks flooded the country with inadequately secured bank notes and stimulated reckless borrowing on the part of the industrialists and farmers for the purpose of expanding their enterprises.[40] Western Pennsylvania also participated in this orgy of unsound banking, and its people, as a result, witnessed frequent foreclosures, heavy discounting, and a general growing distrust of the banking system. A contributor writing under the pseudonym of "Scediasm" suggested in the *Gazette* of March 2, 1816, that anyone desiring to enrich himself should establish a bank, name himself president, induce a friend to serve as cashier, procure a copper plate from the local engraver, and start issuing paper money. His advice was tardy, because many men in western Pennsylvania had already acted upon the idea.

The chartering of the second United States Bank in 1816 as a part of the general program of the National Republicans met with approval in western Pennsylvania. Findley and Gallatin finally found themselves in step with popular opinion on the question. The younger Scull, who took over the editorship of the *Gazette* in 1816, and his successor, Morgan Neville, who served as its editor from 1818 to 1820, favored the rechartering of the bank. But before many months had passed the men of the western country realized that the second United States

[39] *Crawford Weekly Messenger* (Meadville), February 18, 1811.
[40] Sharpless, *Two Centuries of Pennsylvania History*, 256, 273.

Bank would not relieve their financial difficulties—on the contrary, it called a halt upon the reckless issuance of unsecured bank notes and drove many local banks out of existence. Its policy of holding the bank notes of the unstable banks and presenting them with a request that they be redeemed in specie was fatal to the weaker banks. As a bank was driven out of an isolated community by this practice of the national bank, the people of the community became increasingly opposed to the national bank. Regardless of the unsound principles upon which the local banks had been established and conducted, they had rendered a service to their patrons in that the bank notes had served as a circulating medium, although the notes may have been little more than scrip.

Though some of the western people resented the action of the second United States Bank in demanding specie payment, many of them realized by 1817 that the indiscriminate expansion of banks and inflation of money were dangerous. The more conservative ones preferred to call a halt upon their unwise finances. The *Pittsburgh Gazette* suggested such a policy and on January 24, 1817, printed a signed statement of some thirty Pittsburgh merchants announcing that "with a view to suppress the circulation of certain paper of chartered associations, purporting to be *Bank Notes* which have of late inundated this place to the exclusion of chartered *Bank Notes*" they would not accept the paper of some specified associations or of any others operating on similar principles. Two Pennsylvania banks, the Farmers' Bank of New Salem and the Youghiogheny Bank of Pennsylvania at Perryopolis, were among those so designated.

On February 5 a bill was reported for consideration in the lower house of the state legislature to establish a bank at Waynesburg. It was claimed that there were no banks closer than thirty miles and that the people of Greene County faced a great inconvenience in banking transactions. That reply to the argument maintained that there were two banks in Washington County and one in Fayette County that might be used by citizens in that section. One legislator stated that "perhaps money would be a relief to the people of Greene; but they could only obtain it upon principles which it was well known, had been destructive of the prosperity of the people of the state." Another member opposed to the formation of the bank in Greene County asserted that there were evils in the banking system and that "to avoid the poison of a viper, he should not deem it safe to plant it in the bosom"; he further explained that banks were like ancient baronies with their trains of vassals—all who dealt with them became, in some degree, their dependents. In the same issue of the paper the editor declared that great expectations had been excited from the establishment of the national bank; that it was a great colossus extending from Maine to Louisiana bestriding the United States and trampling on the Constitution; and that like Midas it changed everything it touched to gold specie.[41]

The depression that swept western Pennsylvania from 1817 to 1821 increased the opposition and bitterness of the people to the second United States Bank. The bank, together with the importation of cheap foreign goods, was held responsible for the economic stagnation in the region. The *Pittsburgh Gazette,* traditionally Federalist, was reluctant to place the responsibility on the bank, but on September 15, 1818, its new editor, Morgan Neville, admitted that the whole western country was confronted by general bankruptcy. A few months later he frankly stated in an editorial on the bank on February 22, 1819: *"The western country is decidedly opposed to the United States bank."* The announcement of the decision in the famous McCullough *v.* Maryland case, which denied the right of a state to tax the branch banks of the national bank, did not excite Neville greatly, but neither did it assuage the resentment of western men toward the bank.[42]

The opposition to the national bank continued unabated throughout the next two years. Many local banks crumpled

[41] *Crawford Weekly Messenger* (Meadville), February 28, 1817.
[42] *Pittsburgh Gazette,* March 29, 1819.

under the pressure that was brought to bear upon them to redeem their notes in specie. In February of 1820 the Erie *Gazette* reported that the Bank of Washington, the Farmers' and Mechanics' Bank of Pittsburgh, and the Farmers' and Mechanics' Bank of Greencastle had forfeited their charters.[43] In 1822 the Northwestern Bank of Pennsylvania at Meadville was forced to liquidate, although the creditors and depositors lost no money. By this time is was obvious that western Pennsylvanians were definitely opposed to the banking phase of the program of the National Republicans. They were still convinced that the United States Bank was inimical to their interests and they believed that it gave the eastern financiers an undue advantage over them. While the industrial recovery, beginning in 1821, alleviated their condition to a great extent, it did not cause them to feel kindly toward the bank; it merely served to make them less outspoken in their opposition. They were ready to join the followers of a great antagonist of the bank when he appeared in 1829.

The National Republicans' advocacy of internal improvements completely captivated western Pennsylvanians. From the days of the French and Indian war the people in the western counties had been consumed with the desire to build roads and to develop arteries of transportation that would link them with the American seaboard. Also they had contended without cessation for the unrestricted navigation of the Mississippi River. The purchase of Louisiana, which had removed the interference of foreign nations in the navigation of the Mississippi; the aid that the national government gave in the building of the Cumberland Pike, in the building of forts, and in the improvement of the harbor at Erie; and the assistance of the state government of Pennsylvania in building roads and turnpikes had proved insufficient for the transportation needs of the western counties. The National Republicans' program for the development of roads, canals, harbors, and river transportation strongly appealed to western Pennsylvanians.

[43] *Erie Gazette*, February 12, 1820.

The earliest road building west of the mountains was accomplished during the French and Indian War as a part of the British military program. The Braddock Road and the Forbes Road were built for the specific purpose of facilitating the movement of troops and supplies, but they eventually proved to be even more valuable as means of promoting westward migration, and for many years they served as the chief means of egress from the West. These roads were improved at various times, and other roads were built connecting with them, but the difficulty of constructing a network of roads in the new western counties was so great that comparatively little progress was made before 1790.

The number of settlers in the western country at that time and the establishment of the state government under a new constitution stimulated the building of additional roads and bridges to join western Pennsylvania to the seaboard for the purposes of migration, commerce, and the improvement of military defense. Legislators were aware of the necessity of opening roads and improving waterways in the state to enable Philadelphia to compete with New York for the inland trade. Their attention to the improvement of transportation was directed to that problem by unceasing appeals from western settlers, and there was not a single year between 1790 and 1825 when the state legislature did not consider measures to build roads or to improve river transportation.

During the last decade of the eighteenth century the chief concern of the western people and their representatives in the state legislature was the construction of a road or roads that would unite Pittsburgh with Philadelphia. Apparently all were agreed that such a road was desirable, but there was disagreement upon the route that it should follow; the settlers of various communities naturally preferred that the road should be built where they could utilize it. In February of 1791 the committee on inland roads and navigation reported the results of its investigation and indicated that the route in the straightest line from Frankstown to Pittsburgh appeared to

THE AMERICAN SYSTEM 253

be the best. The members of the committee estimated the cost of developing the road at three hundred pounds. They had also considered a road from Bedford to Pittsburgh, estimating the cost at five hundred pounds, and another road from Bedford to the Youghiogheny.[44] The people of Westmoreland County immediately petitioned the legislature to grant money to complete the road from Bedford to Pittsburgh.[45] A month later the lower house voted to postpone the bill for the improvement of the road to the West, and but a single western representative concurred with the postponement.[46] In September of the same year every western legislator in the house concurred upon the passing of a bill to declare Chartiers Creek in Allegheny County a public highway.[47] The governor in his communication to the legislature in December attempted to summarize the reports of the committee on roads and said:

If their opinion is sanctioned by your approbation, the proposed roads to *Pittsburgh,* to *Poplar Run,* and to the *Little Conemaugh,* being blended and formed into one great road, leading from *Frankstown* to *Pittsburgh,* the projected canal between the *Quitapahilla* and Tulpehoccon being opened, and a few easy portages established in proper situations, a certain foundation will be laid for connecting the western waters of the *Ohio* and the great lakes with the eastern streams, flowing into the *Atlantic,* particularly with the tide-waters of the *Delaware,* in the neighbourhood of *Philadelphia.*[48]

The governor's ambitious program was not carried out by the legislature, however, nor were any roads to the West completed before 1794, when the turnpike to Lancaster was constructed. The delay in the building of the roads was caused by the jealousies of the people in different localities and of the legislators from different sections of the state. But neither the people nor their representatives ceased to plan and to clamor for roads. A petition from a number of citizens from Fayette, Westmoreland, and Bedford counties was read on January 13, 1794, imploring the legislature to appoint men to survey the

[44] Pennsylvania, *House Journal,* 1790-91, p. 208.   [45] *Ibid.,* p. 225.
[46] *Ibid.,* p. 339, 340.   [47] *Ibid.,* p. 521, 522.   [48] *Ibid.,* 1791-92, p. 13.

road from Spiker's at the foot of the Allegheny Mountains to Cherry's Mill on Jacobs Creek; an act declaring the Allegheny River a public highway was passed; and the committee on inland roads and navigation recommended the building of a road from Berlin in Westmoreland County to the west side of Laurel Hill at an estimated cost of four hundred dollars.[49] At the same time Adamson Tannehill complained about the delay in the plans for the road to Pittsburgh.[50]

Two years later, in 1796, the legislature became interested in the construction of a road from Philadelphia to Presque Isle by way of the Tioga, and at the same time the committee was instructed to include a clause authorizing the governor to contract for the opening of a road from Pittsburgh to Le Bœuf by way of Franklin. The following day, February 1, a petition from Washington County urged the construction of a road through the southern part of that county from the Monongahela toward the Ohio, preferably from the head of Whitley Creek to the settlement of Wheeling. At the same time another group sought the building of a road from Somerset to Washington and thence to Wheeling.[51]

The improvements of roads and the building of new ones continued during the next century but with results that were only a little more satisfactory. Some roads were completed, but even their completion did not satisfy the people who were not immediately touched by them. The settlers in the northwestern counties were more aggressive in their demands for internal improvements during this period. They sought a road that would unite Pittsburgh and Lake Erie, and they pressed hard for the building of the road by state aid. They did not, however, hesitate to build turnpikes that were privately owned by companies established under an act of the legislature. In 1806 a committee of seven men including Henry Baldwin, Roger Alden, and Wilson Smith attempted to raise money

[49] Pennsylvania, *House Journal,* 1793-94, p. 99, 258, 309.
[50] *Pittsburgh Gazette,* June 21, 1794.
[51] Pennsylvania, *House Journal,* 1795-96, p. 180, 184; 1796-97, p. 225.

for an Erie-Waterford turnpike.[52] The *Crawford Weekly Messenger* of April 2, 1807, reported that the previous legislature had granted five hundred dollars for the improvement of navigation on French Creek; but more pleasant was the news contained in the columns of May 28, 1807, which indicated that the legislature had granted three thousand dollars for the improvement of roads in western Pennsylvania and had apportioned the money as follows: for the road from Beaver to Mercer, $450; from Pittsburgh to Butler, $300; from Butler to Mercer, $400; from Butler to Franklin, $400; from Franklin to Meadville, $400; and from Meadville to Waterford, $450. Evidently the internal improvement program as carried on by the state of Pennsylvania was well established by this time. But even these improvements did not satisfy the people of northwestern Pennsylvania because there was still no direct convenient outlet for their products. In 1811 a long memorial to the legislature proposed a road from Northumberland to Waterford by way of Franklin, which was at the junction of French Creek and the Allegheny River, and Meadville, with the explanation that New Orleans and Montreal were unsatisfactory as trading terminals. It held that Philadelphia was the natural outlet for the beef, pork, flour, cheese, butter, spirits, hemp, and linen cloth produced in that region.[53]

In southwestern Pennsylvania the building of the Cumberland Road, which had been begun in 1807, created a controversy between the people of Pittsburgh and those of Uniontown and Wheeling. Albert Gallatin, whose home was located a few miles to the southwest of Uniontown, was secretary of the treasury when that federal project was contemplated. Undoubtedly his influence was thrown on the side of those people who preferred to have the road from Uniontown to Wheeling rather than those who desired the national road to go through Pittsburgh. A beautifully drawn map among his papers indicates that he had given the matter considerable attention.[54]

[52] *Crawford Weekly Messenger* (Meadville), January 12, 1806.
[53] *Ibid.*, November 20, 1811.   [54] Gallatin Papers, vol. 15.

Furthermore, the fact that Badollet, Gallatin's business partner, was placed in charge of the construction of a part of the road indicates that Gallatin's interest may have been quite personal. Pittsburghers were alarmed because the road did not touch their city. As soon as the construction of the road was resumed after the Treaty of Ghent, editorials in the *Pittsburgh Gazette* pointed out that goods might go directly from Baltimore or Alexanderia to Wheeling and thence down the Ohio River, entirely missing Pittsburgh. This project greatly increased the commercial rivalry between Pittsburgh and Wheeling.[55]

Despite the activities of the state legislature in fostering the building and improvement of roads from 1790 to 1815, despite the great industry of the building of roads by turnpike companies incorporated by acts of the state legislature, and regardless of the fact that the national government was constructing the Cumberland Road through southwestern Pennsylvania at that time, there was still great dissatisfaction among the people because of inadequate transportation facilities. This dissatisfaction is indicated clearly by William Reynolds in his summary of the condition of roads in northwestern Pennsylvania in 1821. He stated:

> Roads had been opened from Franklin to Meadville and Waterford by the creek route, and from the latter point to Erie the turnpike was in use. The state road had been cut out for part of the distance, and other rude ways extended to the various centers of settlement. These, while passable, were of the most primitive character, as may be believed, when it is stated that the entire amount expended by the county for roads and bridges for the five preceding years was less than $2,000, and for 1818 but $98.67. Neither of the turnpikes connecting with the town had been completed. French creek was the chief artery of commerce. Upon its surface the exports were carried to the market by flat boats or rafts and imports brought by keel boats from Pittsburg.[56]

[55] See Crall, "A Half Century of Rivalry between Pittsburgh and Wheeling," in *Western Pennsylvania Historical Magazine*, 13:237-255 (1930).
[56] Reynolds, "Crawford County. A History of Its Growth and Development," in *Daily Tribune-Republican* (Meadville), centennial edition, May 12, 1888. p. 5.

In the face of the unsatisfactory roads in the western counties, the proposal of the National Republicans to develop channels of commerce by federal aid was alluring to the majority of the western Pennsylvanians, but the Pittsburghers were wary. The Cumberland Road would give a commercial advantage to southwestern Pennsylvania and to Wheeling, and western commerce might find its way to the Atlantic seaboard with very little benefit to the merchants of Pittsburgh. Furthermore, the project of the Erie Canal frightened them. There was the possibility that with its completion, western Pennsylvania would be isolated commercially. The Pittsburgh merchants and the *Pittsburgh Gazette,* however, were the center of a limited circle of opponents to the policy of federal internal improvements, and had the Cumberland Road been directed through Pittsburgh they undoubtedly would have been whole-hearted in their support of the program.

Curiously enough the *Pittsburgh Gazette* was almost silent upon the congressional appropriations that were made for the building of the road in 1816 and 1817. But in 1818 Neville opened a barrage against the project. He condemned the spending of $1,200,000 by Congress on a road that followed no recognized route. He asserted that its completion was the aim of certain rival towns and states rather than a national objective.[57] By the close of the year, however, the Cumberland Road was an accomplished fact, and the editor could only deprecate the fact that there was a noticeable decrease both in the number of people who passed through Pittsburgh and in the number of boats that plied their way down the river from that point.[58] He lost little time in regrets, however, and continued his editorials in behalf of internal improvements. Throughout the years 1818 and 1819 he struggled to awaken the people of both eastern and western Pennsylvania to the necessity of combating the effect of the Cumberland Road and the future effects of the Erie Canal by the improvement of

[57] *Pittsburgh Gazette,* October 2, 1818. [58] *Ibid.,* September 17, 1819.

turnpikes between Philadelphia and Pittsburgh and the clearing of the Ohio River from Pittsburgh to Wheeling.[59] Pentland of the *Statesman* and Snowden of the *Mercury* gave him no support.[60] Their opposition led to a lively interchange of recriminations, which may have had some influence in promoting a more vigorous advancement of internal improvements in the state.

The state of Pennsylvania, swept by this fervor for internal improvements, had appropriated large sums of money for such improvements in northwestern Pennsylvania in 1817. Thirty-five thousand dollars had been allotted for a road from Pittsburgh to Waterford by way of Mercer and Meadville; three thousand dollars was allowed for a road from Meadville through Warren County to the northern boundary of the state; two thousand dollars was set aside for a road from Mercer to the state line in the direction of Warren, Ohio; and twenty-six hundred dollars were appropriated to improve the navigation of the Allegheny River, French Creek, and the Conewango.[61] Turnpike connections between Pittsburgh and Erie were completed in 1821 when the Mercer and Meadville Turnpike was opened.[62]

Western Pennsylvania's politicians championed the American System in all its phases in the years 1815 and 1816. They supported the tariff with substantial unanimity in the hope that it would increase the manufacturing of iron, glass, and textiles and even with the anticipation that it would aid the farmers. They supported the establishment of the second United States Bank, but because their local banks failed in increasing numbers, by 1818 their ardor for that institution had cooled. And, finally, western Pennsylvanians and their representatives sponsored a huge program of internal im-

---

[59] *Pittsburgh Gazette*, June 30, 1818; November 26, 1819.
[60] *Statesman* (Pittsburgh), December 7, 1819; *Pittsburgh Mercury*, December 10, 1819.
[61] *Crawford Weekly Messenger* (Meadville), April 4, 1817.
[62] Reynolds, "Crawford County, A History of Its Growth and Development," in *Daily Tribune-Republican* (Meadville), centennial edition, May 12, 1888, p. 5.

provement, although the Pittsburgh merchants were worried by the fact that the Cumberland Road did not go through Pittsburgh. It is true that the emphasis was placed upon internal improvements by the state rather than by the federal government, but even so, the improvements coincided with the comprehensive program of the young nationalists who dominated the policies in Washington. So great was the hold of this national American System upon the people of western Pennsylvania that only one party, a National-Republican party, existed in the region from 1815 to 1823.

THE END OF AN ERA

CHAPTER ELEVEN

THE story of local politics and annual elections in western Pennsylvania for the years from 1816 to 1823 is drab and dull in comparison with that of the stirring years from 1787 to 1790, the period of the Whiskey Insurrection, the election of 1799, or that of 1805. The Federalist party, relatively ineffectual since 1800, had no organization worthy of the name after the disastrous election of 1816, and candidates ceased to use the name in western Pennsylvania after 1823. The National Republicans, practically unanimous in their attitude toward the American System and faced by little competition from the Federalists, were free to quarrel and wrangle among themselves over the distribution of local and state offices. The former Democratic-Republican organization was permitted to deteriorate, and, with a few exceptions, petty personalities entered into the conduct of the political campaigns in the various counties.

The election of 1816 was a mere routine so far as the presidential election was concerned. James Monroe encountered little opposition in the region; his electoral ticket carried the usual western counties, with the exception of Allegheny and Erie.[1] His failure to carry Allegheny County was probably due to the popularity of Baldwin, formerly a radical Republican but now grown conservative and highly acceptable to the Federalists.[2] Baldwin's success in this elec-

[1] *Crawford Weekly Messenger* (Meadville), November 29, 1816.
[2] *Ibid.*, October 19, 1816.

tion and the retirement of William Findley were the most significant features of that year's political activities in western Pennsylvania. The one put on the mantle of leadership that the other had relinquished after thirty-four years. Dr. David Marchand of Greensburg, Robert Moore of Beaver County, Christian Tarr of Brownsville, and Thomas Patterson of West Middletown in Washington County were Baldwin's colleagues in the fifteenth Congress, which lasted from March 4, 1817, to March 3, 1819. These men formed a delegation that was completely new to Congress; but it was a delegation experienced in local politics.

An unusual incident occured in 1817 to create at least a temporary excitement in political circles. James Monroe, in his good-will tour of the country, paid a visit to Pittsburgh. It was made the occasion for much rejoicing on the part of the Republicans, and even the editor of the *Gazette,* young Scull, who could not refrain from rebuking the Democrats for their sycophancy, admitted that "on occasions like the present, party feeling should be laid aside, and all classes join in paying him [*the president*] those respectful attentions which are his due."[3]

Monroe's visit aided the Republicans at an opportune time, because the year 1817 was a gubernatorial election year and, as usual, political interest rose above that of congressional elections or of years in which only the members of the state legislature were elected. Governor Snyder, whose campaign of 1805 against McKean and whose election in 1808 had created much agitation, reached the end of his term of eligibility at this time. The available candidates to succeed him were not as effective as he had been either in building up a political organization or in exciting public attention. The two candidates, William Findlay of Mercersburg, state treasurer from 1807 to 1817, and Joseph Hiester of Reading, then a member of the House of Representatives, were the rival candidates. Findlay had been nominated by a caucus

[3] *Pittsburgh Gazette,* July 1, 1817.

of 113 Republicans, whereas Hiester was reported to have received the nomination from 39 Republicans who met behind closed doors.[4]

The campaign was conducted primarily upon the basis of personalities. The electorate was asked to vote for Findlay because Hiester had opposed the ratification of the federal Constitution in the ratifying convention of 1787 and because he was accused of cowardice in running away at the battle of Brandywine. The friends of Hiester appealed for votes on his behalf because Findlay had been accused of misappropriating funds from the state treasury.[5] One contributor to the *Crawford Weekly Messenger* asserted that a change of officeholders would be the only result of the election as both candidates were Republicans.[6] William Findley of Westmoreland from his retirement at Youngstown penned an endorsement for his old friend, Hiester. He asserted that "Joseph Hiester has capacity to discharge the duties of governor to advantage, a solid and decisive judgement, firmness to sustain with prudence and decision *any siege of office,* and is the *last old revolutionary character who is likely to be a candidate for governor.*"[7] The endorsement apparently did very little to aid Hiester, however, because he carried Allegheny County by a majority of only thirty-seven votes and Crawford County by the meager margin of six votes and was unsuccessful in every other western county.[8] His victory in Allegheny County was the result of the stanch support of the *Pittsburgh Gazette,* which had been been remaining aloof from politics since 1815. This aloofness was indicative of the general apathy toward politics that existed in western Pennsylvania, although the *Gazette* itself should have been enlivened by the success of Baldwin and the Federalists in the county offices in the previous year.[9]

[4] *Crawford Weekly Messenger* (Meadville), August 29, 1817.
[5] *Ibid.,* September 5, 19, 1817.   [6] *Ibid.,* August 29, 1817.
[7] *Ibid.,* September 5, 1817.   [8] *Ibid.,* October 31, 1817.
[9] *Pittsburgh Gazette,* October 15, 1816; October 28, 1817.

Yet the next year the congressional elections provoked no issue or controversy, with the possible exception of Baldwin's election in Pittsburgh. The tariff was made a definite issue, and Baldwin won by a decisive majority. Every congressman from western Pennsylvania, moreover, was returned to his seat in the lower House. Nor was there interest in politics of any appreciable nature until 1820 when the presidential, gubernatorial, and congressional as well the state elections occurred. Monroe's success was assured in that election, but in the state Hiester once more appeared as a candidate against Governor Findlay, who stood for reëlection.

Findlay had made use of the patronage to build up his following, but the fact that the people in the state were undergoing a depression tended to offset anything he may have done. Unfortunately for him, he could not rid himself of the odium which grew out of the charge that he had misappropriated state funds while in the treasury office. He was finally "white-washed" of the charge by a vote of sixty-two to thirty-one in the state house of representatives.[10] But such political "white-washings" often serve only the purpose of giving more publicity to the charges, which seemed to be the case in this instance. A long article in the *Harrisburg Chronicle* was reprinted in the *Crawford Weekly Messenger* for August 25, 1820, denouncing Findlay and defending Hiester. It maintained that Findlay did not defend the country; as state treasurer he had manipulated the funds; as governor he had sold offices, imposed clerks upon the appointees to the offices, appointed hosts of justices of the peace, and opposed the wishes of the people, who had recommended a reduction in the fees for public officials. On August 25 a group of Republicans in Washington County met at the home of John Chambers, resolved not to vote for Findlay, charged that his nomination was accomplished by a union of officeholders, and accused him of multiplying the offices. A meeting of Republicans in Beaver reported that it could find no eminent qualities in

[10] *Crawford Weekly Messenger* (Meadville), March 10, 1820.

Findlay.[11] And William Findley of Westmoreland once more endorsed Hiester, his erstwhile colleague. Hiester defeated Findlay in this election, but he carried only two of the counties in western Pennsylvania—Allegheny and Beaver—the former by a margin of 39 votes and the latter by a majority of 243 votes.[12] Hiester's conservatism had little appeal to a section that was traditionally democratic in its Republicanism.

Baldwin of Pittsburgh and Thomas Patterson of West Middletown were reëlected to their seats in Congress, but Andrew Stewart of Uniontown supplanted Christian Tarr of Brownsville; George Plumer of Robbstown succeeded David Marchand of Greensburg; and Patrick Farrelly of Meadville defeated Robert Moore of Beaver County. The men newly elected to Congress did not change the complexion of western Pennsylvania's delegation, because they were all Republicans, nor was the quality of the representation from the western counties lowered. Farrelly was an especially able and cultured lawyer, who could hold his own in any argument or debate. Plumer of Westmoreland was a prominent farmer, and Stewart was a lawyer and business man who was to serve eighteen years in the House intermittently from 1821 to 1849, when he declined to stand for renomination.[13]

Baldwin, still the most brilliant of western Pennsylvania's representatives, became ill in 1822 and was forced to resign his seat. His work as chairman on the committee on manufactures had made him very popular with his constituents, and upon his arrival in Pittsburgh on August 16, 1822, the citizens greeted him with a salute of thirteen guns, after which the mayor, city officials, and a great number of citizens received him. He was later tendered a banquet by the manufacturers of Pittsburgh for the work he had done on the tariff.[14] In the election that followed, Walter Forward, Henry Baldwin's

[11] *Crawford Weekly Messenger* (Meadville), September 15, 1820.
[12] *Ibid.*, October 24, 1820.
[13] United States Congress, *Biographical Directory*, p. 1569.
[14] *Pittsburgh Mercury*, August 21, 1822; Boucher, *A Century and a Half of Pittsburgh and Her People*, 2:380.

former law associate and stanch friend, was elected to succeed him; he received 2,004 votes against the 1,364 votes cast for his opponent, Ephraim Pentland.[15] Forward was not as prominent a leader in Congress as his predecessor had been, nor did he receive appointments to committees as significant as those on which Baldwin had served, but he was alert to the interests of his constituents, who indorsed him and reëlected him in 1822. In that election the entire delegation of western Pennsylvania men were returned to their seats in Congress.

The interest of the electorate of the western counties was probably at its lowest ebb during this and the following year. The people were on their way to economic recovery; the Federalist party was long since dead, and there were but few people who would refer to themselves as Federalists. In 1823 there was a gubernatorial election in which Andrew Gregg ran on a Federal Republican ticket against John Andrew Schulze, who obtained a majority of 25,350 votes in a smashing victory over his Federal Republican rival. Only Warren County of western Pennsylvania gave Gregg a majority—a majority of only twenty-one. The remainder of the western counties rolled up a majority of 14,194 for Schulze.[16] Federalism was virtually annihilated in western Pennsylvania—no representatives and only three senators from the region were listed as Federalists in the legislature.[17] Republicanism unopposed and with a prosperous constituency was forced to look within its own ranks for controversies to enliven politics. Theoretically, the people were National Republicans, favorably disposed toward protectionism, advocates of internal improvement, both state and national, and supposedly adherents to the second United States Bank. Yet actually, at the close of this era in politics in western Pennsylvania, a strong antipathy to the bank already existed, and an undercurrent of opposition, particularly among the farmers, was arising to the

[15] *Pittsburgh Mercury,* October 16, 1822.
[16] *Crawford Weekly Messenger* (Meadville), October 28, 1823.
[17] *Ibid.,* November 11, 1823.

tariff. Even before the close of this era, there were evidences of the beginning of a new one.

As early as 1820 there was a faint murmur in favor of Andrew Jackson, who was to capture the hearts and obtain the votes not only of western Pennsylvania but also of the entire state in the ensuing election. Atkinson, editor of the *Crawford Weekly Messenger,* who had seemed to lose interest in politics after 1817, indicated his preference for "Old Hickory" at the time that James Monroe was receiving an almost unanimous electoral vote in 1820.[18] Unfortunately the editor did not indicate his reason for this shift to Jackson, and his assertion of allegiance at that time stands as a lone cry in the wilderness. Within two years, however, the sentiment for Jackson spread in the western counties.

The swing to "Old Hickory" seemed to emanate from Westmoreland County. The friends of Jackson were invited to meet in Greensburg in December of 1822 to consider and adopt measures preparatory to the presidential election. which was almost two years in the future. They met on December 28, established a committee of correspondence, and instructed that committee to correspond with like committees throughout the state. On November 14 of the following year, a meeting of devotees of Jackson was held in Pittsburgh at which a committee of correspondence was selected and a delegate chosen to attend the convention on March 4 of the next year. On January 8, 1824, a second meeting was called in Greensburg in the interests of Jackson, and early in that year similar meetings were called in Crawford, Beaver, Erie, and Venango counties.[19] The movement for Jackson was sweeping western Pennsylvania like wildfire, but it did not envelop all of the leaders of the region. Walter Forward of Pittsburgh, then a member of the House of Representatives, and Walter Lowrie of Beaver, in the United States Senate, attended the

[18] *Crawford Weekly Messenger* (Meadville), September 17, 1820.
[19] *Ibid.,* December 24, 1822; January 27, November 23, 1823; January 20, 27, February 10, 17, 23, 1824.

THE END OF AN ERA 267

caucus that nominated William H. Crawford in February and cast their votes for him.[20]

The swing to Jackson continued with accelerated momentum as the summer approached, and Mercer County joined the procession.[21] In Pittsburgh, the *Allegheny Democrat,* a pro-Jackson newspaper, was founded by John McFarland, who pledged his support to Jackson. Atkinson observed that the *Democrat* was patently a campaign newspaper;[22] but it existed for many years as a strong Democratic organ. The movement for Jackson would not be denied, and in the presidential election he carried western Pennsylvania in a landslide. Every county west of the mountains gave him an overwhelming majority. The vote stood as follows: Jackson, 6,869; Adams, 637; Crawford, 1,083; Clay, 264.[23] The old era had closed and the new one had begun; the first half century of western Pennsylvania politics was completed.

A panoramic view of this first half century of western Pennsylvania politics, from 1773 to 1823, encompasses a pioneer agricultural people striving to alleviate their difficulties and to improve their social conditions by legislative measures and political methods. At the beginning of the period, western Pennsylvania was merely an aggregate of some fifty thousand pioneers living in a section of the American frontier, which was segregated from the Atlantic seaboard by the Appalachian Mountains. These people, comprising English, Scotch, Scotch-Irish, German, and other racial stocks, were struggling to adjust themselves to each other and to the conditions of the American wilderness. The great majority of them were farmers of the small-scale system who owned three or four hundred acres of land; a few of them, such as General John Neville, owned large tracts and had many slaves; but in the

---

[20] *Crawford Weekly Messenger* (Meadville), March 2, 1824.
[21] *Ibid.,* March 30, 1824.   [22] *Ibid.,* June 25, 1824.
[23] *Erie Gazette,* November 18, 1824; *Crawford Weekly Messenger* (Meadville), November 18, 1824.

main they constituted an agrarian society of small farmers. It was the era of the ax, the hoe, and the gun.

As the years passed, small towns arose. Pittsburgh, Washington, Greensburg, Meadville, and Erie were among the thriving towns of the first half century. Enterprising townsmen fostered manufacturing and commerce with the result that by 1790 commercial activities tended to produce political rifts between the merchants of Pittsburgh and Washington, who bought their commodities from houses in Philadelphia or Baltimore, and the farmers of southwestern Pennsylvania, who sold their products down the Mississippi. Manufacturing was well under way by the close of the century and increased with accelerating speed during the next twenty-five years. Nevertheless, western Pennsylvania, because of the belated settlement and occupation of the region between the Allegheny River and Lake Erie, remained predominately agricultural.

The problems of the people in the region were those germane to a pioneer agrarian society. They wanted cheap land and clear titles to it; they sought protection against Indian raids; they needed roads for the facilitation of travel and commerce; they desired paper money because they were in debt; and they clamored for greater representation in the state legislature because governmental assistance was essential to the solution of their problems. Their political philosophy and behavior were determined by these problems and by the fact that they were pioneers with the traditional pioneer traits of emotionalism, provincialism, and individualism.

The organization of Westmoreland County in 1773 was the signal for the official beginning of politics in western Pennsylvania. Thereupon, two struggles began and continued concurrently during the period of the American Revolution. The first was a controversy between the Virginia settlers who made their homes along the Monongahela and Youghiogheny rivers in Washington and Fayette counties under the impression that they occupied Virginia territory and the Pennsylvania settlers in the region around Fort Ligonier and Hannastown, who believed that the land belonged to the Quaker colony. The Virginia-Pennsylvania boundary dispute was settled in 1780, but the political controversy between the two groups was not brought to an end until the formation of Washington County in 1781 and of Fayette in 1783, which enabled the Virginia adherents to conduct their own local government. The second struggle arose between the democratic patriots of the western counties and the conservative group of the East. The revolutionary party east of the mountains, opposed to the conservative Tory group, effected an alignment with the western men to control the government and establish the new state constitution of 1776. For the next ten years until the backwash of the Revolution swept the democratic group from power, western Pennsylvania representatives belonged to the majority party.

During those ten years a vigorous back-country democracy developed, and strong leaders came to the front. William Findley, William Todd, Thomas Baird, and Christopher Lobenger, of Westmoreland; John Smilie, Nathaniel Breading, and Edward Cook, of Fayette; and James Marshel, James Edgar, and David Redick, of Washington, were outstanding democratic leaders. General John Neville and John McDowell of Washington County and Hugh Henry Brackenridge of Pittsburgh were able men but not susceptible to the party regimentation of the so-called radicals. They were interested in problems of local concern, however, and increased the political weight of the western counties. The western democrats held the balance of power in the state legislature between 1783 and 1786; they dominated the council of censors in 1783 and 1784 and so prevented the calling of a convention to make a conservative constitution; and they aided in rescinding the charter of the Bank of Pennsylvania in 1786. Killing the bank charter proved to be a tactical mistake, however, and that action together with the general conservative backwash of the Revolution swept the democratic group from office in 1786.

For the ensuing decade, back-country democracy was in the opposition party in the state, although it was not in the minority in the western counties. The farmers opposed successively and unsuccessfully the ratification of the federal Constitution in 1787, the revision of the democratic state constitution in 1789 and 1790, and the federal excise on spirituous liquors in 1791. They were dissatisfied with the federal government's ineffectual attempts to eradicate the Indian menace in 1790 and 1791; and they were disappointed with its lack of interest in the navigation of the Mississippi; its determination to enforce the tax on whiskey in 1794 brought to a head the frustration and exasperation of back-country democrats. The Whiskey Insurrection was the high point of their opposition.

Federalism seriously challenged the supremacy of the western radicals during the period from 1790 to 1799. National political parties arose in that decade, and the friends of Hamilton increased in numbers in western Pennsylvania. General John Neville and his son Presley, Abraham Kirkpatrick, Isaac Craig, John McDowell, Senator James Ross of Washington and Pittsburgh, John Woods, and Judge Alexander Addison of Washington led the Federalist forces in the region. But the addition of the "Young Giant," Albert Gallatin, to the democratic ranks, and the reëntry of the wily Brackenridge into politics at the time that the Federalists blundered in passing the Alien and Sedition Acts in 1798 turned the tide. The following year Thomas McKean, a Republican of the Jeffersonian stripe, was elected governor of Pennsylvania.

A month later the organization of Jeffersonian Democracy was begun in western Pennsylvania. Brackenridge was appointed a justice of the state supreme court; eight new frontier counties were established in March of 1800; the *Herald of Liberty,* a newspaper for the Democratic Republicans, was set up by August 16 of the same year; a committee to aid in the naturalization of aliens was formed in Pittsburgh; committees of correspondence for each county and for the townships were organized; a committee to preserve order at elections was instituted to get out the votes; Judge Alexander Addison was impeached; and the purchase of Louisiana, which guaranteed the free navigation of the Mississippi to western men, was accomplished. The Federalist party could not cope with this Democratic organization and virtually disappeared west of the mountains except in the towns of Pittsburgh, Washington, and Meadville, where Federalists continued to control the local offices. The Democratic Republicans, relieved of a strong opposition party, fought among themselves. In 1805 the contest was sharp and revolved around the issues of a revision of the state constitution and the clearing of land titles. The supremacy of the Jeffersonian party was not seriously challenged until 1812, however, when DeWitt Clinton gathered up the loose ends of political opposition to worry Madison for a time.

The politics of the period of the War of 1812 were interesting and confused. The Democratic Republicans had favored the embargo and they had retained an antipathy to the English commanders at Detroit and elsewhere, but they were not anxious to have their militiamen march out of Pennsylvania. The militia companies held a rendezvous at Meadville, where the Republicans, who were in the majority, harassed Samuel Lord and other Federalists by destroying their property. A hitherto untold story of what was nearly a pitched battle at the bridge in Meadville between two companies of the militia, one Republican and the other Federalist, is indicative of the political animosities of the times. When the British approached Erie, however, the people forgot their political differences for the time being and concentrated on defending the territory.

From 1814 or 1815 the development of manufacturing in the region made its mark on commerce. Steamboats, iron, glass, rope, and many other products were manufactured. Banking facilities were increased—the Northwestern Bank of Pennsylvania was chartered in 1813 and opened in Meadville. Pressure was brought to bear on transportation problems. Clay's American System was attractive to western Pennsylvania business men because it provided for improving transportation and increasing tariff rates and because these men had visions, even then, of a great manufacturing region. Henry Baldwin, a Pittsburgh lawyer, met the demand for a tariff leader and became a prominent exponent of business. The years from 1815 to 1825 are filled with efforts to obtain state and national aid to build roads and canals, to improve the harbor at Erie, and to clear the Ohio River of snags and rocks. The farmers were never completely converted to the American System, however, and in 1823 and 1824, when the movement to elect Andrew Jackson began, they quickly fell in line. Western Pennsylvania did not "go democratic" then—it had always been democratic. Jackson merely revived the spirit of a frontier democracy that had been lulled into inactivity for a time by visions of industrial affluence.

BIBLIOGRAPHY

BIBLIOGRAPHY

MANY lacunae exist in the original sources covering the history of western Pennsylvania during the years that fall within the purview of this work. Few organized manuscript collections of the letters and writings of the political leaders are available. Except for the papers of Albert Gallatin, William Irvine, and Arthur St. Clair, only incomplete collections of a few such men as Hugh Henry Brackenridge, Alexander Addison, William Findley, James O'Hara, and Ephraim Douglass were located.

Printed sources and newspapers, however, in sufficient quantities to give a clear account of the political activities of the region were available. The official publication of the records of various conventions and the journals of both houses of the state and national legislatures record the official action of western Pennsylvania men in those bodies. Newspapers, after 1786, reveal the local events and reflect the opinion of the people at home. The *Pittsburgh Gazette,* the Greensburg *Farmers' Register,* and the *Crawford Weekly Messenger* proved to be of the greatest value. The latter was particularly useful because it was the most significant newspaper in northwestern Pennsylvania during its lifetime (1805-31). Moreover, Thomas Atkinson, its founder, reprinted political items from the journals of Uniontown, Washington (Pennsylvania), Greensburg, Pittsburgh, and Erie, thus making it a virtual repository of political information for the whole region. Every issue printed is extant and available, a fact not true of any other regional paper of the period, and for that reason extensive use was made of it.

A great number of secondary works were consulted for background and for actual information. They are included here as an aid to students of western Pennsylvania history even though they may not have been referred to in the footnotes. The theses of graduate students in history at the University of Pittsburgh deserve special mention because in them is collected, digested, and made available a great mass of scattered but important material.

SOURCE MATERIAL

MANUSCRIPTS

Brackenridge, Hugh Henry. Letters. There are some seventeen letters in the possession of the Darlington Library, University of Pittsburgh.

Denny-O'Hara Papers. In the custody of the Historical Society of Western Pennsylvania. Pittsburgh.

Gallatin, Albert. Papers. New York Historical Society. The Gallatin Papers in the library of the New York Historical Society comprise twenty-three folio volumes of letters, diaries, accounts, and various other documents. The Historical Society of Western Pennsylvania has photographic reproductions of many of those papers relating to western Pennsylvania.

Irvine, William. Papers. Historical Society of Pennsylvania. Philadelphia.

NEWSPAPERS

Baltimore. *Niles' Weekly Register,* 1811-49. 75 vols.
Bedford Gazette, weekly, 1805-15.
Brownsville Gazette, weekly, 1809-10.
Brownsville. *Western Palladium,* weekly, 1812.
Brownsville. *Western Repository,* weekly, 1810.
Erie Gazette, weekly, 1820, 1824.
Erie. *Mirror,* weekly, 1808-11.
Greensburgh & Indiana Register, weekly, 1812-15. A continuation of the *Farmers' Register,* with no change in serial numbering.
Greensburg. *Farmers' Register,* weekly, 1799.
Meadville. *Crawford Democrat,* weekly, 1809-15.
Meadville. *Crawford Weekly Messenger,* 1805-12, 1814, 1816-18, 1820, 1822-24.
Meadville. *Daily Tribune-Republican.* Centennial edition. May 12, 1888.
Mercer. *Western Press,* weekly, 1811-38.

Philadelphia. *Democratic Press,* daily, 1821, 1825.
Philadelphia. *Pennsylvania Packet, and Daily Advertiser,* 1787, 1788.
Pittsburgh. *Allegheny Democrat, and Farmers' & Mechanics' Advertiser,* weekly, 1824-26
Pittsburgh. *Commonwealth,* weekly, 1805, 1807.
Pittsburgh Gazette, weekly, 1786-89, 1793, 1794, 1796, 1798-1805, 1807-09, 1811-19.
Pittsburgh Mercury, weekly, 1815, 1818, 1819, 1822.
Pittsburgh. *Statesman,* weekly, 1819.
Pittsburgh. *Tree of Liberty,* weekly, 1800, 1801, 1803, 1805.
Somerset Gazette, weekly, 1806-07.
Somerset Whig, weekly, 1813-15.
Uniontown. *Fayette and Greene Spectator,* weekly, 1811-14.
Uniontown. *Fayette Gazette and Union Advertiser,* weekly, 1797-1805.
Uniontown. *Genius of Liberty and Fayette Advertiser,* weekly, 1805-18.
Washington. *National Intelligencer,* 1800.
Washington, Pa. *Herald of Liberty,* weekly, 1798-1801.
Washington, Pa. *Reporter,* weekly, 1805-15.
Washington, Pa. *Western Corrector,* weekly, 1810-11.
Washington, Pa. *Western Register,* weekly, 1817-18.
Washington, Pa. *Western Telegraphe, and Washington Advertiser,* weekly, 1795-1811.

OTHER PRINTED SOURCES

Adams, John Quincy. *Memoirs.* Edited by Charles F. Adams. Philadelphia, 1874-77. 12 vols.
Addison, Alexander. *On the Alien Act. A Charge to the Grand Juries of the County Courts of the Fifth Circuit of the State of Pennsylvania . . . 1798.* Washington, 1799. 21 p.
Addison, Alexander. *Rise & Progress of Revolution: A Charge to the Grand Juries of the County Courts of the Fifth Circuit of the State of Pennsylvania . . . 1800.* Philadelphia, 1801. 36 p.
Addison, Alexander. *Reports of Cases in the County Courts of the Fifth Circuit, and in the High Court of Errors and Appeals, of the State of Pennsylvania.* Washington, Pa., 1800. x, 396, xxiv p.
Address of the Democratic Republican Committee of the Borough

of Pittsburgh and Its Vicinity, Favourable to the Election of De Witt Clinton to the Presidency of the United States at the Ensuing Election. Pittsburgh, 1812. 25 p. A pamphlet in the possession of the Historical Society of Western Pennsylvania.

Annals of Congress; the Debates and Proceedings in the Congress of the United States ... from March 3, 1789 to May 27, 1824; compiled by Joseph Gales, Sr., and W. W. Seaton. Washington, 1834-56. 42 vols.

Ashe, Thomas. *Travels in America Performed in 1806.* London, 1809. 316 p.

Bates, Frederick. "Letter of Frederick Bates to A. B. Woodward," in *Michigan Pioneer and Historical Collections,* 8:557-563 (1886).

Birkbeck, Morris. *Notes on a Journey in America.* Philadelphia, 1817. 189 p.

Brackenridge, Henry M. *Recollections of Persons and Places in the West.* Philadelphia and Pittsburgh, 1868. 331 p.

Brackenridge, Hugh H. *Gazette Publications.* Carlisle, 1806. 348 p.

Brackenridge, Hugh H. *Incidents of the Insurrection in the Western Parts of Pennsylvania, in the year 1794.* Philadelphia, 1795. 3 vols. in 1.

Crumrine, Boyd, ed. "Minute Book of the Virginia Court Held at Fort Dunmore (Pittsburgh) for the District of West Augusta," in Carnegie Museum of Pittsburgh, *Annals,* 1:525-568 (1901-02).

Crumrine, Boyd, ed. "Minute (or Order) Book of the Virginia Court Held for Ohio County, Virginia, at Black's Cabin (Now West Liberty, W. Va.), from January 6, 1777, until September 4, 1780, when Its Jurisdiction over any Part of Pennsylvania Had Ceased," in Carnegie Museum of Pittsburgh, *Annals,* 3:5-78 (1904-05).

Crumrine, Boyd, ed. "Minute Book of the Virginia Court Held for Yohogania County, First at Augusta Town (Now Washington, Pa.), and Afterwards on the Andrew Heath Farm near West Elizabeth; 1776-1780," in Carnegie Museum of Pittsburgh, *Annals,* 2:71-429 (1903-04).

Crumrine, Boyd, ed. "The Records of Deeds for the District of West Augusta, Virginia, for the Court Held at Fort Dunmore (Pittsburgh, Pa.), 1775-1776," in Carnegie Museum of Pittsburgh, *Annals,* 3:237-327 (1904-05).

Davis, Mrs. Elvert M. "The Letters of Tarleton Bates, 1795-1805,"

in *The Western Pennsylvania Historical Magazine,* 12:32-53 (1929).
Dick, John. "Recollections of an Early Settler," in *Daily Tribune-Republican* (Meadville). Centennial edition, 9-13 (May 12, 1888).
Doddridge, Joseph. *Notes on the Settlement and Indian Wars of the Western Parts of Virginia & Pennsylvania.* Wellsburgh, Va., 1824. 316 p.
Egle, William H. "Minutes of the Board of Property and Other References to Lands in Pennsylvania," in *Pennsylvania Archives,* third series, 1:1-807; 2:1-158.
Findley, William. "An Autobiographical Letter," in *The Pennsylvania Magazine of History and Biography,* 5:440-450 (1881).
Findley, William. *History of the Insurrection in the Four Western Counties of Pennsylvania.* Philadelphia, 1796. xv, 328 p.
Fithian, Philip V. *Philip Vickers Fithian, Journal and Letters, 1767-1774.* Edited by John R. Williams. Princeton, 1900. xxi, 320 p.
Fithian, Philip V. *Philip Vickers Fithian; Journal, 1775-1776.* Edited by Robert G. Albion and Leonidas Dodson. Princeton, 1934. xviii, 279 p.
Hamilton, Alexander. *Works.* Edited by Henry Cabot Lodge. New York and London, 1904. 12 vols.
Hamilton, William. *Report of the Trial and Acquittal of Edward Shippen, Esquire, Chief Justice, and Jasper Yeates and Thomas Smith, Esquires, Assistant Justices of the Supreme Court of Pennsylvania.* Lancaster, 1805. 491, 96 p.
Huidekoper, Alfred. "Holland Land Company." Typescript in possession of Mr. John E. Reynolds of Meadville, Pa. 21 p.
Hutchins, Thomas. *A Topographical Description of Virginia, Pennsylvania, Maryland, and North Carolina.* Reprint, edited by Frederick C. Hicks. Cleveland, 1904. 143 p. Hutchins, who had made two journeys through the region, gives a brief description of the topography of the land at the headwaters of the Ohio and of the plant and animal life there.
Jones, Samuel. *Pittsburgh in the Year Eighteen Hundred and Twenty-six.* Pittsburgh, 1826. 152 p.
Lloyd, Thomas. *The Trial of Alexander Addison, Esq.* Second Edition, Lancaster, 1803. 154, 14 p.
McMaster, John B., and Frederick D. Stone, eds. *Pennsylvania and*

the Federal Constitution, *1787-1788*. Lancaster, Pa., 1888. viii, 803 p.

Madison, James. *Writings*. Edited by Gaillard Hunt. New York, 1900-1910. 9 vols.

Niles' Weekly Register. See NEWSPAPERS, Baltimore.

Pennsylvania Archives. First series, Philadelphia, 1852-56. 12 vols. Second series, first edition, Harrisburg, 1874-93. 19 vols. Third series, Harrisburg, 1894-99. 30 vols. Fourth series, Harrisburg, 1900-02. 12 vols. Ninth series, Harrisburg, 1935. 10 vols.

[*Pennsylvania Colonial Records.*] Harrisburg, 1851-53. 16 vols. The Minutes of the Provincial Council constitute the first ten volumes of this set.

Pennsylvania. Constitutional Convention, 1776. *The Proceedings Relative to Calling the Conventions of 1776 and 1790. The Minutes of the Convention that Formed the Present Constitution of Pennsylvania, together with the Charter to William Penn, the Constitutions of 1776 and 1790, and a View of the Proceedings of the Conventions of 1776, and the Council of Censors.* Harrisburg, 1825. v, 382, iv p.

Pennsylvania. General Assembly. *Minutes of the First Session of the Eleventh General Assembly*. Philadelphia, 1787.

Pennsylvania. General Assembly. *Proceedings and Debates of the General Assembly of Pennsylvania*. Philadelphia, 1787.

Pennsylvania. *House Journal,* 1790-97, 1803-04.

Pennsylvania. *Laws of the Commonwealth of Pennsylvania from October 14, 1700, to March 20, 1810*. Philadelphia, 1810. 4 vols. This collection of laws was edited by Judge Charles Smith and is commonly known as Smith's laws.

Pennsylvania. *Senate Journal,* 1790-91, 1794-95, 1816.

Pennsylvania. Supreme Court. *Reports of Cases Adjudged in the Supreme Court of Pennsylvania*. Edited by Horace Binney. Philadelphia, 1809-15. 6 vols.

St. Clair, Arthur. *The St. Clair Papers*. Arranged by William H. Smith. Cincinnati, 1882. 2 vols.

United States. Bureau of the Census. *Heads of Families at the First Census of the United States Taken in the Year 1790. Pennsylvania.* Washington, 1908. 426 p.

SECONDARY MATERIAL

Adams, Henry. *The Life of Albert Gallatin*. Philadelphia, 1879. v, 697 p.

Agnew, Daniel. "Address to the Allegheny County Bar Association, December 1, 1888," in *The Pennsylvania Magazine of History and Biography*, 13:1-60 (1889).

Agnew, Daniel. *A History of the Region of Pennsylvania North of the Ohio and West of the Allegheny River*. Philadelphia, 1887. vii, 246 p.

Albert, George D., ed. *History of the County of Westmoreland, Pennsylvania*. Philadelphia, 1882. 727 p.

Albig, W. Espy. "Early Development of Transportation on the Monongahela River," in *The Western Pennsylvania Historical Magazine*, 2:115-124 (1919).

Allegheny County, Pa. Centennial Committee. *Allegheny County: Its Early History and Subsequent Development*. Pittsburgh, 1888. 133, 144 p.

Ambler, Charles H. *A History of Transportation in the Ohio Valley*. Glendale, Calif., 1932. 465 p.

American Council of Learned Societies. "Report of Committee on Linguistic and National Stocks in the Population of the United States," in American Historical Association, *Annual Report*, 1:103-441 (1931).

Anderson, D. R. "The Insurgents of 1811," in American Historical Association, *Annual Report*, 1:165-176 (1911).

Andrews, J. Cutler. *Pittsburgh's Post-Gazette*. Boston, 1936. 324 p.

Armor, William C. *Lives of the Governors of Pennsylvania*. Philadelphia, 1872. 528 p.

Armor, William C. *Scotch Irish Bibliography of Pennsylvania*. Nashville, Tenn., 1896. 38 p.

Babcock, Charles A. *Venango County, Pennsylvania*. Chicago, 1919. 2 vols.

Baldwin, Leland D. "Shipbuilding on the Western Waters, 1793-1817," in *The Mississippi Valley Historical Review*, 20:29-44 (1933).

Baldwin, Leland D. "Whiskey Rebels: The Story of a Frontier Uprising." Manuscript in the possession of the University of Pittsburgh Press.

Bates, Samuel P. *History of Greene County, Pennsylvania.* Chicago, 1888. 898 p.

Bausman, Joseph H. *History of Beaver County, Pennsylvania.* New York, 1904. 2 vols.

Beals, Ellis H. "Arthur St. Clair in the History of Western Pennsylvania." Master's thesis, University of Pittsburgh, 1928.

Beaumariage, Alexander. "The Hoge Family in Politics." Master's thesis, University of Pittsburgh, 1937.

Bell, Albert H. *Memoirs of the Bench and Bar of Westmoreland County, Pennsylvania.* Batavia, N. Y., 1925. 302, iii p.

Bell, Edmund H. "Echoes of Early Brownsville," in *The Western Pennsylvania Historical Magazine,* 7:10-23 (1924).

Bining, Arthur C. "The Rise of Iron Manufacture in Western Pennsylvania," in *The Western Historical Magazine,* 16:235-256 (1933).

Bining, William J. "The Glass Industry of Western Pennsylvania." Master's thesis, University of Pittsburgh, 1936.

Boucher, John N., ed. *A Century and a Half of Pittsburgh and Her People.* New York, 1908. 4 vols.

Boucher, John N. *History of Westmoreland County, Pennsylvania.* New York, 1906. 3 vols.

Boucher, John N. *Old and New Westmoreland.* New York, 1918. 4 vols.

Bowman, James L. "Some Historical Notes of South-West Pennsylvania," in *The Western Pennsylvania Historical Magazine,* 10:48-57, 117-125, 187-190 (1927).

[Brackenridge, Henry M.] "Biographical Notice of H. H. Brackenridge," in *The Southern Literary Messenger,* 8:1-19 (1842).

Brackenridge, Henry M. *History of the Western Insurrection in Western Pennsylvania.* Pittsburgh, 1859. 336 p.

Brigham, Clarence S., comp. "Bibliography of American Newspapers, 1690-1820. Pennsylvania," in American Antiquarian Society, *Proceedings,* 30:81-150; 32:346-379 (1920, 1922).

Brownson, James I. *The Life and Times of Senator James Ross.* Washington, Pa., 1910. vi, 52 p.

Buck, Solon J. "The Planting of Civilization in Western Pennsylvania." Manuscript in the possession of the University of Pittsburgh Press.

Caley, Percy B. "Child Life in Colonial Pennsylvania," in *The West-*

ern Pennsylvania Historical Magazine, 9:33-49, 104-121, 188-201, 256-275 (1926).

Caley, Percy B. "The Life and Adventures of Lieutenant-Colonel Connolly," in *The Western Pennsylvania Historical Magazine,* 11:10-49, 76-111, 144-179, 225-259 (1928).

Campbell, Alton G. "Pioneer Iron Industry," in Sons of the American Revolution, Pennsylvania Society, Fort Necessity Chapter, Uniontown, *Fort Necessity and Historic Shrines of the Redstone Country,* 109-125. Uniontown, Pa., 1932.

Carnahan, James. "The Pennsylvania Insurrection," in New Jersey Historical Society, *Proceedings,* 6:113-152 (1851-53).

Carson, Hampton L. *The Genesis of the Charter of Pennsylvania.* Philadelphia, 1919. 57 p.

Carson, W. Wallace. "Transportation and Traffic on the Ohio and the Mississippi before the Steamboat," in *The Mississippi Valley Historical Review,* 7:26-38 (1920-21).

Centenary Memorial of the Planting and Growth of Presbyterianism in Western Pennsylvania and Parts Adjacent. Pittsburgh, 1876. 445 p.

Commemorative Biographical Record of Washington County, Pennsylvania. Chicago, 1893. 1486 p.

Conner, Martha. "Hugh Henry Brackenridge, at Princeton University, 1768-1771," in *The Western Pennsylvania Historical Magazine,* 10:146-162 (1927).

Cox, Isaac J. "Western Reaction to the Burr Conspiracy," in Illinois State Historical Society, *Transactions,* 29:73-87 (1928).

Craig, Neville B. *Exposure of a Few of the Many Misstatements in H. M. Brackenridge's History of the Whiskey Insurrection.* Pittsburgh, 1859. 79 p.

Craig, Neville B. *The History of Pittsburgh.* New edition, annotated by George T. Fleming. Pittsburgh, 1917. xxiv, 310 p.

Crall, F. Frank. "A Half Century of Rivalry between Pittsburgh and Wheeling," in *The Western Pennsylvania Historical Magazine,* 13:237-255 (1930).

Creigh, Alfred. *History of Washington County.* Washington, Pa., 1870. 368, 121 p.

Crumrine, Boyd, ed. "The Boundary Controversy between Pennsylvania and Virginia; 1748-1785," in Carnegie Museum of Pittsburgh, *Annals,* 1:505-524 (1901-02).

Crumrine, Boyd, ed. *The Centennial Celebration of the Incorporation of Washington, Pa.* Washington, Pa., 1912. iv, 103 p.

Crumrine, Boyd. *The Courts of Justice Bench and Bar of Washington County, Pennsylvania.* Washington, Pa., 1902. xii, 352 p.

Crumrine, Boyd, ed. *History of Washington County, Pennsylvania.* Philadelphia, 1882, 1002 p.

Dahlinger, Charles W. "Fort Pitt," in *The Western Pennsylvania Historical Magazine,* 5:1-44, 87-122 (1922).

Dahlinger, Charles W. *Pittsburgh, A Sketch of Its Early Social Life.* New York and London, 1916. vii, 216 p.

Davis, Elvert M. "Elbridge Gerry, Jr., Visits Pittsburgh, 1813," in *The Western Pennsylvania Historical Magazine,* 12:257-262 (1929).

Dinsmore, John W. *The Scotch-Irish in America.* Chicago, 1906. iv, 257 p.

Douds, Howard C. "Merchants and Merchandising in Pittsburgh, 1759-1800." Master's thesis, University of Pittsburgh, 1936.

Downes, Randolph C. "Problems of Trade in Early Western Pennsylvania," in *The Western Pennsylvania Historical Magazine,* 13:261-271 (1930).

Durant, Samuel W. *History of Mercer County, Pennsylvania.* Philadelphia, 1877. vi, 156 p.

Eakin, Myrl I. "Hugh Henry Brackenridge—Lawyer," in *The Western Pennsylvania Historical Magazine,* 10:163-175 (1927).

Eastman, Frank M. *Courts and Lawyers of Pennsylvania; A History, 1623-1923.* New York, 1922. 3 vols.

Eiselen, Malcolm R. *The Rise of Pennsylvania Protectionism.* Philadelphia, 1932. 287 p.

Ellis, Franklin, ed. *History of Fayette County, Pennsylvania.* Philadelphia, 1882. 841 p.

Ewing, Robert M. "Hon. Walter Forward," in *The Western Pennsylvania Historical Magazine,* 8:76-89 (1925).

Ewing, Robert M. "Life and Times of William Findley," in *The Western Pennsylvania Historical Magazine,* 2:240-251 (1919).

Felton, Margaret M. "General John Neville." Master's thesis, University of Pittsburgh, 1932.

Ferguson, Russell J. "Albert Gallatin, Western Pennsylvania Politician," in *The Western Pennsylvania Historical Magazine,* 16:183-195 (1933).

Field, Alston G. "The Press in Western Pennsylvania to 1812," in *The Western Pennsylvania Historical Magazine*, 20:231-262 (1937).

Fleming, George T. *History of Pittsburgh and Environs*. New York and Chicago, 1922. 5 vols.

Ford, Henry J. *Scotch-Irish in America*. Princeton, 1915. viii, 607 p.

Ford, Paul L. *The Origin, Purpose and Result of the Harrisburg Convention of 1788*. Brooklyn, 1890. 40 p.

Forrest, Earle R. *History of Washington County, Pennsylvania*. Chicago, 1926. 3 vols.

Fullerton, James N. "Squatters and Titles to Land in Early Western Pennsylvania," in *The Western Pennsylvania Historical Magazine*, 6:165-176 (1923).

Gibson, John. "General John Gibson," in *The Western Pennsylvania Historical Magazine*, 5:298-310 (1922).

Gray, Juliet G. "Early Industries and Transportation in Western Pennsylvania, 1800-1846." Master's thesis, University of Pittsburgh, 1919.

Gregg, Alan C. "The Land Policy and System of the Penn Family in Early Pennsylvania," in *The Western Pennsylvania Historical Magazine*, 6:151-164 (1923).

Gresham, John M., ed. *Biographical and Portrait Cyclopedia of Fayette County, Pennsylvania*. Chicago, 1889. 602 p.

Guffey, Alexander S. "The First Courts in Western Pennsylvania," in *The Western Pennsylvania Historical Magazine*, 7:145-177 (1924).

Hadden, James. *A History of Uniontown, the County Seat of Fayette County, Pennsylvania*. Akron, O., 1913. viii, 824 p.

Hailperin, Herman. "Pro-Jackson Sentiment in Pennsylvania, 1820-1828." Master's thesis, University of Pennsylvania, 1926.

Harding, Samuel B. "Party Struggles over the First Pennsylvania Constitution," in American Historical Association, *Annual Report*, 371-402 (1894).

Hassler, Edgar W. *Old Westmoreland: A History of Western Pennsylvania during the Revolution*. Pittsburgh, 1900. vi, 200 p.

Hayward, W. J. "Early Western Pennsylvania Agriculture," in *The Western Pennsylvania Historical Magazine*, 6:177-189 (1923).

Hazen, Charles D. *Contemporary American Opinion of the French Revolution*. Baltimore, 1897. x, 315 p.

Higby, Clinton D. *The Government of Pennsylvania and the Nation.* Revised, Boston and New York, 1912. vi, 266 p.

Hildeburn, Charles S. R. *A Century of Printing. The Issues of the Press in Pennsylvania, 1685-1784.* Philadelphia, 1885-87. 2 vols.

"Historic Canonsburg," in *Daughters of the American Revolution Magazine,* 50:12-13 (1917).

History of Allegheny County, Pennsylvania. Chicago, 1889. 758, 790 p. 2 parts in 1 vol.

History of Butler County, Pennsylvania. 1895. 1360 p.

History of Crawford County, Pennsylvania. Chicago, 1885. 1186 p.

History of Erie County, Pennsylvania. Chicago, 1884. 1006, 239 p.

History of Indiana County, Pennsylvania. Newark, O., 1880. 543 p.

Hockett, Homer C. *Western Influences on Political Parties to 1825.* Columbus, O., 1917. 157 p.

Hoge, Mary R. "Salt on the Frontier." Master's thesis, University of Pittsburgh, 1931.

Hogg, J. Bernard. "Presley Neville." Master's thesis, University of Pittsburgh, 1935.

Holdsworth, John T. *Financing an Empire; History of Banking in Pennsylvania.* Chicago, 1928. 4 vols.

[Hopkins, John H., Jr.] *The Life of the Late Reverend John Henry Hopkins, First Bishop of Vermont.* New York, 1875. 481 p.

Houtz, Harry. "Abner Lacock." Master's thesis, University of Pittsburgh, 1937.

Hughes, George W. "The Pioneer Iron Industry in Western Pennsylvania," in *The Western Pennsylvania Historical Magazine,* 14:207-224 (1931).

Huidekoper, Alfred. "Incidents in the Early History of Crawford County, Pennsylvania," in Historical Society of Pennsylvania, *Memoirs,* vol. 4, part 2, 113-163 (1850).

Hulbert, Archer B. *The Old Glade (Forbes's) Road.* Cleveland, O., 1903. 205 p. (*Historic Highways,* vol. 5).

Hulbert, Archer B. "Western Ship-Building," in *The American Historical Review,* 21:72-733 (1915-16).

James, Alfred P. "Early Property and Land Title Situation in Western Pennsylvania," in *The Western Pennsylvania Historical Magazine,* 16:197-204 (1933).

James, Alfred P. "The First English-speaking Trans-Appalachian Frontier," in *The Mississippi Valley Historical Review,* 17:55-71

(1930). Contains a brief, good account of the settling of the Monongahela and Pittsburgh regions.
Jenkins, Howard M., ed. *Pennsylvania, Colonel and Federal.* Philadelphia, 1903. 3 vols.
Johnson, Roy H. "Frontier Religion in Western Pennsylvania," in *The Western Pennsylvania Historical Magazine,* 16:23-37 (1933).
Jordan, John W., ed. *Genealogical and Personal History of Beaver County, Pennsylvania.* New York, 1914. 2 vols.
Jordan, John W., ed. *Genealogical and Personal History of Fayette and Greene Counties, Pennsylvania.* New York, 1912. 3 vols.
Killikelly, Sarah H. *The History of Pittsburgh, Its Rise and Progress.* Pittsburgh, 1906. xix, 568 p.
Konkle, Burton A. *George Bryan and the Constitution of Pennsylvania, 1731-1791.* Philadelphia, 1922. 381 p.
Konkle, Burton A. *The Life and Times of Thomas Smith, 1745-1809.* Philadelphia, 1904. 303 p.
Kovar, Daniel R. "Social Life in Early Fayette County as Seen Especially in Church and Court Records." Master's thesis, University of Pittsburgh, 1929.
Kussart, Mrs. S. "Colonel George Woods, Pittsburgh's First Surveyor," in *The Western Pennsylvania Historical Magazine,* 7:73-87 (1924).
Lee, Alfred M. "Trends in Commercial Entertainment in Pittsburgh as Reflected in the Advertising in Pittsburgh Newspapers (1790-1860)." Master's thesis, University of Pittsburgh, 1931.
Libby, Orin G. *The Geographical Distribution of the Vote of the Thirteen States on the Federal Constitution, 1787-88.* Madison, 1894. vii, 116 p. (University of Wisconsin, *Bulletin. Economics, Political Science, and History Series.* vol. 1).
Lincoln, Charles H. *The Revolutionary Movement in Pennsylvania 1760-1776.* Philadelphia, 1901. 300 p. (University of Pennsylvania, *Publications ... in History,* no. 1).
Lloyd, William H. *The Early Courts of Pennsylvania.* Boston, 1910. 287 p.
McKinney, William W. "Eighteenth Century Presbyterianism in Western Pennsylvania," in *Journal of the Presbyterian Historical Society,* 10:57-83, 97-112 (1919).
McWilliams, S. Elizabeth. "Democratic Party in Pittsburgh and the

Vicinity, 1800-1816." Master's thesis, University of Pittsburgh, 1915.

McWilliams, S. Elizabeth. "Political Activities in Western Pennsylvania, 1800-1816," in *The Western Pennslyvania Historical Magazine*, 7:225-234 (1924).

Martin, John H. *Martin's Bench and Bar of Philadelphia*. Philadelphia, 1883. xvi, 326 p.

Miller, Annie C. *Chronicles of Families, Houses and Estates of Pittsburgh and its Environs*. Pittsburgh, 1927. 133 p.

Miller, Mrs. Carroll. "The Romance of the National Pike," in *The Western Pennsylvania Historical Magazine*, 10:1-37 (1927).

Miller, Florence G. *Our Own Pioneers*. Meadville, Pa., c1929. 210, 2 p.

Miller, John. *A Twentieth Century History of Erie County, Pennsylvania*. Chicago, 1909. 2 vols.

Newlin, Claude M. *The Life and Writings of Hugh Henry Brackenridge*. Princeton, 1932. vi, 328 p.

Oberholtzer, Ellis P. *The Literary History of Philadelphia*. Philadelphia, 1906. xv, 433 p.

"Pittsburgh in 1761," in *The Pennsylvania Magazine of History and Biography*, 6:344-347 (1882).

Reid, Ambrose B. "Early Courts, Judges, and Lawyers of Allegheny County," in *The Western Pennsylvania Historical Magazine* 5: 185-202 (1922).

Reynolds, William. "Crawford County. A History of Its Growth and Development," in *Daily Tribune-Republican* (Meadville). Centennial edition, 1-9 (May 12, 1888).

Reynolds, William. *Fifty Years of the Bench and Bar of Crawford County*. n.p., 1904. 39 p.

Rodgers, Thomas L. "The Last Duel in Pennsylvania," in *The Western Pennsylvania Historical Magazine*, 12:54-57 (1929).

Schenk, J. S., ed. *History of Warren County, Pennsylvania*. Syracuse, N. Y., 1887. 692, cvx. p.

Schramm, Callista. "William Findley in Pennsylvania Politics." Master's thesis, University of Pittsburgh, 1936.

Schramm, Eulalia C. "General James O'Hara: Pittsburgh's First Captain of Industry." Master's thesis, University of Pittsburgh, 1931.

Scrivenor, Harry. *A Comprehensive History of the Iron Trade, throughout the World, from the Earliest Records to the Present Period.* London, 1841. xii, 453 p.

Searight, Thomas B. *The Old Pike. A History of the National Road.* Uniontown, Pa., 1894. 384 p.

Selsam, J. Paul. *The Pennsylvania Constitution of 1776.* Philadelphia, 1936. x, 280 p.

Sessa, Frank B. "Walter Forward." Master's thesis, University of Pittsburgh, 1934.

Sharpless, Isaac. *Political Leaders of Provincial Pennsylvania.* New York, 1919. vii, 248 p.

Sharpless, Isaac. *Two Centuries of Pennsylvania History.* Philadelphia, 1900. 385 p.

Shepherd, William R. "The Land System of Provincial Pennsylvania," in American Historical Association, *Annual Report,* 115-125 (1895).

Slick, Sewell E. "The Life of William Wilkins." Master's thesis, University of Pittsburgh, 1931.

Smith, W. Roy. "Sectionalism in Pennsylvania during the Revolution," in *Political Science Quarterly,* 24:208-235 (1909).

Stanwood, Edward. *A History of the Presidency.* New edition, revised by Charles K. Bolton. Boston and New York, 1928. 2 vols.

Sterrett, Mary M. "Pioneer Women of Western Pennsylvania." Master's thesis, University of Pittsburgh, 1931.

Swank, James M. *Introduction to a History of Ironmaking and Coal Mining in Pennsylvania.* Philadelphia, 1878. 125 p.

Thurston, George H. *Allegheny County's Hundred Years.* Pittsburgh, 1888. 312 p.

Thwaites, Reuben G. "The Ohio Valley Press before the War of 1812-15," in American Antiquarian Society, *Proceedings,* 19:319-368 (1908-09).

United States Congress. *Biographical Directory of the American Congress, 1774-1927.* Washington, 1928. 1740 p.

Veech, James. *The Monongahela of Old.* Pittsburgh, 1858-92. 259 p.

Volwiler, Albert T. *George Croghan and the Westward Movement, 1741-1782.* Cleveland, 1926. 370 p.

Wagner, Pearl E. "The Economic Conditions in Western Pennsylvania during the Whiskey Insurrection." Master's thesis, University of Pittsburgh, 1926.

Walsh, Mary L. "The Legal and Public Career of Alexander James

Dallas." Master's thesis, University of Pittsburgh, 1935.

Ward, Townsend. "The Insurrection of the Year 1794 in the Western Counties of Pennsylvania," in Historical Society of Pennsylvania, *Memoirs*, 6:117-182 (1858).

Warfel, Harry R. "David Bruce, Federalist Poet of Western Pennsylvania," in *The Western Historical Magazine*, 8:175-189, 215-234 (1925).

White, John W. F. "The Judiciary of Allegheny County," in *The Pennsylvania Magazine of History and Biography*, 7:143-193 (1883).

Wiley, Richard T. "Ship and Brig Building on the Ohio and Its Tributaries," in *Ohio Archæological and Historical Publications*, 22:54-64 (1913).

Wiley, Richard T. *Sim Greene and Tom the Tinker's Men*. Philadelphia, 1929. 386 p.

Wiley, Richard T. *The Whiskey Rebellion*. Elizabeth, Pa., 1912. 59 p.

Williams, Mildred M. "Hugh Henry Brackenridge as a Judge of the Supreme Court of Pennsylvania, 1799-1816," in *The Western Pennsylvania Historical Magazine*, 10:210-223 (1927).

Wilson, Erasmus, ed. *Standard History of Pittsburgh, Pennsylvania*. Chicago, 1898. 1074 p.

INDEX

INDEX

The chronological sequence of events has been consistently adhered to in this book, and the reader who uses this index will find the following outline helpful:

Chapter I	1773	pages 1-19		Chapter VI	1794-99	pages 132-154
Chapter II	1773-83	pages 20-37		Chapter VII	1799-1801	pages 155-175
Chapter III	1783-86	pages 38-62		Chapter VIII	1801-1808	pages 176-208
Chapter IV	1786-88	pages 63-100		Chapter IX	1808-15	pages 209-230
Chapter V	1788-94	pages 101-131		Chapter X	1812-23	pages 231-259

Chapter XI 1816-23 pages 260-267
summary pages 267-272

Acheson, David, 135
Adams, Henry, 221
Adams, John, 144, 145, 149, 150, 210
Adams, John Q., 230, 231, 267
Adams, Samuel, 63, 155, 210
Addison, Alexander, 48, 124, 130, 137, 139, 146, 147, 151, 156, 178, 271; on state constitution, 102-105, 107; impeachment, 113, 168-171, 79; sketch, 115
Agnew, Samuel, 174
Agrarian society, 1-19, 267, 268
Agriculture, 203, 219
Alden, Roger, 159, 222, 223, 247, 254
Alien and Sedition Acts, 149, 168, 270
Allegheny County, 9, 13, 15, 25, 137, 145, 150, 178, 195, 201, 238, 260; established, 66, 68, 158; election results, 103, 133, 135, 148, 152, 173, 207, 262, 264; Federalist party, 122, 174, 175
Allegheny College, 160
Allegheny Democrat (Pittsburgh), 267
Allegheny River, 4, 141, 258
Allison, James, 47, 65, 76, 147
Alshouse, Henry, 174
American System, 231-260, 272
Anti-Constitutionalists, 32, 35, 51-62, 66
Anti-Federalists, 75, 80, 86, 90, 96, 104
Armstrong County, 15, 159, 174

Articles of Confederation, 63, 73
Atkinson, Thomas, 185, 187, 206, 266
Augusta County, 25. *See also* Virginia-Pennsylvania controversy

Badollet, 217, 256
Baird, Absalom, 133
Baird, John, 38, 40, 65, 84, 85, 117, 122, 126, 161
Baird, Thomas, 165, 167, 269
Bakewell, Thomas, 238
Bakewell, Page and Bakewell, 238, 241
Baldwin, Henry, 188, 191, 212, 213, 231, 254, 260, 262-265; sketch, 165, 166; on tariff, 242-244, 246, 272
Bank of North America, 51, 52, 56, 59, 60-62, 65, 73; charter, 35, 66, 69, 74
Bank of Pennsylvania, 34, 57, 219, 246, 269
Bank of Pittsburgh, 220
Bank of the United States. *See* United States Bank
Banking, 219, 220, 246-251. *See also* various banks
Barr, James, 65, 76, 79
Barr, Thomas, 29, 41
Bates, Edward, 144
Bates, Frederick, 144, 200

INDEX

Bates, Tarleton, 144, 147, 165-167, 170, 185, 188, 189, 191, 195
Beaver County, 75, 159, 160, 174, 194, 198, 201, 264
Bedford County, 14, 20, 55, 150, 253
Beelen, Anthony, 217
Biddle, Owen, 62
Bill of Rights, state, 30; federal, 94, 98, 100
Bingham, William, 121, 211
Birkbeck, Morris, 237
Bouquet, Henry, 7
Bower Hill, 8, 42, 113, 127
Boyd, Maj.——, 77, 79, 85
Brackenridge, Hugh Henry, 9, 13, 17, 39, 42, 114, 133, 137, 138, 212, 269, 270; in legislature, 64, 65, 67-73; and federal Constitution, 75, 78, 80-85, 93-98; during Whiskey Insurrection, 125, 128-130; anti-federalist activities, 146-148, 153, 154, 156, 157, 161-163, 270
Braddock Road, 3, 7, 8, 252
Bradford, David, 47, 120, 126, 127, 130
Bradford, James, 47
Bradford, William, 42, 128
Brady, James, 174
Breading, Nathaniel, 44, 45, 84, 99, 211, 269
Brendel, W., 187
Brice, James, 133, 135
Brison, James, 157
Brownsville, 14
Bryan, George, 32-35, 52, 54, 57-59, 211
Bryan, Samuel, 54, 61
Buchanan, James, 244, 245
Bucks County, 19
Burd, James, 7
Burr, Aaron, 155, 210; conspiracy, 176, 199, 200
Bushy Run Battle, 7
Butler, Richard, 117, 119, 120
Butler County, 159, 201

Calhoun, John C., 211, 230, 231
Cambria County, 15
Canals. *See* Internal improvements
Canon, Daniel, 99
Canon, James, 33
Canon, John, 27, 48
Canonsburg, 14
Canonsburg Academy, 142
Capital of Pennsylvania, 139
Carlisle, 139
Carmichael, John, 30
Carpenter's Hall Convention, 28-31
Caucus, 185, 227

Cavet, James, 26
Centre County, 159
Chambers, John, 263
Chartiers Creek, 253
Chase, Samuel, 42, 171, 177
Cheeves, Langdon, 211
Chester County, 19
Churches, 11, 12, 17, 46
Claiborne, William, 199
Clapboard Junto, 164-167
Clare, Thomas, 45, 112
Clark, George R., 33
Clarke, R., 76, 77
Clay, Henry, 211, 230, 231, 267, 272
Clinton De Witt, 226, 227, 271
Clymer, George, 34, 61, 76, 78
Cochran, William, 126
Coercive Acts of *1774*, 25
College of Philadelphia, 57, 59
Colmery, John, 224
Colt, Jabez, 159, 200
Colt, Judah, 160
Commerce, 3, 13, 71, 231, 236, 256, 268, 271; effect of Embargo Act, 177, 203, 214-216
Committees of Correspondence, 25-27, 185, 186
Committee of Order and Activity, 167
Commonwealth (Pittsburgh), 188, 193
Conewango Creek, 258
Congress, 234, 235, 261
Connolly, Dr. John, 23-25
Conservative Republicans. *See* Democratic-Republican party, *1801-1808*
Constitution (Pa.), *1776*, 28-31, 52-60, 100, 101, 106; *1790*, 101-110; revision, 188, 189, 192, 193, 222
Constitution (U.S.), 66, 100, 234; ratification, 73-91, 104, 270; amendments, 99, 232
Constitutionalists, 30-34, 52-62
Continental Congress, 28
Cook, Edward, 27-29, 44, 211, 269
Copper and Tin Ware Manufactory, 217
Coroner, 50
Council of censors, 31, 35, 52, 57-59, 100, 101, 269
County commissioners, 50
County organization, 48-51, 186
Courts, *1783*, 49
Coxe, Tench, 152
Craig, Isaac, 114, 123, 151, 164, 166, 216, 270
Crawford, William, 27, 211, 244, 267
Crawford County, 140, 159, 174, 189, 201, 262, 267
Crawford Weekly Messenger (Mead-

INDEX

ville), 187
Croghan, George, 23, 24, 27, 41
Cumberland County, 20, 39
Cumberland Pike, 251, 255-259
Cunningham, John, 133, 135, 174
Currency problems, 35, 37, 60, 67, 219, 249, 250

Dallas, Alexander J., 122, 123, 155, 166, 170, 177, 240
Darragh, John, 226
Democratic party, organized, 122-125; *1794-95*, 129-132, 134, 135
Democratic-Republican party, 102, 110, 138, 144, 148, 150, 233, 260, 270, 271; organization, 152-175; in power, 176-230
Democratic societies, 125
Democrats, 38-62, 110-113, 117-122, 261
Denny, Ebenezer, 241
Depreciation certificates, 67, 69, 73
Dickerson, Joshua, 224
Divesting Act of *1779*, 67
Dixon, James, 189
Donation lands, 159
Douglass, Ephraim, 45
Dreisback, Simon, 53
Duane, William, 177, 178, 202, 203
Dunmore, John Murray, Earl, 21, 23-25

Economic conditions, 213, 214; *1817-21*, 236-239
Edgar, James, 48, 52, 84, 90, 91, 138, 269
Education, 17, 142
Election results, *1784*, 60; *1789-90*, 109, 117; *1794-99*, 132-135, 142, 146-148, 150, 152; *1799-1801*, 163, 173; *1801-1808*, 178, 185, 189-196, 201, 203, 207; *1808-15*, 223-226, 229; *1816-23*, 260-263, 265, 267
Emancipation Act, 34
Embargo Act, 177, 202, 214, 223, 271
England, 177, 202, 223, 225; commercial treaty, 136-139
Era of Good Feeling, 232
Erie, 268; harbor, 205, 251, 272
Erie Canal, 257
Erie County, 159, 174, 178, 189, 194, 201, 260; land problems, 140, 160, 197
Erie-Waterford Turnpike, 255
Ewalt, Samuel, 113, 135, 139, 142, 148, 165, 171, 173, 174, 192
Ewing, James, 23

Farmers' and Mechanics' Bank, 220

Farmers' Bank of New Salem, 249
Farmers' Register (Greensburg), 161, 187
Farrelly, Patrick, 198, 200, 213, 264
Fayette County, 9, 15, 43-45, 55, 112, 148,158,174,178,195,234,238,249,253, 269; organized, 22, 25, 35, 38; election results, 84, 103, 132, 135, 148, 152
Fayette Gazette and Union Advertiser, (Washington), 161
Federal-Republican party, 173, 202, 234, 265
Federalist party, 63; *1788-94*, 122, 123, 129-131; *1794-99*, 132-136, 138, 143-154; *1799-1801*, 155-175; *1801-1808*, 176-208; *1808-15*, 209-230, 233; *1816--23*, 260, 262, 265, 271, 272
Federalist, 64, 110; and federal Constitution, 75, 79, 85, 86, 90, 96; *1788-94*, 113-122
Fenno, John, 120, 121
Findlay, William, 261-264
Findley, William, 36, 38, 39, 48; council of censors, 51-62; in legislature, 65, 68-70, 72, 113, 117-119, 161-174; ratifying convention, 74-76, 79-86; 88, 89, 93, 94; on state constitution, 103, 105-109; in Congress, 122, 124, 126, 130, 133, 136, 138, 148, 149, 152, 154, 191, 192, 194, 201, 207, 212, 213, 223, 246-248, 261, 262, 264
Finley, James, 45, 99, 116, 117, 119
Finnie, Alexander, 7
Fitzsimons, Thomas, 52, 53, 58, 76, 234
Flennicken, John, 65, 76, 103
Forbes Road, 7, 8, 252
Foreign affairs, 136, 177, 221, 223
Forster, Alexander, 159, 205, 206
Fort Bedford, 7
Fort Burd, 14
Fort Ligonier, 7, 22
Fort Necessity, 7
Fort Pitt, 7, 23, 25, 42, 114
Forward, Walter, 165, 166, 188, 191, 212, 244, 264, 266
Foster, Samuel, 159
Foulkes, William, 198
Fowler, Gen.——, 165
Frame of government, 30
France, 8, 20, 22, 143-145, 177, 202
Franchise, 28, 30, 108, 110
Franklin, Benjamin, 66, 67, 85, 210
Franklin County, 39, 160
Frankstown Road, 142
Fraser, John, 30
French and Indian War, 20, 22, 252
French Creek, 255, 256, 258
French Revolution, 143

INDEX

Freneau, Philip, 42, 120
Friedt, William, 223
Friendship Hill, 112
Frontier life, 12, 15-18, 51

Gallatin, Albert, 45, 48, 99, 100, 164, 176, 212, 217, 270; and state constitution, 102, 103, 107; in legislature, 117-120, 122-24; during Whiskey Insurrection, 126, 128, 130; sketch, 111-113; Jay Treaty, 133-138; *1796-98* elections, 145-149, 154; on American System, 235, 246-248, 255
Gazzam, William, 165, 170, 194
Gehr, Baltzer, 53
Gênet, Citizen, 120, 122
Geography of western Pennsylvania, 1-6
Gerry, Elbridge, 143-145, 158, 227
Gerrymandering, 158
Gibson, James, 184
Gibson, John, on committee of correspondence, 27, 41, 139, 145, 147, 211
Gilchrist, John, 65, 76
Giles, William B., 210
Gilkison, John C., 158, 166
Gilmore, John, 226
Glass industry, 216, 217, 236, 237, 241, 243, 244, 246
Governor, powers in *1800*, 160
Grant's Hill, 97
Greene County, 15, 142, 143, 158, 173, 174, 178, 195, 249, 250
Greensburg, 14, 268
Gregg, Andrew, 265
Griffin, Isaac, 213, 224
Grundy, Felix, 211

Hamilton, Alexander, 38, 63, 74, 113, 120-122, 128, 129, 149, 155, 176, 210, 220, 231
Hamilton, David, 127, 133
Hamilton, James, 198
Hamilton, John, 194, 201
Hancock, John, 210
Hand, Edward, 105, 108
Hanna, Robert, 26
Hannastown, 14, 15, 41; during Virginia-Pennsylvania controversy, 22-29
Harris, Ephraim, 226
Harrisburg Convention, 98-100
Hart, Joseph, 52
Hartford Convention, 229, 232, 233
Henry, Patrick, 210
Herald of Liberty (Pittsburgh), 151, 161, 187
Hermitage Furnace, 238

Hiester, Joseph, 261-264
Hill, Riese, 224
Hoge, David, 113, 147
Hoge, David, Sr., 47
Hoge, John, 103, 113, 117, 119, 120, 147, 201, 212, 213
Hoge, Jonathan, 47
Hoge, William, 113, 173, 174, 201, 212, 213
Holland Land Company, 140, 159, 182-184, 197
Hopkins, Thomas, 224
Huidekoper, Harm Jan, 159, 182n., 183
Hull, John, 226
Hunter, James, 58
Hunter, John W. 205
Hurst, Henry, 191
Hutchinson, James, 124

Indian menace, 13, 14, 20, 24, 32, 37, 45, 74, 119, 136, 137, 140, 159, 182, 268, 270
Indiana County, 15
Industrial development, 219, 233, 268, 271
Internal improvements, 141, 231, 233, 251-257, 272. *See also* various canals, roads, etc.
Irish, Nathaniel, 165, 192
Iron industry, 216, 218, 234, 238, 240, 243-245
Irvine, William, 53, 105, 124
Israel, Isaac, 33
Israel, John, 151, 161, 162, 173, 188

Jackson, Andrew, 211, 223, 229, 232, 234, 266, 267, 272
Jacobinism, 125, 153, 168
Jay, John, 136
Jay Treaty, 136-139, 143
Jefferson, Thomas, policies, 120-122, 128, 144, 153-155, 168, 172, 176, 190, 202, 203, 210, 220
Johnson, Richard M., 211
Johnston, John, 189
Judiciary, 107, 168, 178-181, 196, 199, 222
Justices of the peace, 48-50, 196

Kennedy, Joseph, 187
Kentucky and Virginia Resolutions, 168
Kerr, James, 174
Kirkpatrick, Abraham, 114, 123, 164, 270

INDEX

Lacock, Abner, 173, 174, 180, 188, 193, 213, 224
Lake Erie, Battle of, 216, 228
Lancaster Turnpike, 253
Land problems, 8, 13, 20, 37, 45, 50, 62, 65-69, 81, 119, 140, 141, 222, 268; northwestern Pennsylvania, 182-184, 195-199
Lane, Presley Carr, 135, 174, 180, 207, 224
Lawrence, John, 224
Lee, Henry, 157
Leet, Daniel, 33
Leib, Dr. Michael, 177, 178, 201, 203
Lenox, David, 127
Lewis, William, 105
Linen industry, 244
Lobenger, Christopher, 30, 41, 224, 269
Lobenger, John, 223, 224, 247
Lodge, Benjamin, 132, 142
Lord, Samuel, 160, 197, 228, 271
Louisiana Purchase, 171, 176, 251, 271
Lowndes, William, 211
Lowrie, Walter, 241, 242, 244, 267
Lucas, John B. C., 113, 115, 156, 157, 169-171, 174, 189, 211
Lyle, Aaron, 213, 224
Lyle, John, 174
Lytle, John, Jr., 174

McAllister, Richard, 58
McArthur, William, 180, 184, 191, 194
McCalmont, James, 76, 78, 79, 85
McCandless, William, 189
McClelland, John, 30
McClure, William, 226
McClurg, Joseph, 167, 216
McCullough, John, 27
McDowell, James, 65
McDowell, John, 33, 47, 52, 102, 124, 169-171, 269, 270
McFarland, Abel, 224
McFarland, John, 267
McFarlane, Andrew, 24
Mackay, Aeneas, 24
McKean, Thomas, 39, 43, 69, 86, 89, 104, 105; Democratic-Republican activities, 150-156, 158, 165, 169, 173, 174; as governor, 177-181, 185-190, 192-196, 201, 203, 208
McKee, David, 197, 206
Maclay, Samuel, 186
McLean, James, 58, 77, 85
McMaster, John, 173, 174
McMillan, Rev. John, 46, 48, 115, 116, 123, 130, 133, 134, 137, 139
McNair, Dunning, 133, 135, 139
Madison, James, 42, 74, 144, 203, 208, 210, 223, 226-228
Marchand, David, 213, 261, 264
Marks, William, 224
Marshall, John, 143-145, 183
Marshel, David, 126
Marshel, James, 33, 46, 84, 90, 91, 99, 102, 124, 127, 128, 130, 174, 211, 269
Marshel, John, 174
Mead, David, 160, 194
Meadville, 159, 160, 178, 217, 228, 235, 268, 271
Meason, Isaac, 36
Mercer County, 160, 174, 178, 189, 201, 267
Mercer-Meadville Turnpike, 258
Mifflin, Thomas, 26, 61, 104, 211
Miles, Samuel, 52, 53, 57
Miley, Jacob, 76, 78, 79
Militia, 50, 145, 157, 271
Miller, Henry, 105
Miltenberger, George, 217
Minor, John, 117, 135, 139
Mirror (Erie), 205
Mississippi River, navigation, 45, 62, 65, 70, 136-138, 172, 215, 251, 270, 271
Monongahela country, 7-9
Monongahela River, 4
Monongalia County, 15, 25, 112. *See also* Virginia-Pennsylvania controversy
Monroe, James, 143, 177, 210, 260, 261, 263, 266
Montgomery, James, 174
Montgomery, William, 124
Moore, John, 30, 41, 58, 133, 135
Moore, Robert, 213, 261, 264
Morris, Robert, 32, 34, 35, 38, 52, 63, 68, 69, 73, 121, 211
Morrow, William, 226
Morton, John, 211
Morton, Thomas, 120, 173, 180
Muhlenberg, Frederick, A., 52, 53, 55, 60, 73, 124
Muster days, 50

National-Republican party 231-261, 263, 265, 272. *See also* Democratic-Republican party
Nationalism, 35, 63, 73, 232
Negley, John, 224
Nemacolin Trail, 3
Neville, John, 8, 16, 25, 27, 41, 42, 45, 46, 84, 90, 151, 164, 211, 267, 269, 270; *1788-94*, 113, 117, 119, 123, 127, 130
Neville, Morgan, 248
Neville, Presley, 114, 123, 130, 133, 139, 146, 147, 151, 164, 211, 257, 270
Neville political alliance, 9, 114, 115, 139

INDEX

New England, 176, 232
New York, 155
Newspapers, 108, 161, 163, 187
Northwestern Bank of Pennsylvania, 220, 271

O'Hara, James, 116, 123, 164, 175, 192, 205, 216, 218, 237, 238
Ohio, 176
Ohio country, 15, 25
Ohio River, 4, 172, 215, 258, 272
Otis, Harrison G., 210

Paine, Thomas, 172
Parkinson's Ferry meeting, 128
Party organization, 48-51, 116, 120-122, 132, 143, 186, 209-230
Passmore, Thomas, 179
Patronage, 263
Patterson, James, 224
Patterson, Thomas, 261, 264
"Peace Ticket," 226
Peebles, Samuel, 202
Penn family, land, 13, 24, 34, 66, 67
Pennsylvania, 19, 108, 109, 155
Pennsylvania Assembly, 51-62, 66-80, 74, 76-86
Pennsylvania Legislature, 54, 55, 107, 109, 117, 136, 170, 179
Pennsylvania Population Company, 140, 159, 184, 198, 200
Pennsylvania Public Works System, 253
Pennsylvania Road, 142
Pennsylvania Supreme Court, 43, 54, 110, 150, 156, 198; impeachment of judges, 179, 180
Pentland, Ephraim, 188, 207, 258, 265
Perry, Oliver H., 216, 228
Perry, James, 28-31
Philadelphia, 3, 19, 139
Philips, Theophilus, 65
Phillips, John, 224
Pinckney, C. C., 143-145, 210
Pinckney Treaty, 136-138
Piper, John, 76, 79, 85, 180
Pittsburgh, 8, 13, 41, 64, 65, 90, 96-98, 142, 147, 160, 215, 256, 268, 271
Pittsburgh Academy, 17, 44, 68, 157, 158
Pittsburgh Eagle Foundry, 217
Pittsburgh Fire Company, 165
Pittsburgh Gazette, 17, 64, 92; political alignment, 116, 144, 161, 162, 187, 188
Pittsburgh Manufacturing Company, 220
Plumer, George, 264
Pollock, Thomas, 223
Pontiac's Conspiracy, 7

Population of western Pennsylvania, 7, 8, 11, 12, 14, 19, 22
Porter, Charles, 174
Porter, Peter B., 211
Potomac River, 3
Potter, James, 58
Presbyterian Church, 11, 17, 46, 68
Proclamation of *1763,* 7, 20, 22
Prothonotary, 50

Quakers, 19, 109
Quids, 177, 204

Radical Republicans. *See* Democratic-Republican party, *1801-1808*
Randolph, John, 176
Read, James, 53, 58
Reading, 139
Redick, David, 47, 65, 69, 95, 103, 115, 130, 137, 147, 269
Redick, John, 170
Reed, Joseph, 26, 33
Reed, Robert, 189, 191, 192
Republicanism, 117
Revolutionary War, 21, 25-28, 32, 34; results, 36, 37, 213, 269
Reynolds, William, 188n., 256
Richardson, Andrew, 165, 173
Riddle, James, 167
Rights of Man Doctrine, 37
Ritchie, Craig, 133, 142
Ritchie, Matthew, 60, 117
Rittenhouse, David, 122
Roads and highways, 119, 141, 215, 268; to the West, 3, 8-10, 68, 73, 251-254. *See also* Internal improvements, various roads
Roberts, Jonathan, 244
Rogers, John, 197
Ross, James, 48, 115, 128, 130, 238, 270; on state constitution, 103-108; candidate for governor, 150, 151, 164, 173, 204-207, 212
Rugh, Michael, 113, 132
Rush, Benjamin, 122
Russell, Benjamin, 158

St. Clair, Arthur, 23, 24, 52, 58, 123, 148, 211, 238
Savary de Valcoulon, 111, 112
Schulze, John A., 265
Scott, Dr. Hugh, 164
Scott, Samuel, 224
Scott, Thomas, 33, 45, 46, 84, 90, 116, 117, 120, 124, 133, 211, 224, 234, 235

INDEX

Scull, John, 125; and *Pittsburgh Gazette*, 17, 64, 212; Federalist activities, 144, 148-151, 153, 156, 172, 175, 205, 225; attack on Israel, 161-164; on American System, 217, 218, 220
Scull, John I., 248
Second Continental Congress, 26
Sectionalism, 3, 25, 32
Seeley, Michael, 197
Semple, James, 226
Semple, Samuel, 23, 27, 41
Semple, Steele, 147
Settlement, 7-12, 22
Shays, Daniel, 63
Shays's Rebellion, 63
Sheriff, 50
Shipbuilding, 218
Shippen, Edward, 171, 179, 180, 183
Smilie, John, 36, 43, 45, 48, 77; in council of censors, 51-62; and Bank of North America, 65, 69, 72, 74; ratifying convention, 84-86, 88; in legislature, 103, 113, 117, 118, 120, 122, 124; during Whiskey Insurrection, 126, 130, 135, 142; in Congress, 148, 149, 154, 164, 174, 191, 192, 194, 201, 207, 212, 213, 224, 246, 247, 269
Smith, Abraham, 85
Smith, Charles, 105
Smith, Devereaux, 24
Smith, George, 132
Smith, James, 30
Smith, Robert, 177
Smith, Samuel, 52, 177, 192-194, 197, 201, 205, 212
Smith, Thomas, 171, 179, 180, 183
Smith, Wilson, 191, 192, 254
Smur's Tavern, 153
Snowden, John M., 161, 258
Snyder, Simon, 196; *1805* and *1808* campaigns, 185, 186, 188, 191, 203, 204, 207; as governor, 221, 222, 224, 261
Social life and conditions, 213, 214; on frontier, 16, 18, 20, 21, 49
Society for the Encouragement of Manufactures and Arts, 235
Society of Cincinnati, 38, 121
Somerset County, 174, 194
Spayd, John, 204
Spoils System, 158
Springer, Zadock, 99
Stewart, Andrew, 245, 264
Stokely, Thomas, 116, 120, 133, 138, 139
Stuart, Gilbert, 158
Supreme Executive Council, 31, 50, 51, 54, 55, 61, 65, 108

Susquehanna River, 3
Sutton, Andrew, 224

Tannehill, Adamson, 165, 189, 194, 212, 226, 254
Tannehill, Josiah, 141
Tariff, protective movement, 213, 214, 231, 233, 235-246, 258, 263; of *1816*, 234, 239-242; *1819-24*, 242-246
Tarr, Christian, 224, 261, 264
Taxation, 37, 55, 73, 119
Thompson, Charles, 25, 210
Thompson, William, 170
Todd, William, 38, 40, 60, 62, 84, 103, 122, 126, 133, 140, 161, 211, 244, 269
"Tom the Tinker," 127
Torbett, Samuel, 205, 220
Tories, 21, 25, 34, 36
Torrence, Joseph, 99
Treaty of Fort Stanwix, 8
Treaty of Ghent, 229, 232
Treaty of Greenville, 159
Treaty of Paris, 8
Tree of Liberty (Pittsburgh), 161, 162; political alignment, 187, 188
Trevor, Samuel, 174, 224
Turtle Creek, 24
Tyler, John, 167

Uniontown, 14, 15, 142
United States Bank, first, 120, 121, 246, 247; second, 231, 233, 236, 248, 249, 258, 265; office of discount and deposit, 219, 246, 258
University of Pennsylvania, 57

Vance, Joseph, 174
Venango County, 159, 174, 178, 189
Virginia-Pennsylvania controversy, 14, 15, 21-25, 32, 268
Virginians, in western Pennsylvania, 20, 22, 36
Virginia and Kentucky Resolutions, 168

Wallace, William, 133
War of *1812*, 140, 203, 211, 216, 221, 225, 227, 229, 231-233, 236, 271
Warren County, 159, 174, 178, 189, 265
Washington, 14, 90, 98, 147, 160, 268, 271
Washington Academy, 142
Washington County, 9, 15, 25, 55, 66, 84, 178, 194, 195, 238, 249, 254, 269; organized, 22, 33, 38, 142; political

INDEX

leaders, 45-48; election results, 99, 103, 122, 133, 135, 148, 152, 173
Washington, George, 38, 143, 149, 210
Wayne, Anthony, 53
Waynesburg, 143
Waynesburg Bank, 249
Weaver, Isaac B., 174
Webster, Daniel, 211, 214
Western Pennsylvania, described, 1-19, 32, 36, 37, 71
Western Telegraphe and Washington Advertiser, 161
Westmoreland County, 14, 15, 26, 32, 55, 65, 145, 238, 253, 266, 268; organized, 20, 23; and state constitution of *1776*, 28-31; political leaders, *1783*, 38-43; election results, 84, 99, 103, 124, 132, 135, 148, 152, 174
Westmoreland Democrat (Greensburg), 161
"Westmoreland Whigs," 204
Wheeling (W. Va.), 256
Whig party, 21, 27
Whiskey Insurrection, 125-132, 134, 146, 176, 260, 270
White, Benjamin, 133, 135
Whitehill, John, 52, 53, 55-57, 59, 74, 86
Whitehill, Robert, 32, 33, 52, 76, 77, 79, 104
Wilkins, John, Sr., 116, 123, 139, 147, 151, 164
Wilkins, John, Jr., 173, 201, 218, 219
Wilkins, William, 213, 218, 220
Wilkins family, 9
Williams, Ennion, 198
Willing, Thomas, 121, 211
Wilson, James, 32, 34, 39, 52, 63, 73, 101, 121, 211; ratifying convention, 86-89; on state constitution, 104-109
Wilson, Thomas, 213
Wirsthoff, William, 189
Woods, George, 114, 115
Woods, John, 124, 133, 139, 146, 148, 212, 226, 229, 270
Woolen industry, 217, 218, 238, 241
Wright, Alexander, 180
Wynkoop, Gerardus, 76, 102

XYZ Affair, 144

Yazoo land affairs, 177
Yeates, Jasper, 128, 171, 183, 198; impeached, 179, 180
Yohogania County, 15, 25. See also Virginia-Pennsylvania controversy
Youghiogheny Bank of Pennsylvania, 249
Youghiogheny River, 3

ERRATA

Page 27, line 14 *For* The following day *read* The same day
Page 58, line 17 *For* James M'Lene *read* James McLean
Page 65, line 30 *For* James McDowell *read* John McDowell
Page 147, line 19 and footnote 32. *For* August 26 *read* August 25
Page 152, line 6 *For* Tenche Coxe *read* Tench Coxe

THIS BOOK has been printed from Caslon type for the University of Pittsburgh Press by Davis & Warde, Inc., Pittsburgh. The paper used is Dill & Collins Suede Wove. The portraits have been reproduced in aquatone.